D1583553

The Medical Diaries

ALSO BY DAVID IRVING

Hitler's War

The Trail of the Fox

The War Between the Generals: Inside the Allied High Command

The War Path: Hitler's Germany

Adolf Hitler:
The Medical Diaries

THE PRIVATE DIARIES OF
DR THEO MORELL

EDITED BY
DAVID IRVING

SIDGWICK & JACKSON
LONDON

First published in Great Britain in 1983
by Sidgwick & Jackson Limited

Copyright © 1983 by David Irving

ISBN 0–283–98981–5

Designed by Jack Meserole

Printed in Great Britain by
R.J. Acford, Chichester, Sussex
for Sidgwick & Jackson Limited
1 Tavistock Chambers, Bloomsbury Way
London WC1A 2SG

Contents

I

AN INTRODUCTION

II

THE DIARIES OF THEO MORELL

EPILOGUE

The Cast

BLASCHKE, PROFESSOR HUGO. Hitler's dentist.

BRANDT, PROFESSOR DR. (of Medicine) KARL. Surgeon. Born 1904, entered Nazi Party in March 1932, Hitler's escort doctor (Begleitarzt) from 1934 to October 1944. From the summer of 1942 General Commissioner (1944: Reich Commissioner) of Public Health and Sanitation. Backed only by Hitler's favorite architect Albert Speer, and himself in decline, Brandt was sentenced to death in March 1945 for having sent his family to where they would be overrun by advancing American troops. Through Speer's intervention he escaped the noose, only to be hanged by the Americans in 1947.

BRINKMANN, PROFESSOR E. Medical Diagnostic Institute, Berlin.

CHAOUL, PROFESSOR HENRY. Leading Berlin X-ray specialist, a Syrian.

CONTI, DR. LEONARDO. Swiss born; Reich health chief; party veteran; suicide in American captivity.

EICKEN, PROFESSOR CARL VON. Ear, nose and throat specialist at Berlin University's famed Le Charité hospital.

EXNER, FRAU MARLENE. Hitler's dietician. Appointed by Morell in summer of 1943, she had to quit early the next year because of partly Jewish blood.

GIESING, PROFESSOR ERWIN. Army medic, ear, nose and throat specialist at Field Hospital II, Lötzen, East Prussia. Born 1907, entered Party and SA relatively early (August 1932), tended Hitler after the bomb plot of July 1944 and became quite close to Hitler until his sudden dismissal in October 1944 after the doctors' intrigue.

HAASE, PROFESSOR DR. WERNER. Surgeon, Berlin University hospital.

HASSELBACH, PROFESSOR DR. HANSKARL VON. Army doctor, Brandt's assistant as surgical escort doctor to Hitler from 1936. Born 1903, died 1981.

KERSTEN, FELIX. Faith healer and masseur, treated Himmler, Ribbentrop and others.

LAVES, PROFESSOR WOLFGANG. Pharmacologist, formerly Göttingen University, director of the "Professor Theo Morell Private Research Laboratory" at Olmütz.

LÖHLEIN, PROFESSOR DR. WALTER. Director of the University Eye Clinic, Berlin.

MAKKUS, CORPORAL DR. ROLF. From 1939–45 Morell's clerk and orderly, today a lawyer in Frankfurt am Main.

MANZIARLY, FRAU CONSTANCE. Hitler's dietary assistant, 1944–45. Missing in Berlin, May 1945.

MORELL, PROFESSOR DR. THEODOR GILBERT. Hitler's personal physician, 1937–1945.

MULLI, DR. KURT. Chief chemist at Morell's Olmütz factory.

NISSLE, PROFESSOR A. Forensic analyst. Chief of a research institute at Freiburg in southern Germany.

RIEDEL, DR. GÜNTHER. Director designate of Morell's Institute of Electron Optics in Bavaria.

RÖSSLE, PROFESSOR R. Director of Pathological Institute of the University of Berlin's Le Charité hospital.

SCHENCK, PROFESSOR ERNST-GÜNTHER. Colonel and Inspector-General of Nutrition in the Waffen SS during the war, today a noted pharmacological authority.

STUMPFEGGER, DR. LUDWIG. Hitler's last escort doctor. Described by Giesing as "conscientious and clinical, but very ambitious, reserved, cool."

WEBER, PROFESSOR A. Cardiologist at a Bad Nauheim clinic.

WEBER, DR. RICHARD. An assistant doctor in Morell's Kurfürstendamm practice in Berlin from January 1941.

WOHLGEMUT, DR. WOLFGANG. Richard Weber's predecessor.

ZABEL, DR. Director of the Institute of Nature Healing in Berchtesgaden.

ZACHARIAE, DR. Army doctor, Morell's medical representative treating Mussolini.

I

AN INTRODUCTION

How the Diaries Were Found

OBVIOUSLY, he had once been a corpulent and imposing figure, this elderly man lying on a stretcher in an empty room of the Red Cross facility at Munich station. But his hair was awry, his face was pale and he was sobbing quietly to himself. A figure which had once been clad in a magnificent uniform was now outfitted in cast-off American battledress, American socks and a GI shirt several sizes too small for him.

These were the clothes he had been allowed to take with him when he was thrown out of the American Civilian Internment Camp No. 29, better known as Dachau Concentration Camp. It was June 30, 1947. The American authorities had no further use for prisoner number 21,672—he himself had been cleared of war crimes charges, and the Doctors' Trial at Nuremberg had ended without his having been able to give evidence. So they had driven him to this railroad station, given him his discharge papers and left him for the Bavarian Red Cross to find.

Two hours passed before a nurse, Eva Meier, spotted the tragic figure and saw how ill he was. She arranged for an ambulance to take him into hospital—the auxiliary district hospital, Alpenhof, at Tegernsee.

At the hospital they listed his papers and possessions. His passport showed him to be Professor Theo Morell, doctor of medicine, sixty years old. He looked much older. A discharge report drawn up by the Dachau camp hospital on the previous day stated that he had serious cardiac trouble, that he was unable to work and was suffering "aphasic speech disorders."

The release papers showed the reason for his internment: "Hitler's personal physician."

IN THE HOSPITAL at Tegernsee, Morell made no statement about Hitler's health. He was a physical wreck. The American investigators had abused him and treated him with contempt. "Dr. Morell," an early interrogation summary noted, "has been the subject of a large number of intelligence reports, all of which refer to him in a most uncomplimentary manner. Some reports describe him as a shrewd, money-crazed quack doctor who believes in his own quackery; others describe his hygienic habits as being those of a pig. This interrogator has very little to add, and can only agree with the writers of the earlier reports."[1] He wept each time his young wife, Johanna, visited him. She had heard from his fellow prisoners that at Oberursel Interrogation Camp near Frankfurt the American authorities had used bright lights and the heating system in an attempt to break his powers of resistance—as though this mountain of flab had ever had any. His captors were convinced that Morell was keeping secrets about Hitler from them. Once when she visited him, he told her of his experiences. "They pulled out my toenails one by one to try to make me talk," he feebly said. Johanna Morell could not listen. "Don't work yourself up over it," she said. "I don't want to hear about that now. When you get better."[2]

But Morell never left that hospital. He died at 4:10 A.M. on May 26, 1948, without revealing the full story of what he knew. His personal papers had been confiscated by the American authorities. His widow had only the letters that Morell wrote to her from his internment. "How often I have thought back to that fiftieth birthday," he reflected in one letter. "How swiftly the years have gone, and how sorry I am that I could not devote myself more to you. I've often wished I was standing at that turning point in our lives again."[3]

Now his entire Hitler dossier has surfaced, and is in this author's hands. It has been a long search. By 1974, when I completed my biography of Hitler,[4] I had collected most of the other papers of Professor Theo Morell, and all of the interroga-

---

[1] Headquarters, United States Forces European Theater Military Intelligence Service Center: OI/CIR (Consolidated Interrogation Report) No. 4, 29 Nov 1945: "Hitler as seen by his Doctors."

[2] Frau Morell, interviewed by Otmar Katz, June 1967. These transcripts were made available to me by her attorney, Dr. Heinz-Lebrecht Herrmann.

[3] Morell to his wife, July 1, 1946.

[4] David Irving, *Hitler's War* (New York: Viking Press, 1977).

tion reports prepared on him by the British and Americans at the war's end. From the medical records, the electrocardiograms, the X rays, the urinalyses, the blood serologies and the neurological reports on "Patient A," "M. F.," "Adolf Müller," and whatever other pseudonyms were given to the Patient Hitler by his doctors, it was already possible to challenge most of the rumors and legends that had been circulated about him.

Then, in September 1981, I obtained access in the National Archives in Washington to a large cardboard box containing Morell's diaries and the dossier he had kept lest something befall his top patient—and hence himself too: he would need to provide the Gestapo with detailed records of his treatments and sessions with Hitler.

The history of the Morell diaries is this: they were carried in an officer's personal trunk out of Berlin to the supposed safety of Bad Reichenhall in southern Germany. There they were buried near a wall of the bunker building housing Morell's brand-new electron microscope. A Dr. Riedel ran this institute for Morell. Riedel confirmed in a note dated December 3, 1958, that early in 1945 Morell's driver Stelzer had arrived from Berlin with several crates containing Morell's precious carpets and other goods, and these had been stacked inside the bunker. On April 10 two trucks had arrived from Morell's Hamma Inc. at Olmütz carrying seventy crates of glandular secretions that Morell's pharmaceutical processes needed. The secret files had been buried like the earlier trunk in the courtyard, and thus survived the initial crisis of defeat.

When Frau Morell arrived at Reichenhall on July 8, 1945, with her sick husband, the Riedels did not welcome her. "My husband was unable to go the whole way with me because of his weak heart, so he stayed behind sitting on a bench," described Frau Morell in a note of October 2, 1945. "And he also told me not to be surprised if I found a lot of our Berlin property in Dr. Riedel's household." Frau Riedel opened the door to her but did not invite her in. "While I stood on the doorstep she fetched the key to the bunker and explained that a lot of our things were missing, either stolen or taken away by the Americans. I was rather surprised at that as the bunker was locked and only they had the keys. . . . I hope," she continued, "that when my husband is released from captivity the Riedel family

will give us precise information about where my husband's personal property is."

According to Morell's assistant, Dr. Rolf Makkus, now
(1983) a lawyer in Bad Homburg, a female French journalist
had visited Morell in the first hospital at Bad Reichenhall during
May 1945 and had learned of the cache. American troops then
raided the institute. Riedel, it seems, traded the valuables to
them in return for being left unmolested. "In my plight," Riedel
said in one report, "I asked the American occupation troops who
had meanwhile arrived to put a guard on the laboratory. They
were very considerate and immediately provided four soldiers
who made themselves at home in the bunker. After a while these
sentries got bored and ransacked the entire Morell crates."

The papers were shipped to the Military Intelligence Service
Center, formerly the Luftwaffe's notorious Dulag Luft interrogation camp, at Oberursel im Taunus. They too had kept their
eyes open for Morell's files. Dr. Karl Brandt, a rival Hitler doctor,
had told them under interrogation during June that since 1943
Hitler had received almost daily injections, the composition of
which Morell refused to reveal. "Morell kept a notebook which
he surely has with him," stated Brandt, "in which he regularly
noted names and treatments administered."[5] The American
authorities now had those notes, and American officers headed
by Captain Walter H. Gruendl, a former research chemist, began
to interrogate Morell and the dozen other physicians who had
treated Hitler over the years.

Morell's memory was genuinely shaky. An early interrogation report on him states, "Some of his information is produced
from memory; some is based on documentary evidence found in
his papers. . . . It should also be noted here that . . . on some
occasions he does recall things which he later is unable to
confirm."[6] The Morell documents were subsequently shipped to
the United States and vanished for nearly forty years (thus
sharing the fate of Eva Braun's diaries and her correspondence
with Hitler, and of the diaries of Hans Lammers, Karl Wolff and
a score of other personalities). Other journalists kept up the
search for them. On June 10, 1967, the German journalist

[5] CCPWE No. 32, Ashcan, Report DI-30, dated 12 July 1945: "High Nazi
Personalities. Information and Suggestions of Medical Interest."
[6] OI/CIR/4.

Otmar Katz asked Morell's widow, Johanna, "Do you think the Americans—that's what people are saying—might have found the medical records? The authentic medical files?" "Maybe," she answered. Katz pressed her: "Did your husband ever say anything about it? Where can the medical files have been?" She could not say. Nobody could say with certainty. In 1968, when Professor Hugh Trevor-Roper made available his British intelligence files to me for *Hitler's War*, it became clear to me from them that the Americans *had* captured the Morell diaries and his Hitler dossier. But my search of American archives failed to locate it.

This was no wonder, as the papers had gravitated into a classified medical library outside Washington, D.C. Then, out of the blue, in March 1981 Washington archivist Robert Wagner received a telephone call from the Department of Health, Education and Welfare (HEW): they had found the Morell files; would the National Archives like to accession them? From the original transmittal letter attached to them it appeared that Major R. G. Seelig, chief of the German Military Documents Section at the Military Intelligence Division of the Pentagon had sent them to the Office of the Surgeon General on June 28, 1946, listing them as "Dr. Morell's medical records, appointment booklets, medical account of Hitler's health, photographs, personal correspondence." On October 4, 1946, Seelig had sent further unspecified Morell documents to a Dr. Turner of Medical Intelligence at the Pentagon. The Pentagon had later loaned them out to the Army Medical Library, subsequently known as the National Institutes of Health, a division of HEW based at Bethesda, Maryland; and it was from here on March 18, 1981, that Dr. John B. Blake, chief of the institutes' History of Medicine Division, sent them over to George Wagner at the Modern Military Branch of the archives. "As you will see," he wrote, "it also includes X rays of some of the other Nazi leaders, some photographs, etc."

Papers attached to the files indicate that in about March 1946 an unnamed American officer had toyed with the idea of publishing them, but evidently gave up: the job of deciphering the manuscripts had beaten him. He noted, "I am sorry that I am not yet able to present the material in a more refined form. As soon as I have dug out the English meaning, I plan to list all drugs which Dr. Morell used. . . . The material is not my property thus I do not like to show it to too many people. Mr. Sheets my partner and the man who found the documents still plans to issue the material as a book. Do you think that such [a] book would gain enough attention or interest in the medical profession?"

By September 1981 these new Morell papers had been accessioned and largely microfilmed on National Archives (NA) microcopy T-253, roll 62. The filmed portion comprises the correspondence files including 72 pages of private letters, a spring binder including 122 pages of records on Hitler's health from July 1942 to April 1945, a folder of documents on Benito Mussolini's health dated from November 1, 1944, to March 23, 1945, a desk diary covering the final weeks from November 1944 to the end of the war, a bundle of medical data cards on which Morell noted his almost daily sessions with "Patient A" from 1942 to 1944, and a sheaf of loose notes detailing individual crises since August 1941. Some items have not been filmed, including an important but unphotogenic diary for 1944 and a thick pack of large filing cards on which Hitler's daily diet for 1943–1945 was meticulously recorded. Together with my secretary, Jutta Thomas, who had already excelled with her transcription of the shorthand diaries of Field Marshal Erwin Rommel,[7] I this spring completed the task of deciphering all the annotations, cross-checking them, determining the precise meanings of the exotic medications used (see Appendix) and obtaining expert opinion on both Hitler's problems and Morell's methods.

So the medical picture of the world's most infamous dictator, Adolf Hitler, is now complete. A picture emerges of the remarkable relationship that developed with his medicine men and with Morell in particular—the doctor who reigned supreme from his introduction to Hitler in the winter of 1936 until his dramatic leave-taking from him in the last days before the collapse of the Third Reich, when Hitler snapped at him: "Get out of that uniform, put on some plain clothes and go back to being the doctor of the Kurfürstendamm!"

[7] David Irving, *The Trail of the Fox* (New York and London, 1977).

The Relationship

FOR AS LONG as the attention of modern historians remains rooted to the curse of Adolf Hitler, they will also be mesmerized by the relationship between him and that shadowy figure in the background: his personal doctor, Theo Morell.

This is natural. Since history began, man has been hypnotized by visions of power and influence, by the mental and physical peculiarities of those who wield those instruments, and by the doctors whom these men of power attract to their sides. Winston Churchill retained as physician Lord Moran—a man not unsimilar to Morell—and Lord Moran wrote an equally fastidious diary in which he jotted down sufficient detail to reconstruct, in his declining years, a memoir of Britain's great wartime prime minister, a book that would arouse furious controversy. Joseph Stalin kept a whole court of doctors, many of whom he eventually terminated with considerable prejudice in a fit of anti-Semitic paranoia.

Nobody should underestimate the influence that such doctors can secretly wield. They are indispensable and know it. Great events can be affected by the illness of their leaders. International conferences, like Yalta, have been overshadowed by the physical decline of the statesmen present. Battles can be lost because of one general's debility: Napoleon was plagued by hemorrhoids and obliged by a painful attack of diarrhea to desert the field at Waterloo for several hours at the height of that battle, and forfeited victory. In Morell's diaries we find proof that Hitler was similarly weakened by dysentery for weeks at the height of the Battle for Russia in the summer of 1941, and again bedridden with hepatitis shortly before the Battle of the Bulge in 1944; we learn too that he was oppressed by the knowledge that he had a heart ailment—rapid progressive coronary sclerosis, which might at any moment write finis to all his schemes for Germany.

The similarity with Napoleon was only superficial. Napoleon abhorred doctors and spurned medicines until shortly before his death. Hitler was the opposite, the typical hypochondriac. From his earliest youth he rarely traveled without his medicine cabinet, and willingly believed himself almost incapable of survival without pills, injections and battalions of attendant doctors. Senior among them was Morell, his personal physician for the last eight years of his life.

"Morell," wrote Dr. Karl Brandt, one of his less flattering rivals in American captivity, "comes from somewhere near Darmstadt, is about fifty-six years old, very fat, has a bald head, a round and very full face, dark-brown complexion and dark-brown eyes, is near-sighted and wears glasses, has very hairy hands and chest. Approximately five feet seven inches tall." He added the perhaps unremarkable corollary: "Married, no children." And one of Hitler's private secretaries has rendered us this even less appetizing description of a typical soirée with Morell: "With his heavy, hairy hands clasped across a podgy paunch, Morell would fight back his drowsiness. He had the odd characteristic that when he closed his eyes he did so from the bottom upward—it looked hideous behind the thick pebble glasses. . . . Sometimes Colonel von Below would give him a nudge and he'd wake up with a start and chuckle out loud in case the Führer had just told a joke."

No, Morell was not popular in Hitler's circle. He was teetotal and did not smoke. Worse: "He didn't eat," recalled Brandt's associate, Dr. Hanskarl von Hasselbach. "He munched like a pig at a trough." One of the headquarters secretaries put it this way: "Morell had an appetite as big as his belly, and he gave not only visual but audible expression to it." When Hasselbach once remarked on Morell's body odors, Hitler snapped: "I don't employ Morell for his fragrance but to look after my health." Despite Hitler's loyal backing, the doctor was ostracized by most of the adjutants. This hostility, his friend Dr. Aloys Becker stated, manifested itself in petty indignities inflicted on Morell and his wife. When they were invited to the Wagner household at Bayreuth, for instance, one of the younger SS adjutants exclaimed in an insulting tone, "What are you doing here! Who invited you!"

It remains a matter for some wonderment that Hitler should have allowed this obese, middle-aged doctor to dose him with the extraordinary volume and variety of medicines that he did. Hitler's staff were in despair. His perennial housekeeper, Frau Anni Winter, explained, "Once Morell started on him, all sorts of medicines began popping up on Hitler's table, and their number and potency increased at the same rate as the dietary regulations multiplied, the restrictions on certain foods were intensified and his overall food intake declined. It began around the winter of 1937–38 with one little medicine bottle. Over the next seven years there were enough to fill an attaché case." Morell administered tablets and dragées, uppers and downers, leeches and bacilli, hot compresses and cold poultices, and literally thousands of injections—liters of mysterious fluids that were squirted into his grateful but gullible Führer each year, so often that even Morell sometimes could not find anywhere to slide the needle into his chief's scarred veins.

Since the end of the war, there has been speculation about Morell and his methods. How great was his influence on the Führer? What were his treatments of this man determining the destinies betimes of two hundred million Europeans? Dr. Erwin Giesing, the ear, nose and throat doctor who studied Hitler at close quarters after the assassination attempt of 1944, was infuriated that Hitler could not see through Morell. "Morell," he commented in a November 1945 manuscript, "converted the largely healthy man that Hitler had earlier been into one constantly plied with injections and fed with tablets which made Hitler more or less dependent on him; he played on Hitler's neuropathic nature by spouting utter rubbish about how Hitler's extremely heavy work load meant that he was burning energy at the same rate as people in the tropics, and that the lost energy had to be immediately replaced by all sorts of injections like iodine, vitamins, calcium, heart- and liver-extract, and hormones."[1]

[1] Erwin Giesing, M.D., "Report on my Treatment of Hitler." A daily record prepared in June 1945. I have donated a copy to the Institut für Zeitgeschichte (Institute of Contemporary History) in Munich, along with all other documents used for this volume.

Yet there were educated people who had been treated by Morell, before his elevation to Hitler's physician, and who claimed that he had benefited and even cured them where other physicians had failed. But to other doctors Morell's methods seemed haphazard and nonantiseptic. Here is how Giesing recalled one 1944 episode: "Morell then went into the bunker's ante room and gave Hitler his injection, as usual in the presence of Linge [Hitler's valet]. I waited in the office. After about five minutes Morell came back with the used syringe in his right hand and some empty ampoules in his left—I recall there was one large one and two smaller ones. When he put the empty ampoules on the desk for a moment I saw they were unlabeled. Then Morell took them into the orderlies' bathroom, rinsed out the syringe and disposed of the empty ampoules by tossing them into the toilet."

We shall later investigate the medicines administered by Morell. First we should examine Hitler's clinical personality. Dr. Giesing would suggest: "From Hitler's psychopathic constitution and the associated conviction that he always knew better, there developed a marked neuropathic disorder. His intense contemplation of his own bodily functions, and particularly his preoccupation with his gastrointestinal and digestive tracts, were only one token of this. Others were the frequency with which he took his own pulse when I gave him a checkup, and then asked me to confirm it; and his ever-present fear of an imminent death—in the fall of 1944 he repeatedly said that he had only two or three years to live. Of course, he was convinced that he would by then not only have attained final victory but have given the German people such leadership and have consolidated their position so enormously that 'others will be able to take up where I leave off.' Other significant tokens were his addiction to medication like sleeping pills, all manner of indigestion tablets, bacterial compounds and 'general-purpose fortifier' pills and injections. Not that Hitler was your common drug addict; but his neuropathic constitution led to his finding certain drugs, like the strychnine and atropine contained in the anti-gas pills, and the cocaine in the sinus treatments I gave him, particularly pleasurable; and there was a clear inclination toward becoming a habitual user of such medications, as he himself admitted to me."

In a 1951 study Professor von Hasselbach also questioned Morell's injection treatments. "None of us other doctors knew what was in those jabs of his," said Hasselbach. Brandt shared a prison cell for a brief time with Morell—he would later say that those few days were worse than everything he had suffered so far at American hands and than anything they could yet do to him—and Morell assured him that he had never injected morphine, but only hormones, vitamins and glucose. But could such massive treatments really be innocuous? Captain Heinz Assmann, who was a navy staff officer attached to the High Command from August 1943 and as such stood at Hitler's side daily until April 23, 1945, talked to experts who regarded these thousands of glucose injections as anything but harmless. "They talked of the danger of premature arteriosclerosis," he wrote, "with all its side effects like premature senility." Assmann maintained, "There are also grounds to believe that the shots A.H. got were beefed up with stimulants like Pervitin [a notorious amphetamine-type compound], because several observers who were witness to A.H.'s collapses told of how he revived dramatically after getting tablets or jabs from Morell."

It must be said that Morell's dossier shows no evidence that he administered Pervitin to Hitler. In fact it is unlikely. Pervitin —chemical designation 1-Phenyl-2-methylaminopropanehydrochloride—was a substance capable of pharmacologically reproducing the effect of a stimulation of the vegetative sympathetic nervous system. But it was addictive; moreover, it was found to cause serious permanent damage and was restricted under the Germany Narcotics Act in 1941. Pervitin does appear a very few times in Morell's papers, for example in his agenda for October 15, 1943 ("Pervitin prescription for Engel Pharmacy") with the handwritten postscript, "Out of stock." The Engel Pharmacy supplied all medical stores to Hitler's headquarters. And on January 27, 1944, he wrote: "Prescription Eupaverin + Pervitin, heating pads." But Morell was familiar with the dangers of Pervitin. He wrote to one patient on December 1, 1944, "You can get Intelan and bars of Vitamultin with the enclosed prescriptions from the Engel Pharmacy at No. 63 Mohren Strasse 63, Berlin W8. But let me warn you against Pervitin. This does not replace lost energy, it is not a carrot but the stick! For a general pick-me-up it might be good to have an injection of 5 cc of Homoseran every two or three days."

Dr. Giesing was frustrated by not knowing precisely what Morell was injecting Hitler with. "For instance," he wrote, "I don't know if he injected hormones. It might be important to know whether or not massive hormone doses were having an effect on Hitler's physique in the sense of suppressing female stigmata."

Reich ministers and Nazi Party officials also brooded on Morell. In June 1943 Joachim von Ribbentrop came out into the open and tackled him about the treatment. Morell, it will be seen, wrote a painstaking record of the conversation. "Reich Foreign Minister von Ribbentrop had invited me to lunch at Fuschl. . . . After lunch he invited me upstairs to talk something over. Now it came out why he had asked me to lunch—to speak to me about the Führer's health and my treatment of him." Ribbentrop had, noted Morell, inquired whether it was a good thing for Hitler to get so many injections. "Whether he was getting anything other than glucose? Whether I was giving him anything else?" Morell answered laconically, even cryptically, "I give him what he needs."

He could afford to snub these powerful inquirers. He knew he had enjoyed Hitler's unqualified confidence. Didn't Hitler keep telling him, again and again, how much he needed him? In July 1944 Hitler was to fob off the fuming Dr. Giesing with this explanation: "It's like this. It was Morell who healed me. I know that Morell's newfangled methods are still not recognized internationally, and that even out here Morell is still researching in many fields without having reached firm conclusions. But isn't that how it always has been with innovations in medicine? It has always taken a finite time before new methods are accepted. I haven't the slightest doubt that Morell will see things through. And the moment he needs financial support for his researches he'll get it from me."[2]

Morell could boast of similar utterances by Hitler. There was one significant episode in the fall of 1944 a few weeks after

[2] Giesing, manuscript of June 1945.

the Doctors' Intrigue failed to dispose of him. After midnight on November 8, when Hitler was planning the Ardennes Offensive, Morell was called to him. "The Führer had suddenly been seized by pains in his sternal region coupled with a violent gaseous buildup in his abdomen," the doctor inscribed in his diary a few hours later. "From what he told me, the patient is at present facing some of the biggest decisions of his life, and this is causing him mounting nervous problems." Once again Morell brought swift blessing through his hypodermic needle. "The Führer kept thanking me for this immediate relief. After retching several times, bringing up the air and gases he had swallowed, the Führer became completely relaxed and was just about as pleased as could be. He told me I would never believe the aggravation the recent intrigue against me had caused him. 'Those dunderheads didn't pause to consider the damage they would have inflicted on me by their action!' he said. 'I would have suddenly found myself without a doctor, although they know how often you've already saved my life in the eight years you've been with me. Look how things stood before! All the doctors they roped in were failures. I'm not an ungrateful man, my dear doctor, and if we both get through the war and if fortune smiles on us, you'll see how magnificently I'm going to reward you after it!' "

Morell seized the opportunity. "Mein Führer," he wheedled, "if a normal doctor had had to treat you, you would have been off the job so long that the Reich would have gone on the rocks because of it. I have had to undertake crash cures and prescribe maximum doses, I have had to go to the very limits of the permissible even though I may be reproached for this by many colleagues. I bore the responsibility—but I can take it, because if you had ever had to quit, for however long, Germany itself would have come to grief." Hitler took Morell's hand, pressed it warmly and gave him a lingering, grateful look. "My dear doctor," he said, "I am glad and lucky to have you." [Diary.]

SMALL WONDER that the other doctors envied Morell's position, particularly Hitler's escort doctor, Karl Brandt, a good-looking young surgeon whom the Americans would hang in 1947 (his last grim words on the gallows in Landsberg jail were: "I—am —ready").

Brandt racked his brains over the Morell enigma: under interrogation in September 1945, he tried to answer how and why Morell managed to maintain his position for eight years. Was he subject to some external pressure to keep Hitler under his influence? Was he somebody else's tool? Or was Morell himself seeking to enslave Hitler for his own political or commercial ends? Eventually Brandt gave up. Although Morell had his measure of animal cunning, Brandt had to accept that he was "too dense" for political intrigues; besides, he would never get involved in anything that might expose his quivering frame to personal risk. Perhaps Morell influenced Hitler in the way that doctors do, until Hitler could not do without his treatments and eventually came to regard himself as owing some kind of obligation toward Morell as a person? Hasselbach, Brandt's assistant since 1936, drew attention to Hitler's evident dependence on Morell. "I just couldn't get over the influence Morell had on Hitler in medical respects," he wrote. Brandt surmised three possible ways in which Morell might have snared Hitler: by some narcotic like morphine; or by hormone treatments; or by less specific means—perhaps by playing on the gratitude that patients feel toward doctors who have cured an illness or stimulated their personal performance.

Why did Hitler elect to stay with Morell? His reasons were probably both complex and irrational. His choice was governed by the antipathy shown during the Third Reich toward all true experts. Most of the top Party officials favored doctors of dubious repute. Himmler and Ribbentrop were devoted to nonmedical practitioners and masseurs like Felix Kersten; Hess was dedicated to herbal medicine and astrology. The dilettante was king, in a dictatorship where the leader hated specialists. And of Hitler's inclinations there could be no doubt. On August 30, 1944, he snarled at his new chief of air staff, Lieutenant-General Werner Kreipe—who had just ventured the expert view that the Messerschmitt-262 jet plane would make a better fighter than bomber—"Experts are only good at one thing: explaining why something will not work!" And Hitler's aversion to the military brains of the General Staff was equally notorious: he called it an establishment for lying. What more natural than that the busy Führer should engage a physician who could work instant "miracle cures" through a hypodermic needle?

Morell's actual treatment of Hitler will be analyzed later. Probably only clinical experiments can establish how far Hitler's unquestioned capacity for sustained effort derived from Morell's medication. Morell unquestionably influenced Hitler by his use of stimulants. "By stimulants," Brandt wrote, "I am thinking not just of the daily intake of Vitamultin but of the massive glucose injections, which are bound to have had an effect on Hitler's sense of vitality." Hasselbach was more robust in his indictment of the physician's methods. "In many cases he suggested to patients that they were suffering from a serious malady which he then successfully 'cured,'" he claimed. "I will say," he admitted however, "that he often displayed a healing hand with nervous complaints." Morell had treated the propaganda minister: Dr. Goebbels had contracted dermatitis over virtually his entire body and was unable to sleep because of the irritation; twenty-two doctors tried to cure it and failed. Morell's course of Homoseran injections worked, and Goebbels never forgot it. "I'm happy to be able to withstand these present burdens," he recorded on March 10, 1943. "I attribute this primarily to Morell's treatment." Hitler, impressed, loaned his doctor to other VIPs, including Mussolini.

The dossier on "Patient A" destroys many legends cherished by historians. Former OSS-adviser William C. Langer's speculation about Hitler's exotic sexual and psychological problems are exposed for the bunkum that they were. Charles Heston's recently published theories in *The Hitler Casebook*, about Hitler's addiction to narcotics, are also contradicted. American myths about Hitler's "congenital syphilis" and Soviet whispers about his "impotence" are slain by the urinalyses and blood serologies reproduced in the Appendices. However, there does now seem evidence to support the persistent suggestions that by 1945 Hitler was a victim of *paralysis agitans*—also known as Parkinsonism. Morell certainly suspected it. There is no other explanation for the medication which he initiated (daily doses of Homburg 680), a prescription which he left his doomed patient still taking while he fled to Bavaria on April 22, 1945.

One thing is certain. Many of Morell's medicines were quite harmless, and he injected the others in such minute quantities that they would have been virtually useless. Modern experts have described Morell's many hormone preparations, like

Orchikrin, a so-called youth elixir, as trash. Of course, Morell may have realized this: he may have administered them as placebos to keep the pill-crazy Führer contented. The same charitable view cannot be taken of his lavish use of inferior proprietary sulphonamides like Ultraseptyl long after they had been publicly exposed as toxic by experts, nor of his use on Hitler of his own still-experimental penicillin.

It is unlikely that Morell will be adjudged one of the great physicians of this century. History will term him a doctor with an unjustified sense of his own capabilities—a man who was less wicked than negligent, perhaps, but above all a man of monumental jealousy and vulnerability.

Theodor Morell

SECOND SON of a primary school teacher of Huguenot blood, Theodor Gilbert Morell first saw the light of day on July 22, 1886, at Trais-Münzenberg, a village in Upper Hesse. That made him nearly three years older than his future famous patient. His mother came from a wealthy Hessian farming family. He had an elder brother Adolf, and a sister Emilie was born after him. His final passport would describe him as having "medium build, oval face, gray eyes." From his papers we know that he was overweight, tipping the scales at 224 to 230 pounds. So there is little wonder that in the final years of his life he suffered kidney and heart ailments. As a child he was already plagued by recurring stomach cramps, and this affliction prevented him from attending the local primary grade school.

At school he shone. His General Certificate of Education, dated February 16, 1907, stated he had been excused from oral examinations on account of his year's performance and his written work. For a while, from sixteen to nineteen, he attended a teachers' seminary at Friedberg in Hesse. He went on to teach for a year at Breizenheim near Mainz, and then began more serious studies at Giessen, where he matriculated, and read medicine at Heidelberg University. The examining body handed down its results on July 26, 1909. Anatomy: very good; physiology: very good; physics: very good; chemistry, zoology and botany: good. Morell went on to France, where he studied at Grenoble and Paris—as a visiting student in the "Institut D'accouchement Tornier" he read parasitology from December 1909 to the middle of the following year—and then returned to Germany and Munich. His papers began to fill with testimo-

nials won as a probationer in immunology, psychiatry, at an ear
clinic, and in August 1910 in a gynecological clinic too.

He did not complete his specialist training. In 1913 he wrote
a gynecological Ph.D. thesis, "The displaced transverse presenta-
tion and its treatment on the basis of sixteen cases observed in
Munich University gynecological clinic." The Royal Bavarian
State Ministry issued him a license as a medical practitioner
under § 29 of the Reich Professional Code on May 23, 1913, in
Munich. Theo Morell began to earn a living as an assistant
doctor at Bad Kreuznach. But after only a brief stay there he
embarked as a ship's doctor with the Woehrmann line, then
moved to the Hamburg–South America and the North German
Lloyd lines. In later years he would hint mysteriously that his
more abstruse treatments were a product of his experience as
a ship's doctor in the tropics.

After a while he became something of a specialist on urinary
diseases. He acquired a little practice at Dietzenbach near
Offenbach. During World War I he served briefly as a battalion
medic on the western front, and then as army doctor in a
prison camp at Ohrdruf in Thuringia. In January 1919 he
purchased a practice in Berlin, and there he would stay, in
Bayreuther Strasse, for the next seventeen years. In 1920 he
married a well-to-do actress, Johanna Möller. The marriage bore
no children; the real fruits were those he earned in his Berlin
practice. His ability was noised far and wide. Many patients
came from the Inter-Allied Commission. There were many Jews
too—particularly after he bought a villa at Heringsdorf, an
explicitly Jewish watering place on the Baltic coast, in about
1925. In this villa he set up a sanatorium, but it did not pay and
he later converted it into a small hotel. With his wife's substantial means he was able to equip a very luxurious practice.
In the following years he was offered—and turned down—
positions as court doctor to the Shah of Persia and the King of
Romania. He turned them down, because life in Berlin was
sweet enough. He was able to dispense with panel patients
altogether and take only the private ones, with means to pay
his fees.

By the early thirties, Theo Morell was already a prominent
and fashionable doctor. A 1932 prescription pad among his
papers bears the printed legend: "X rays, high frequency,

diathermy, radiation, galvanic treatments, urinalyses and blood serologies." His annual income was about 150,000 Reichsmarks. The Crown Prince gave him a signed photograph. The rich and famous of postwar Germany rubbed shoulders in his waiting room. There was the singer Richard Tauber, heavyweight champion Max Schmeling, Rosita Serrano, Martha Eggert and Hansi Burg, the mistress of Hans Albers. But a more critical analysis of his clientele would show mainly the big names of stage and screen, apart from a number of hypochondriacs and political personalities—people of whom his assistant Dr. Richard Weber would later disparagingly remark: "They could hardly be called very critical or intelligent."

When the Nazis came to power in January 1933, there were disagreeable side effects for Morell. His doctor's nameplate was defaced by the word *Jew*, perhaps because of his Jewish clientele, but later he would suggest that because of his swarthy looks he might himself have been mistaken for a Jew. Whatever the reason, his practice went into decline. The non-Jew Morell rushed to draw the consequences and joined the Party in April 1933. But he continued to treat Jewish patients, for the next five years at least. Two years later he moved across Berlin to the swank Kurfürstendamm, where his new practice at No. 216 specialized in venereal cases. His nameplate here proclaimed the words "General Practitioner," because he was not in fact a specialist. In his home, adjacent to the practice, were all the paraphernalia of a wealthy professional man: an oak dining room, a bedroom designed by the famous Professor Gustav Eberlein of the Berlin Museum of Fine Arts, with carvings that had taken a whole year, and a study. Among his ultra modern equipment were an X-ray room with the latest gadgets, an ultraviolet lamp and three diathermy machines.

N THE SPRING of 1936 his screen friends introduced a new patient to Morell—the Munich intimate of Hitler and his personal photographer, Heinrich Hoffmann. Hoffmann had taken to drink after his first wife's death, and was turning slowly homosexual; he needed Morell as he was suffering from gonorrhea, tactfully referred to by Morell in interrogations as pyelitis. Morell did not really want to go down to Munich, because he had more than enough clients in Berlin. But Hitler sent his personal plane to fetch him to Munich, and thus it came about that the doctor was introduced in Hoffmann's villa in the elegant suburb of Bogenhausen to the Reich Chancellor. Hitler was very melancholy at the time, as his perennial chauffeur Julius Schreck had just died, and he feared he might be losing his friend Hoffmann too. Morell's friend Aloys Becker would later recall, "Hitler was very taken with Morell, and regretted that Morell had not been there to treat Schreck too."

Morell cured the photographer. There were no complications. He stayed in Munich four weeks, and accompanied Hoffmann on a convalescent trip to Venice. In this way he became an intimate of Hitler's too. Early in the summer of 1936, Johanna Morell came on a visit to her husband in the Hoffmann household. Morell pointed out a young girl and said: "See that platinum blond? That's the Führer's girl friend." Eva Braun had been one of Hoffmann's laboratory assistants, and would remain loyal to Hitler until their suicide pact of 1945.

The Hoffmanns invited the Morells to spend Christmas 1936 with them. On Christmas Day, Heinrich Hoffmann suggested that the doctor and his wife drive with them up to the Obersalzberg mountain, where Hitler lived in the "Berghof." The newcomers were quartered in the "Bechstein House," but they were invited up to the Berghof every day.

It was a Christmas that Frau Morell was unlikely ever to forget. "One day," she said, "when everybody was down in the bowling alley, Frau Hoffmann too, I went and sat down on the bench round the fireplace down there, and my husband was with me. All of a sudden, Hitler came and said, 'Can you spare a moment, Morell?'"

The two men strolled off into the conservatory. That evening was to be the turning point in Morell's life. "Bormann and Brandt came in," continued Frau Morell. "They'd evidently got wind of something, I said to myself afterward. They both hurried into the conservatory. But Hitler sent them out with a flea in their ear! And that's when he pinned my husband down!"

The arrangement was that Morell would take over Hitler's medical treatment. Hitler had stomach problems. None of his doctors seemed able to cure them. Probably they were largely hysterical in origin. Morell suspected it; in his diaries are several instances where episodes were associated with "major upsets." The specific reason why Hitler had decided to try a different doctor now was a severe attack of eczema. "I had eczema on both legs," he recalled eight years later. "It was so bad that I was covered in bandages and couldn't get my boots on even." The generous Führer promised the new internist that if his cure worked, he would give him a house.

Johanna Morell was unenthusiastic. She could guess what they had been talking about. Businesslike and temperamental as she was, she ran up to Theo when he returned to the bowling alley and hissed, "What do we need with that! Why come down here of all places! We've got a splendid practice in Berlin." But the temptations were too great for Morell.

Probably on the very next day he gave his new patient a complete checkup. Then he straightened up, adjusted his thick-lensed spectacles, and promised: "I'll have you healthy again in less than a year."

It was a bold promise, but he knew which cure he was going to try.

"I Was Never Ill"

ONE IS TEMPTED to say that until a few years before Adolf Hitler met Morell he had a superb constitution. He had had lung trouble as a child, but this disappeared in later years. So Morell told interrogators. There was a scar on Hitler's left thigh, the result of a World War I injury when he had performed hazardous missions as a runner in the front lines. Dr. Giesing wrote in November 1945, "He had an old, nonirritating bean-size oval-shaped deeply furrowed World War I scar (with its longitudinal axis running from bottom to top) above the middle of the exterior. Hitler was unable to tell me if there was still any shell splinter in it."

But that was all. When Morell once suggested it was time to draw up a medical history, Hitler turned him down. On March 31, 1945, the physician recorded the refusal in his diary. "I was never ill," Hitler had said. "So there's nothing to write up."

Morell was not easily fobbed off and reminded Hitler of how he had fallen heavily during the Munich putsch attempt in November 1923 and injured his left collarbone and upper arm —an injury of which he had only just learned. The arm had been paralyzed for some time, but by rigorous exercises Hitler had regained full use of it again. (He had fractured his left shoulder blade—scapula—in the inferior aspect of the glenoid cavity. Morell told interrogators in 1945 that in consequence the range of abduction and rotation of Hitler's upper left arm was limited for some years after that.) Hitler still insisted that there was nothing to write up—it was quite unimportant, and he had regained complete mobility of the arm.

Hitler regarded himself as normally healthy. When a serious

dysentery forced him into bed in the summer of 1941, he apologized for inconveniencing Morell. "The Führer sent word over by valet this morning," noted the doctor [Diary], "that he has never had a day in bed since being gassed in the World War, so he thinks he's a rotten patient." Other entries suggest a more turbulent picture of this patient's medical history. Morell wrote this on December 1, 1944, after injecting Hitler with the regular daily cocktail of glucose, Vitamultin and liver extract: "Says he always had his worst spasms after violent emotional upsets: the trial in 1924 (life-or-death); overdue bills of credit in 1929 (the *Völkischer Beobachter* newspaper and Eher Publishing Company); untrustworthiness of the military in 1935–1936; on top of this there was the dysbacteria, probably caused by the spasms. More spasms [on July 18] 1943 before his confrontation at Feltre with the Duce and the premonition, for that matter the knowledge, that the Italian army was about to betray them. And in 1944 after the assassination attempt."

Perhaps the 1924 episode was not as bad as the others, because when Morell listed them again on January 10, 1945, he omitted it. "Recently over tea with Frau Christian and Miss Schroeder," he wrote, "the Führer mentioned that he had really bad spasms for the first time in 1929." And on October 3, 1944, Morell again referred only to the later episodes: "I might further mention that the Führer—as he himself stated during this evening—has had such stomach spasms and gas buildups ever since 1929 as a result of the major upsets of that time. Then again he suffered violent spasms after taking capsules recommended by Brückner[1] over a long period (Dr. Grawitz[2] was able to establish the presence of methyl alcohol in the capsules). Since then he has had the spasms again and again after periods of major aggravation such as he has been having a lot of lately."

What did not help matters was that by 1936, when Morell came to him, Hitler was already an extreme and cranky vegetarian. He ate neither fish nor fowl nor meat, nor even eggs. He went so far as to attribute his extraordinary energy to this fad. But others pointed out that before he came to power he had

[1] SA-Gruppenführer Wilhelm Friedrich Brückner, born December 11, 1884, wartime comrade of Hitler and later his chief adjutant.
[2] Ernst Robert Grawitz, M D., born in Berlin on June 8, 1899. Chief surgeon of the SS. Specialist in internal medicine since 1929.

been even more active. Sources close to him have testified that his vegetarianism was of comparatively recent origin, perhaps 1931 or 1932. Secretary of Agriculture Richard Darré later tied Hitler's abstinence from meat and sudden conversion to vegetarianism to the suicide of his beloved niece Geli Raubal in his apartment in September 1931. "It may well be," Giesing conceded when Darré confided this to him in September 1945, "that he felt that he had to repress guilty sexual feelings." Hitler's housekeeper Anni Winter provided support for this belief. "He stopped eating meat after Geli Raubal's death," she told a German historian in 1952. "He used to enjoy fruit, vegetables and pastries. But when Professor Morell became his physician his eating and drinking habits really took a turn for the worse and became unhealthy and abnormal." Frau Winter went so far as to call Morell's influence demoniacal, saying he had slowly but systematically ruined Hitler's health; he had starved the Führer, and then kept him alive artificially with his injections and pills.

THE FIRST doctor to join Hitler's staff was not Morell but a young and unassuming surgeon, Karl Brandt. Brandt was handsome, slender and upright. Born in Mulhouse in the Alsace in 1904, he had studied surgery at Jena, Freiburg, Munich and Berlin before practicing his craft under the famous Professor Magnus in the surgical department of the mining hospital at Bochum. He had first set eyes on the Nazi leader in nearby Essen in the summer of 1932 and entered the Party a few weeks after they came to power. When Magnus was transferred to Berlin in the winter of 1933–34, he asked Brandt to join him in the surgical department of the university clinic there.

Brandt's fateful introduction into Hitler's service occurred indirectly. Hitler's onetime chauffeur, Emil Maurice, had seen a photograph of the good-looking German swimming champion Anni Rehborn while languishing in Landsberg fortress in 1924. He contacted her, and through Maurice she entered Hitler's orbit. When she then married Brandt, the surgeon was sucked into the Führer's wake as well. On August 15, 1933, Brandt was among his entourage as they motored through Bavaria. Near Reit-im-Winkel Hitler's adjutant, Brückner, was injured in a car accident. Brandt gave first aid, took Brückner to the hospital at Traunstein and operated on his fractured leg and skull immediately. Hitler decided it would be prudent to have a doctor with him on all his trips. When he went to Venice in the following year to meet Mussolini, Brandt flew with him.

As these trips multiplied, two more doctors were attached to the staff, both former assistants of Magnus: first, Dr. Werner Haase, and from 1936, Dr. Hanskarl von Hasselbach, who had known Brandt since their student years together and been fetched by him to the Bochum hospital in May 1933.

I T IS NOT without interest to learn that the Röhm Purge of June 1934—the Night of Long Knives—left its mark on Hitler's health. He told one specialist, Professor Carl von Eicken, that he had suffered from *tinnitus aurium,* a ringing in the ears, because of the "general worries" since that day.

But for years even before that he had been plagued by gastrointestinal pains. At first he had innocently dosed himself with a remarkable stuff going by the name of "Neo-Balestol." Balestol was a gun-cleaning oil used by soldiers in World War I. Word must have been passed round the trenches that it was good against stomach pains, and a sharp-eyed businessman had made up a similar oil and marketed it since the armistice under the trade name of Neo-Balestol. Professor Ernst-Günther Schenck, a top medical expert of the German armed forces in World War II, has told this author: "Evidently one of his old soldier comrades tipped off Hitler to take this for his stomach pains. But there was fusel oil in it, and this resulted in poisoning." Later, he says, Neo-Balestol was banned by the Reich health agency. From the medical records we know that immediately after dosing himself with it Hitler suffered headaches, double vision, dizziness and a ringing in the ears. In conversation with Eicken—the senior ear, nose and throat specialist of the famed Le Charité clinic in Berlin—he admitted that Dr. Grawitz had treated him over Christmas 1934 for acute poisoning brought on by this Neo-Balestol, "which," as Eicken also noted in his consultation notes, "contains fusel oil."

By the spring of 1935, at the time of the important negotiations on the Anglo-German naval agreement, Hitler became alarmed at a growing impediment in his throat. In some of his speeches there was an audible squeak, which was particularly unattractive in a demagogue like him. He himself feared a malignant growth. Eicken was again summoned to the Chancery on May 13 to investigate. He diagnosed the cause as a tiny polyp in the larynx, dangling on the right vocal chord. He proposed an operation to remove it, and that Hitler should come to the Charité for that purpose. Hitler insisted on having it done in the Chancery. "Herr Professor," he asked anxiously, "tell me—is it cancerous? Kaiser Friedrich was told, you know, and I must have time to look for a successor."

Ten years later Eicken, interrogated by British officers, recalled that Hitler had been generally alert and lively on this occasion. (How great was the difference when he saw him for the last time in 1944: "His movements and reactions, both physical and mental, had become slower," the professor said, "and he now trembled frequently.") The operation was performed on the Chancellor on May 23, 1935; Hitler, relieved, asked about the fee. The professor gestured dismissively and said: "It was an honor for me." Hitler retorted, "Be reasonable. You've got eight children!" He eventually endowed a foundation set up by Eicken with 200,000 Reichsmarks and enriched Eicken's personal account by a further 60,000 RM. A further lease on life was worth that and more to Hitler. As for Eicken, he jotted a brief account of this routine operation in his file: "Removed polyp with a noose after injecting 0.015 morphium, pantocain spray and daubing."

On the Obersalzberg in August 1935, Hitler contracted a severe cold with subsequent sore throat, causing him a lot of harrumphing and coughing. In the second week of August he again noticed the disturbing "foreign object" feeling in his pharynx. Again he sent for Eicken, who noted, "It occurs to the patient, when his attention is drawn to the symptomatology of the 'swallowed foreign object,' that a thorn got under a fingernail when he was handing over a bouquet and he pulled it out with his teeth and swallowed it, caused him a sharp pain when he swallowed it, but it did not bother him after that." Eicken investigated, and recorded the following: "Mucus matter on the tonsils. Acute pharyngitis. Daubed pharynx with two and a half percent silver nitrate."

Meantime he had sent the polyp he had removed from patient "Adolf Müller" to Professor R. Rössle, of the Pathological

Institute. Rössle sent him his report on August 21: "This was a so-called vocal chord polyp (papilloma). Its benevolence is certain. It has been completely removed, there are signs of chronic inflammation on it with minor hemorrhages and remains of such bleeding in the tissues, as are to be found almost always in such polyps."

DURING 1936 Hitler had further problems of a personal kind. While his political methods triumphed, and his reborn Wehrmacht had successfully remilitarized the Rhineland in March 1936—against the advice of his petrified generals—Hitler the man was not made of such stern stuff as the public believed. On May 16, his personal chauffeur Julius Schreck died after a painful illness, and the death affected Hitler badly. Four days later he again sent for the amiable ENT doctor, Professor von Eicken. Eicken wrote afterward, "He's had that buzzing in his ears again for several days, at night it sounds like a high-pitched metallic ringing in his left ear." Eicken could find nothing clinically wrong with either ear. Audibility was over six meters on both sides. He jotted down a few conclusions: "Obviously overworked. Worried (driver Schreck!). Can't get to sleep and then doesn't get much sleep either." The professor recommended: "Go for walks in the evening, take hot and cold foot baths, light sedatives! Take a break from work." Hitler's response was that his sleep was always better on the Obersalzberg than here in Berlin. He had his own explanation for this, as he told Dr. Giesing in July 1944: "I was born at an elevation of 1,300 feet, and I believe a man should live at the altitude he was born at."

The anger at the generals during the Rhineland crisis had aftereffects, evidently. That summer of 1936 Hitler was victimized by worsening stomach pains, often so agonizing that he could neither work by day, nor sleep by night. Hitler had enough insight to suspect their partly hysterical origin. He was in no doubt that the unreliability of his generals during the Rhineland operations lay behind these abdominal complications. On December 6, 1944, we find Morell recording in his diary Hitler's conviction that all his medical problems had been a consequence of "eleven years of vexation over these generals of the 20th of July."

MANY DOCTORS tried to cure the pains. Despite their often exalted Party ranks, they failed. Dr. Grawitz failed, and so did Professor Bergmann of the Charité. In fact the correct, austere, impeccable Bergmann proposed such a radical treatment that a white-faced Hitler fled the doctor's surgery. He was almost unable to eat. Under Dr. Grawitz's treatment he grew thinner and weaker. That was when Morell appeared on the scene over Christmas 1936 and made Hitler the bold promise: "I'll have you healthy again in less than a year."

"You can never know, doctor, how much I am indebted to Morell," Hitler explained pathetically to Dr. Giesing in 1944. "He saved my life in 1936. I was so far gone that I could scarcely walk. I was given totally wrong treatments. Grawitz and Bergmann too, they both had me starving. Finally I was just drinking tea and eating biscuits. Then came Morell, and he cured me."

Morell suspected that an abnormal bacterial flora of the intestinal tract was causing Hitler's stomach pains. He had done a lot of research on the problem. Intestinal bacteria were important for the active substances they produced and the way they prevented the destruction of other substances in the gastro-intestinal tract. His first step was to send a fecal specimen to Professor A. Nissle in Freiburg in Breisgau. Nissle, a scientist operating in something of a medical backwater in the bacteriological research institute there, had developed a particular strain of *bacillus coli communis* which displayed the useful property of colonizing the intestinal tract; the bacteriological division of the Hageda Pharmaceutical Company in Berlin had begun manufacturing this strain under the trade name "Mutaflor," packed in enteric soluble capsules. It is certainly no coincidence that it occurs in Morell's papers again and again. "Nissle had developed a theory," says Professor Schenck today, "that there are various endemic strains of coli bacilli in the body, some of which promote the digestion of foodstuffs, while others lead to harmful digestive processes. This was the basis of his Mutaflor. The assumption was that the coli strains in the Mutaflor were the beneficial ones, and they were administered in these capsules to overpower and replace the more harmful strains." It is, says Schenck, a controversial theory even today.

Nissle was definitely no charlatan. He had researched for ten years already into possible interrelations between intestinal dysbacteria and cancer. He had carried out Mutaflor trials on advanced cancer cases on the assumption that intestinal poisoning played a significant part in this disease. "Even though I cannot boast of any cures," he wrote subsequently to Morell, on August 5, 1941, "I did find it was possible to prolong the life of these quite hopeless cases and to make their disease at least bearable so that they could enjoy the *prospect* of recovery." When Nissle's critics prevented the publication of his cancer trials in 1933 he began to dose himself with Mutaflor as a means of personal cancer prophylaxis; the result was, he wrote, that he now felt fresh and able to defeat insomnia even after the worst upsets or aggravations. "Even if the only effect was to save a major part of the cancer victims from just inhumanly wasting away and to prolong some kind of tolerable existence, I can feel happy to have helped the human race," Nissle summarized.

What cannot be denied is that Morell's cure worked on Hitler. Nissle's Freiburg tests showed that there were indeed dysbacterial flora in Hitler's intestinal tract. Encouraged by this, Morell began dosing his new patient with the Mutaflor capsules, one or two daily after breakfast. "He gave me coli capsules," Hitler related afterward to Giesing. "And large quantities of vitamins and heart- and liver-extract." After six months Hitler was able to eat properly again, without getting those fearful stomach cramps. He regained his lost weight. "In six months the eczema was gone," said Hitler. "After nine months I was fit again."

As a reward the Morells were given VIP tickets to the Party rally at Nuremberg in September 1937. And in later years Hitler could only say, "That's what Morell said: one year!"

Hitler as Patient

MORELL'S appearance at the Berghof startled Hitler's other courtiers by its suddenness. They did not know whether to hustle him off their territory or to fawn upon him; and when they made up their mind it was too late. He stayed until almost the end as Hitler's court physician.

The Morells became frequent guests on the Obersalzberg. The doctor began his treatment of the dictator while his young wife went off with Eva and Gretl Braun to sun and swim in the lakes around Berchtesgaden. With the success of the cure Morell's future seemed assured. Hitler had promised a villa, but the Morells chose an expensive one on Peacock Island in Berlin's Schwanenwerder district—No. 24–26 Insel Strasse—and bought it on March 28, 1939, at a cost of 338,000 Reichsmarks. Hitler made him an interest-free loan of 200,000 Reichsmarks toward the purchase price and converted it into a gift two years later in lieu of the fees accruing up to then. Morell paid the balance from his own pocket.

Morell's methods were successful, and this medical success was as fateful in its way as Hitler's battlefield triumphs in 1940. Both men became convinced of their own golden touch. Morell doted on Hitler. Hitler in turn trusted him implicitly and turned a deaf ear on the envious rivals who warned against Morell's unorthodox methods.

From Frau Morell's pocket notebook we know that the couple returned to the Berghof for the New Year and stayed until January 3, 1937, together with Hitler's favorite architect, Albert Speer. It was probably now that Morell first formally examined Hitler. "At this time," he later told his interrogators, "he looked his age and was suffering from gastrointestinal disturbance. He weighed about 154 pounds and was about five foot seven inches tall. Temperature, pulse, and respiration were normal, and continued within normal limits for about eight years. His blood classification group was 'A' [Landsteiner]. . . . His psychic state was very complex."

Hitler's chest was pale white and normally sensitive to hot and cold, and to sharp and dull touch. "Hair was absent on both chest and back," Morell testified. "Breasts showed no hypertrophy or other pathology. Supraclavicular, suprasternal, clavicular, sternal, mammary, inframammary, scapular, interscapular, infrascapular, axillary, and infra-axillary regions [were] all found normal on examination. Shape of thorax was sthenic; circumference and diameters were not measured. No retraction or pulsation was observed."

Hitler was long-headed. The skull was slightly dolichocephalic (a term applied to skulls whose breadth is less than four-fifths their length). The hair was dark brown, almost black. The blue-gray eyes betrayed a minimal degree of exophthalmus (protrusion) and moved freely in all directions. The pupillary reflexes were normal, as were the conjunctiva, cornea and sclera. The nose was straight with a slight protuberance on the dorsum; its lower end was thick and fleshy, and the nostrils were rather prominent. The lips were red but rather thin. The teeth were defective and betrayed gingivitis in 1936, which Morell's vitamin C treatment and antiseptic mouthwashes soon cleared up. His tongue had been furred since 1935, a symptom of a gastric disturbance.

In short, the only objective abnormality that Morell detected was in Hitler's gastroenteric region. The abdomen was tender in the epigastric region and around the right kidney. Upon palpation, Morell informed his interrogators in 1945, the left lobe of the liver appeared enlarged and he detected tympanites—the presence of gas in the intestine, which causes the abdomen to ring with a drumlike note when tapped with the fingers—both there and in the umbilical region. When he palpated around the right kidney it caused pain.

None of the doctors who treated him reported any gross sexual abnormalities, although none of them seems to have examined him in detail. Professor Hanskarl von Hasselbach was to testify in 1951: "Hitler had an extreme disinclination to let people see his body. Even I never saw him completely unclothed, let alone checked him over in that state. Probably his former driver and manservant Emil Maurice could give some information as to whether the sex organs were deformed; he dropped hints when we were in captivity. . . . But Hitler's relationship with women manifested . . . a completely natural attitude." Hasselbach stated that Hitler's sex instinct was neither increased nor depressed, and he was neither a pervert nor a homosexual. The 1940 blood serology[1] and particularly the negative outcome of the Wassermann, Meinicke, and Kahn tests prove that he had not contracted syphilis at any time.

Morell evidently examined the lower abdomen in 1936, as he told American investigators that Hitler suffered pain in the region of the right kidney but "none in the regions of the bladder, prostate, testicles, epididymis, urethra or ureters." In fact he seems to have given him a thorough checkup. "There was no disturbance of vesical or rectal sphincter tone," he testified, "and no evidence of prostatic pathology or hemorrhoids." He described Hitler's secondary sexual characteristics as generally normally developed.

Yet it is worth noting that on September 30, 1944, Hitler, afflicted by painful hepatitis, refused to allow Morell to administer an urgently needed enema. "There's been no bowel evacuation for five hours now," recorded Morell irritably that day. "So he's in a lot of discomfort. . . . He flatly refused to allow me to administer an enema of oil or chamomile tea in bed, but on the contrary took an irrigator and tried to administer one to himself in the W.C., the patient sitting upon the toilet bowl for the purpose. I had to wait outside (in fact he even locked me out)." Professor Schenck comments, "This episode indicates that Hitler had a fixation about his intestine and the pain there—that is assuming that he was not suffering from hemorrhoids, which can't be ruled out given his largely sedentary life-style."

A similar shyness was shown on December 8, 1944, when Morell tried to persuade Hitler to allow the new staff doctor,

---

[1] Appendix No. I. Hitler's blood pressure incidentally was usually within normal limits: "Hitler could have passed U.S. pilot tests with these figures," one American medical expert, Major Cortez F. Enloe, told me in 1969.

Stumpfegger, to grope. "I told him," a huffy Morell recorded in his diary, "that Dr. Stumpfegger was waiting outside to inquire about his condition; could he come in and might he also palpate the Führer, so that *he* could see for himself how supple the abdomen was and how good everything looked. But the Führer said it was enough for me to confirm all that, and he did not want other people poking around. I replied that I would have preferred to get a second opinion on his condition from another doctor."

Hitler had liked the company of attractive women particularly during his rise to power, but Morell could see that in later years, with the increase in duties and responsbility, his libido was apparently sublimated. At one time he had been attracted to the beautiful young wife of Philip Bouhler; she lived near the Morells. And according to what the equally eye-catching Magda Goebbels confided to the wife of Otto Meissner, Hitler had even given her a son (Helmuth) in 1934; certainly the blood groups match. Hitler also showed a more than passing interest in the platinum blond wife of the Reich organization leader, Dr. Robert Ley, and was grief-stricken when she committed suicide during the war.

He showed normal jealousies too. When the most eligible bachelor on his staff, Walther Hewel, began dallying with the Führer's beautiful secretary Gerda Daranowski, he put his foot down. Hewel jotted in his diary for June 29, 1941, "Nasty aside by Führer about my employing Miss Daranowski." And again on the following day, "F. annoyed by my use of his ladies for dictation." Morell assured interrogators, though on what evidence we do not know, that Hitler sexually obliged Eva Braun from time to time, although they routinely slept in separate beds. His adjutants have said much the same to this author. As for the apparent deficiency in the male sex hormone (testis) detected in his blood in January 1940, modern experts feel that laboratories then were not capable of measuring this quantity accurately, so too much significance cannot be read into this evidence.

All the doctors considered Hitler neurologically healthy. Answering questions, they testified that he suffered no olfactory hallucinations or impairment of smell, there was no papillo-edema, no double vision, no convergent or divergent strabismus, no deviation of jaw and no motor disturbance of muscle or mastication. The taste sensations along his entire tongue were normal, and when Hitler stuck out his tongue Morell could detect no deviation, fibrillation or atrophy. His lacrimation and salivation were normal; he was able to wrinkle his forehead and shrug his shoulders normally. All these things seemed routine enough.

There was no dysphagia (difficulty in swallowing), and while pressure on an eyeball or on the caratoid sinus slowed the pulse, Morell admitted that he could not recall in which year he had last performed this uncomfortable test on his Führer. As for Hitler's motor area, there were no convulsions, paresis (slight or temporary paralysis), paralysis or aphasia (loss of power of speech) present; his premotor area was also without problem—there was no forced grasping or evident clumsiness. Reporting on Hitler's brain, the temporal area, Morell noted: "No auditory or visual hallucinations. No sensory aphasia. No dream states." It was the same through all the other tests—Patient Hitler's reflex centers and spinal root functions were all uncomplicated and above comment.

Questioned on Hitler's psychiatric data, Morell made these comments:

(a) orientation as to time, place and persons was excellent
(b) memory as to events, both recent and remote, was excellent
(c) immediate retention of figures, statistics, names, etc., was excellent
(d) Hitler's general background was characterized by his lack of university training, for which he had, however, compensated by acquiring a large body of general knowledge through reading
(e) judgment of time and spatial relations was excellent
(f) reaction to environment was normal
(g) he was changeable, at times restless and sometimes peculiar, but otherwise cooperative and not easily distracted
(h) emotionally very labile. Likes and dislikes were very pronounced
(i) flow of thought showed continuity. Speech was neither slow nor fast and was always relevant

(j) globus hystericus [a ball-in-the-throat sensation] was not observed. No amnesia. Epigastric pain may possibly have been of hysterical origin

(k) no phobias or obsessions

(l) no hallucinations, illusions or paranoid trends present.

HASSELBACH, who joined the staff in 1936, would describe Hitler in these early years as robust, ageless, healthy and well built. "Major physical exertions like the big parades were child's play for him," he said, but added: "But even then he had begun living unwisely as he never went to bed before two A.M., and often not until three or four, and got up again around ten. He occasionally took an afternoon nap when he was in the teahouse for five minutes or so." Even this is not quite accurate, because from the diary of orderly Max Wünsche we notice that in June 1938 Hitler would sleep fourteen, eight, ten, and thirteen hours on successive days.

To Hasselbach Hitler complained of having a weak heart. He avoided going up to the Kehlstein House above the Berghof; it was 6,000 feet up, and he said he felt a tightening of the chest there. Hasselbach concluded that these symptoms like the epigastric pains and cramps were of hysterical origin. "During the war," continued Hasselbach, "he dropped his habit of going for half an hour's walk, and he often did not get any fresh air for days or weeks on end. His temperament also underwent a change. In 1936–38 he could still laugh out loud and often did. He was a good-natured man. The stories of his violent tantrums are hugely exaggerated, even for later years. I often had to admire how much he had himself under control, even when he had to face grave decisions or receive unpleasant news."

This strength did not desert him until the end. One of the stenographers who attended Hitler's daily war conferences wrote of the undeniable impression Hitler made on his colleagues: "He appeared a man of indefatigable diligence, scarcely granting himself any respite by day or by night—a man of vast knowledge and experience, gifted with a convincing oratory, while still capable of showing great modesty and kindness toward his associates and collaborators, and understanding for the work of us stenographers."

THE FRIENDSHIP between the two men, Führer and personal physician, deepened.

Hitler liked Morell's company. He sometimes turned up for Sunday tea with the Morells. He liked to wander around their garden and sit at their fireside—he called it the bakehouse, because they baked almond cakes just the way he liked them. (In May 1940 Morell would write from headquarters in France to his wife, "Can you send the Führer one of those almond cakes again? He likes it a lot—said only a few days ago it was the world's finest.") Once Hitler showed up unexpectedly for dinner. A distracted Frau Morell ran around in the kitchen crying: "What on earth can we give him!" They gave him spaghetti and catsup, rounded off with cheese. It occurred to Hitler that cheese was rationed, and he turned to Julius Schaub and commanded: "Give them the coupons!" That, said Frau Morell, was how he was.

Morell was much sought after as a doctor now. Among his papers are consultation notes on the big industrialists like Alfried Krupp and August Thyssen—after Thyssen's death Morell submitted an account for 20,000 Reichsmarks to the estate—and aristocrats like Prince Phillip of Hesse. Hitler's military adjutants were Morell's patients. When Rudolf Hess flew to Scotland in May 1941, he had Morell's patent medicines with him. (Frau Morell later said: "I know that for certain—he had an entire packet of those Vitamultin fortifying tablets . . . we gave them to him for the journey. I never told anybody, but there's no harm in saying it now.")

Reichsmarschall Hermann Göring called Morell the "Meister-Jabber" but rolled up his shirtsleeves for him all the same. Foreign Minister Joachim von Ribbentrop, Economics Minister Walther Funk, Dr. Robert Ley, Alfred Rosenberg, Joseph Goebbels, Gauleiter Erich Koch, Hitler's two top architects Albert Speer and Hermann Giesler—they all crowded into Morell's waiting room, with a host of other gauleiters, Party officials and Wehrmacht generals and of course the leading stars of the stage and screen, while the custom of leading film directors like Leni Riefenstahl went without saying.

Foreign statesmen and diplomats were treated by Morell. Neville Chamberlain was treated for flu in September 1938. The Czech president Emil Hacha inquired about the contents of the miracle injection Morell gave him late on March 15, 1939, when he suddenly fainted in a conference with Hitler. Later, the sick Benito Mussolini was treated by Morell's proxy, Dr. Zachariae, who wrote to Morell on December 3, 1944, full of praise for the Mutaflor treatment ("How right you were with your opinion that the coli flora in the intestine play a major part in everyday digestive processes; I have been able to observe this for myself with several cases here"). Marshal Ion Antonescu sampled Vitamultin, liked it and asked for more. The stout little Japanese ambassador, General Hiroshi Oshima, presented a Samurai helmet to Morell.

All declared themselves satisfied. Luftwaffe general Karl Bodenschatz would write as late as October 1950: "Professor Morell lived very modestly and labored tirelessly on his scientific studies. From my own observations, he was a serious, successful researcher. As a doctor he enjoyed the complete confidence of his patients. I myself was treated by him twice, for influenza and rheumatism." Hitler's Luftwaffe adjutant Nicolaus von Below expressed himself satisfied with the doctor while admitting that he could see why others did not like him. True, some of the more fastidious patients had to steel themselves as Morell's needle approached, wiped on a rag that had wiped countless needles before. And Below felt that Morell was too servile. But when he reproached him in 1944 for allowing Hitler to stuff himself with pills, the doctor retorted: "I'd like to see you treat a patient like the Führer!"

THE PHOTOGRAPHS taken by Hoffmann during the first months of the war show Morell ever at Hitler's side with the other headquarters officers like Erwin Rommel. But he did not like the life of camp follower. He missed his wife and sent her frequent postcards, for instance from Danzig in September 1939. She was an actress with the lead role in a play that was just opening in Würzburg. She wrote back to him on September 29, a bit cross because he had also sent postcards to other ladies at the same time as her. "I had a nice dream about you the other night," she wrote. "Unfortunately only a dream."

Morell took his job seriously. On January 9, 1940, he prepared a series of test samples in the Reich Chancery and made an electrocardiogram as well. He jotted notes on his pad: "Pa-

tient A"—that is, Hitler: "Pulse 72. Blood pressure 172/100
(aged fifty). Second aortic sound today only weakly accentuated. Blood group: A. . . . Blood sedimentation. Blood serology. Blood sugar. Interferometry—Schmidt-Burbach. Vitamins B and C and Cortiron trial (Nordmark Works)."

The detailed reports on these tests showed little out of the
normal. The medical diagnostic institute of Dr. A. Schmidt-
Burbach in Berlin examined to what degree each of the glandular secretions in the blood sample was affected by catabolic
fermentation; the institute reported "slightly discordant reduc-
tions in . . . the sexual hormone values; the values for the
thyroid and pituitary glands, pars post, are also slightly low."
In detail the values recorded by this laboratory's somewhat im-
precise methods were: pituitary, pars post, twelve units (normal
value seventeen); thyroid, fourteen (normal nineteen); testis
♂ nine units (normal twenty). Morell penciled notes on the
hormone medication he was contemplating: "Orchikrin, pituitary from Merck, thyroid."

The urinalysis established, as stated, that Hitler had never
contracted syphilis. A microscopic examination of the fecal
sample by Nissle on January 18, 1940, yielded "an entirely
normal picture, only vegetable fibers being observed." A throat
smear tested on January 23 showed no trace of diphtheria
bacilli.

I N APRIL 1940, the German troops fell upon Denmark and Nor-
way. One month later the Wehrmacht rolled into Holland,
Belgium and Luxembourg. Morell stayed at his patient's side as
the headquarters was moved to the west for the next big push.

In a circle where the comradeship was intense, the fat
doctor found himself something of an outcast. He was older
than most of them. His letters home bristle with references to
his unpleasant and indeed embattled position. He was himself
partly to blame. He had decked himself out in a gray Hollywood-
style fantasy uniform which he had designed for himself, laden
with gold braid, but this made even more enemies. In 1940 he
had to instruct Johanna in a letter, "Have a gold buckle stitched
into the heavy belt like the buckle for political officers. Apparently there are objections to my using the SS buckle." And with
a trace of envy he commented on Hitler's escort doctor, Karl

Brandt, "Dr. B has his army lieutenant-colonel's shoulder straps up, as of today."

The unkindest cut was when Hitler's special photographer Heinrich Hoffmann began cold-shouldering him. He spluttered with fury at "Heini's" unfeeling attitude; worse, the photographer was seen with increasing frequency in Brandt's company. The rage lingered on in the words of his widow talking to a journalist in June 1967: "That was so typical of Brandt and the rest of that gang! And Dr. von Hasselbach too—they were all fine and young and elegant, and they had their dashing SS uniforms. And there was my husband with his gray outfit, and before that the brown one. That was all he had. . . . He didn't have any Party rank."

Morell wrote to her, on paper headed in his handwriting, "General Headquarters, May 13," three days after Hitler launched his armies westward, a letter that unloaded all his unhappiness over Brandt and Hoffmann: "I've got to share a room with Heini. Today he's off somewhere with Dr. B. Let's see how long I can put up with Heini." Three days later he wrote her again. "Quite a pleasant afternoon," he wrote. "Because Heini's away for four days and I went to see him off at the railroad station."

It appears to have irritated Morell that Hoffmann could still rake in money as official photographer, while his own medical practice was going to seed in his absence from Berlin. There was no doubt of Morell's business ambitions, although his acumen was more open to question. Since 1935 he had been half owner of Hamma Inc. in Hamburg, a subsidiary of the Nordmark Pharmaceutical Company. During the war he would become sole owner. He was also a member of the Hageda board (manufacturers of Mutaflor) and of the Chinoin company in Budapest—a company still existing today, but which at that time was turning out an inferior sulphonamide drug much used by Morell under the brand name Ultraseptyl. Morell had also negotiated with Walter Haupt—who had good contacts with the Hungarian business scene and was part owner of a big company in Berlin; with him he set up Walter Haupt & Co., bought an empty factory at Kosolup in the recently "liberated" Sudeten territories, and founded there the Kosolup Dye Company Inc.

He was disarmingly frank about his motives. Writing to

Johanna on June 3, 1940, about his manufacturing plans he explained: "Heini . . . wants a cut of everything and just can't understand why somebody else should earn money without his also getting a share for doing absolutely nothing at all. . . . If only our chemical projects get off the ground! . . . After all, I'll soon be fifty-four. The Heringsdorf villas are not paying, and we can only keep up Schwanenwerder if my income stays large, so I must either earn a lot as a doctor (although my energy is already flagging) or get some kind of income from chemicals and pharmaceuticals."

He watched every penny. In May 1940 he wrote to her, "I get twenty percent off at the Kurfürstendamm pharmacy, but you mustn't let the Fontane pharmacy know that. And the Wittenberg pharmacy also gives me fifteen percent (or is it even twenty?). Ten percent off at Fontane's is too little." He was obsessed with money and toward the end of his life, writing to her from the American camp at Dachau, he belatedly admitted it.

"I shouldn't have been so preoccupied with work," he wrote her. "I should have found more time for you. But I wanted to build a carefree future for us as fast as possible. And now I've done just the reverse!"

His unvarnished mercenary interests won no friends for him at headquarters. Luftwaffe adjutant von Below wrote to him, formally refusing payment for the medical treatment that Morell rendered the adjutants. Disappointed, Morell forwarded the letter to his wife commenting, "Here's the letter from von Below, who's evidently spoken with Brückner. So I'm not to receive any fees for treating the escort unit or the adjutant staff."

Dr. Brandt concluded one unflattering description of Morell with the stinging condemnation that bad as it was, it was still far too good for him. "He was a businessman, not a doctor," wrote Brandt, "very greedy and very stingy. He treated his subordinates wretchedly. . . . Morell once came to me and offered to send patients to operate on. I was then to return the patients to Morell for postoperational treatment. It was a business deal, pure and simple. I turned it down."

Outcast

HITLER'S WESTERN campaign approached its victorious conclusion. Morell wrote on May 16, 1940, to his wife: "The lilac is wonderful, and trees are in full bloom everywhere. . . . I visited some friends and had a fantastic meal of gull's eggs and lox. What a view and what sunshine!—At night we get a bit of enlivenment from the air, and there have been quite a few thumps nearby. What I'd really like is to go to the front. . . . Pity the Volhynians [household help] had to go. You'll find it difficult to get along without them. Should I ask General Keitel for some Poles?"

Morell also mentioned his business interests, and particularly the mass production of his multivitamin tablets for the armed services. "Shouldn't we approach the Army again about Vitamultin? . . . It's doing wonders here. Everybody speaks highly of it, and they're all recommending it to their families back home."

In Flanders the French troops were being marched off into captivity. The British escaped at Dunkirk. On May 26 Morell wrote to Johanna again, still annoyed at the pettiness of Hoffmann and Brandt. "Spent yesterday evening with Heini at the Dreesen's—that is, Frau D was allegedly visiting relatives. Herr D[1] always lays a fine table and won't hear of taking any payment afterward. . . . Heini often goes over there with Dr. B, but he takes care I don't find out or can't go. Can't say he's very forthright, and he's always making fun of me. From time to time I have to give him quite a rap on his knuckles. Dr. B is

[1] Owner of the Rhine Hotel Dreesen at Bad Godesberg.

making friends on every side, at present even with Hewel,[2] and is wooing Bodenschatz whom he sent to a not very distant hospital for shortwave treatment. . . . He's already been over there with Heini to have drinks with the doctors. Yesterday I found out that he has sent Hewel to an ear specialist, a professor in Bonn (but again nobody tells me anything about it). . . . There's hardly anything for a doctor to do around here. I asked the Führer a few days back if he's got any complaints. He said he feels fine apart from one thing: he still has an appetite that's far too large.—He really is getting along famously. He's fresh and lively."

Morell basked in Hitler's radiated glory, and exploited it to the full in his dealings with lesser authority. As in wartime Britain, petty local officials sometimes used scrap iron collections to get even with the rich and powerful. On May 28 Morell learned that the wrought-iron fence around his Schwanenwerder property was to be requisitioned for scrap. He angrily wrote to Johanna, "As far as that iron fence is concerned, evidently Herr Berg has not noticed that it is made of hand-wrought iron. So requisitioning it is out of the question. Anyway, thanks to our invasion of Holland and Belgium we've got so much iron and copper and tin that there'll surely be no more collections.—Besides, has Herr Berg already been over to ask Grand Admiral Raeder [commander in chief of the navy]? Because that fence around the old Bleischröder property is also iron." Then he sprinkled the familiar droplets of jealousy. "How wonderfully peaceful things are," he wrote, "when Heini Hoffmann isn't around and the constant nagging and bitching stops. He's the villain of every mealtime conversation!"

Fortunately Hitler now moved to a new headquarters. It was hutted encampment in Belgium, and Morell was given a room to himself. "Bouhler's[3] adjutant has survived even though his plane crashed in flames," he wrote to Johanna. "He's in the hospital at Maastricht where Werlin's[4] oldest son is, with his left arm amputated. Dr. Brandt has visited them both (again

[2] Walther Hewel, Ribbentrop's permanent liaison officer at Hitler's headquarters, one of Morell's few friends.

[3] Reichsleiter Philip Bouhler, head of the "Chancery of the Führer," committed suicide in May 1945, as he was heavily implicated in the euthanasia and other extermination programs.

[4] Jacob Werlin, general manager of Daimler-Benz.

without my knowledge). . . . Hanke[5] came here the day before yesterday. He seems to be a very brave soldier, he's right out in front everywhere he goes; he's adjutant to Rommel and that's just about the pushiest general we've got, always riding the lead tank of his division!—General Keitel's[6] always pretty decent to me."

On June 1, Hitler entered Brussels. He took his doctor with him. "We were on the road for two days," Morell reported: "Brussels, the Flanders battlefields (Ypres, Loretto, Vimy Ridge, Bensheim, Kortrik and Lille). As these districts were about the most densely populated on earth you can just imagine the devastation. A big square in Lille, piled high with charred tree trunks and automobiles, was littered with dead horses, burned-out tanks and buildings. On the roads along which the British and French retreated there was a higgledy-piggledy tangle of cast-off clothing, abandoned guns, and broken-down tanks, with stragglers streaming back home on both sides of the road, mostly on bicycles, laden with whatever they can carry."

His own position in Hitler's pecking order was evidently of scarcely less importance to Morell than the war itself. On June 3 he poured out his heart yet again to his wife: "Heini's behaving very badly, as he has been all along. Yesterday evening I wanted to go out for a drive and asked him if he'd like to go with me. He said, 'No, and if I do go out it will be with Schaub[7] as I've arranged to go with him.' He didn't go out. In the evening the Führer turned in early, and while Heini was in my room with me an orderly came in carrying a bottle of champagne and three glasses. H[offmann] was rather embarrassed and said, 'No, not in here, take them into Dr. Brandt's room!' It's the same story all the time here. And he keeps trying to make me look ridiculous. But now he knows I've taken all I can stand and next time I'm going to boil over.—Just now he has driven off with Schaub, I think they've gone to the Rhine.—Dr. B went

---

[5] Karl Hanke, gauleiter of Breslau and state-secretary in the propaganda ministry; on November 25, 1944, he married Freda Baroness von Fircks under questionable circumstances (a prenuptial child); was beaten to death in May 1945 in Prague.

[6] Colonel-General, later Field Marshal Wilhelm Keitel, born September 22, 1882, executed at Nuremberg in 1946. The rather supine chief of the Wehrmacht High Command since February 1938.

[7] Julius Schaub, chief adjutant and longtime intimate of Hitler.

off an hour before them.—Whenever there's a picture with me in it, he always finds some fault with it."

What did not help matters was that the photographer talked in his sleep and that these nocturnal Tales of Hoffmann often touched on Morell's sensitive point—his little pharmaceutical empire. "Recently he talked about Dr. B, and said B has spoken with the doctor who has received our Vitamultin to carry out field trials and this man says he's not at all satisfied with it. Afterward he claimed not to know anything about it. On another occasion he was talking about a vitamin-calcium that Dr. B was having manufactured by a company to speed up bone repairs. Apparently he's working with the Henning company in Berlin. . . . In these new quarters we've got separate rooms, thank goodness. As all the other gentlemen have a lot less spare time I'm always by myself. It often seems to me that H goes round everywhere stirring things up against me (and of course he always does it in the most cunning ways). Hewel, who has so much to thank me for, is now as thick as thieves with Dr. B. I'm on very good terms with the pilots like Bauer, Butz and Co. and with the drivers and detectives. But since Hewel and Lorenz[8] are now always eating with the Führer I no longer get invited up so often. There's a lot of pressure on the one remaining place. Often I find out what time they're lunching up there so late that we hardly get anything to eat. If it was not for the Führer, I'd often be glad to be home. . . . Wünsche[9] was here this afternoon; he's got a wound stripe, and the Iron Cross first and second class. It's one A.M. now. Heini's still not back. As SS-Gruppenführer Wolff and General Bodenschatz[10] are asleep next door I can't use the telephone any more."

By the end of the French campaign Morell was virtually out in the cold. When the staff went off on trips they took care he did not find out. "I was hoping to go to Brussels in Dr. Dietrich's

[8] Heinz Lorenz, born August 7, 1913 in Schwerin, was the German Press Agency's representative at Hitler's headquarters until 1945.

[9] SS-Hauptsturmführer Max Wünsche, born April 20, 1914 at Löbau, had been commander of the guard in the Reich Chancery. He was captured by the British in June 1944 in Normandy while fighting in the 12th SS Panzer-Division "Hitler Jugend." Hitler tried to get the British to repatriate him early in an exchange, but it would be 1948 before he returned to Germany.

[10] Major General Karl Bodenschatz, born December 10, 1880 in Upper Franconia. Göring's liaison officer to Hitler.

car," wrote Morell, probably on June 24. "But as they left it until half an hour before they left to tell me I couldn't make it. Speer, Giesler and Breker[11] are here. Speer and Breker are almost always with Dr. B, even on short motor trips. For me there was never a car available. H.H. [Heinrich Hoffmann] is still behaving badly. He's just an old intriguer who doesn't feel right unless he's being insolent and making trouble. He's drunk almost every evening. . . . Yesterday, Sunday, we went to Paris. As the war with France is all but over now, I don't think that [Aloys] B[ecker] will be drafted."

After the fighting stopped, Hitler moved camp again. His new headquarters was up in the Black Forest near Freudenstadt. Morell described it as being in wonderful mountain air with good accommodations and excellent food. "I'm sharing with Heini. As I go for an hour's work every day now, I like to put on long trousers and shoes. . . . How beautiful it must be out in Schwanenwerder now! Our troops are making wonderful progress with hardly any casualties. Today Saturday morning I spent about half an hour alone with the Führer, who's in magnificent health. This aromatic air does wonders for him too. He says he slept longer and better last night than almost ever before."

As we now know, it was in these very days that Hitler took his irrevocable "Barbarossa" decision to launch his armies into the Soviet Union in the coming year.

---

[11] Professor Hermann Giesler, architect and Inspector-General for the Reconstruction of Munich; and Arno Breker, noted sculptor.

Worried Sick

MORELL HIMSELF had suffered his first cardiac episode in 1939 or 1940. His wife would describe it later: "We had been invited to dinner in Wannsee with the Essers, in Berlin. . . . We were in high spirits. Esser cracked a joke, and my husband suddenly stood up and tipped over. He fell on some furniture and hit his head badly. He took to his bed and had an application of leeches. But there was no way he would put his own health before Hitler's."

Their married relationship was evidently one-way. On December 13, 1940, she wrote to her "darling Theokins" from Munich: "It's after eight P.M. now, and I wonder what you're up to? On the way home to Berlin? I've been waiting for your call so much, I'm feeling very lonely, and it makes such a difference if you've got somebody nice with you and you can tell him what's on your heart. Hoffmann telephoned me today; he wants us all to get together next week for a gossip. He couldn't get over to the theater yesterday, unfortunately, as he had so much to do. Perhaps he'll get round to seeing me onstage in January. . . . I've got to sleep alone again tonight and can't snuggle up to you, but it's probably just as well, because then I can put all that longing and desire into my stage performance."

Morell did not write letters as affectionate as that. That winter of 1940–41 his biggest problem was Hitler's refusal to relax even now, in the relatively calm period of planning before Barbarossa. Hitler was obsessed by the idea that he did not have long to live. His naval staff officer, Captain Heinz Assmann, would write, "It is a central factor in the consideration of Hitler's career that he worried constantly over whether he would live to see all his plans put into effect. As a result he was always working under terrific pressure. In my view this did not derive from any private knowledge of some illness or other, but from the realization of the sheer magnitude of the peacetime plans which he regarded as his real mission in future. These included his colossal and all-embracing plans for architectural reconstruction, social welfare, workers' housing, recreational and cultural centers, ports and dockyards, bridges and highways."

Morell's task was to keep this human dynamo alive. For the time being he delegated that job to Professor Nissle's little Mutaflor capsules. That December (1940) he carried out further tests on Hitler, and on December 28 Nissle sent him his findings on the latest fecal analysis. "I'm glad to see," he commented in an accompanying letter, "that the coli bacilli have this time remained typical, in contrast to the last control tests we made, and that no disruptive subsidiary bacilli have turned up. Nevertheless I would be glad if, on account of the shortcomings set out in my report, you would influence your patient, despite the otherwise satisfactory results, to prolong the Mutaflor course for as long as this particular work overload continues. . . . I'm convinced that the patient will find the load easier to carry then, as I know from tests carried out on my own person under fundamentally similar conditions."

The test report stated in detail: "Remarkably sparse growth. Cultures of typical coli bacteria are only moderate in number, and of these only a minority show any extensive identity with the Mutaflor strain. No other germs or worm eggs present."

It is a satisfactory result inasmuch as only coli bacteria were encountered [the report continued]. The fact that these, which are certainly a derivative of the colonizing Mutaflor bacilli, are losing some of their properties during the time they adhere to and pass through the intestine indicates, as does the relatively bacteria-free quality of the fecal sample, that there is some factor operative, capable of inhibiting the normal colonization process of the Mutaflor strain to a certain degree. The most probable such factor is the patient's current work overload. It is therefore advisable, despite the satisfactory composition of the intestinal flora, to continue with the Mutaflor course. (Signed) Nissle.

SOON AFTER Barbarossa began, in June 1941, there was medical
reason to believe that Hitler's life might indeed be entering its
final years. In mid-summer Morell detected a progressive ailment
in his patient's heart, coronary sclerosis. This was nothing un-
usual in a man of fifty-two. Lenin had it at the same age. Morell
explained to his interrogators in 1945: "Percussion disclosed
moderate enlargement of the left ventricle with displacement
of the heart apex to the left of the midclavicular line, though
still within the fifth intercostal space. Under auscultation accentuation of the second aortic sound was heard in second
intercostal space in the right parasternal line."

He took routine electrocardiograms on August 14, 1941, but
this time sent them to Professor A. Weber, director of a university institute in Bad Nauheim. Weber diagnosed a rapidly
progressive coronary sclerosis.[1] Significantly, Morell asked
Weber to supply two letters—one of which would not disclose
the full truth but be suitable for showing to the patient.

Morell kept the finding a secret at first. When Reich Foreign
Minister Joachim von Ribbentrop expressed the view that Hitler
must take more strenuous exercise (Morell diary, June 1943)
the doctor disagreed without however explaining why. For his
own files he noted that he had no right to discuss the cardiological findings with others.

RIBBENTROP: "Why, he's got nothing wrong with his heart, has
he? Or are you thinking of the spasms and circulatory
problems?"
MORELL: "Yes."
RIBBENTROP: "But the Führer should not always *drive* to the teahouse and back. He ought at least to make the return trip,
with its hills, on foot."
MORELL: "You'll have to tell the Führer that."

Some medical episode must have befallen Hitler at the end of
1941. Morell mentioned it in veiled language when talking with
Hitler a year later. "I referred to the episode a year ago (when
his blood press was right up to 200 mm)," wrote Morell; so it
must have been during the army's winter crisis outside Moscow.
Morell also referred, as he subsequently entered in his record of
the conversation, to a second episode during which Hitler had

[1] Appendix No. I.

contracted a kind of influenza (a "brain fever") during an inspection trip to Vinnitsa in the Ukraine. "Brain edema with impairment of vision in right eye and high blood pressure (over 170 mm)," was how Morell recorded it later. That was a reference to Hitler's illness late in July 1942 (see the Morell Diary).

Precisely what happened in the December 1941 episode we still cannot say. Seeking to establish his own indispensability, Morell reminded Hitler of it on December 17, 1942, and recalled how he had refused to consult anybody else "because I said to myself: nobody can do better than me anyway and somebody else might make a botch-up over it. I preferred to take the entire responsibility even though it was tough at the time. I also reminded him of that brain edema at V., and said that—if some improvement had not occurred within twenty-four hours—I would have had to resort to some pretty intensive methods."

Hitler assured the physician once again that he trusted him implicitly, but this time, in December 1942, he insisted on being told the unvarnished truth about his health. The response was not what he expected. Now—as though Hitler did not have enough on his plate with the horrendous Stalingrad crisis— Morell disclosed to him the heart defect discovered in August 1941. "When he told me," noted Morell later that day, "that he always wanted to be told the whole truth about his condition, I referred to the existence of a coronary sclerosis and said this is why I've been giving him iodine for some time now. Subsequent electrocardiograms have confirmed my suspicion, I said. In many people this calcification occurs somewhat faster as a result of intensive hard work, but it usually starts at around forty-five. I added that as the blood vessels of the coronary artery narrow, he may get attacks of angina pectoris. I always have medicine for that at hand, but so must he—in case I am not available—and I left him some nitroglycerine tablets. . . . By the glucose injections, I said, I am doing what I can to strengthen his heart and also to dehydrate the system." (Diary, December 17, 1942.)

From Morell's notes we see that Hitler sent for him that evening to ask about Cardiazol, a heart medicine manufactured by Knoll of Ludwigshafen. He said that Göring had told him he took a tablet of it whenever he felt weak or dizzy. "Wouldn't it do him, the Führer, good too, if he suddenly felt a bit odd during some vital affair?"

Morell advised against it, "Because what Göring has is *low* blood pressure (i.e., his head gets too little blood supply) while he, the Führer, is suffering from too much blood when his temper rises, that is from high blood pressure." This being so, said Morell, if Hitler took a Cardiazol tablet and his blood pressure then went up he might burst a blood vessel. (Notwithstanding this, Morell did then begin prescribing Cardiazol to Hitler.)

The doctor did note one explicit instruction from Hitler on this occasion. "The Führer asked me," he wrote, "to tell him if things should ever look really black for him, as there are some vital decisions he has to take on Germany's account. He says he has no fear of death; that will just be a relief for him. All he has now is just one worry after another and no time that he can call his own. He says he lives only for the fatherland, for Germany." Continued Morell, quoting Hitler: "There is no cure for death, that he knows. But if he should ever fall terminally ill, then I must tell him."

DURING 1943 Hitler's health slipped. Undoubtedly, the military defeats at Stalingrad and in North Africa accelerated the decline. Early in 1943, Morell first noticed a slight tremor in Hitler's left arm and leg, and saw him perceptibly dragging the left leg. He reached for his textbooks, but there was no easy solution. In his diary for December 6, 1944, Morell summarized the history of these trembling fits like this: "At the end of May 1943 the blood sedimentation rate was right down to 2.5 mm. Before the visit to the Duce at Feltre around July 20, 1943, there was a massive attack that began in the Wolf's Lair and continued the next day down at the Berghof. The next attack was a big one, the worst of the lot, after a showdown with the Luftwaffe on or about September 28, 1944, preceded by a number of trembling fits beginning with July 20, 1944."

Morell told his interrogators that the tremor might have been of hysterical nature, but he could not exclude the possibility that it had its origin in the influenza or "brain fever" contracted at Vinnitsa.

He began to step up his own patent medication of Hitler.

On March 14, 1944, he injected Hitler for the first time with shots of his patent multivitamin cocktail, Vitamultin-forte. He assiduously registered that he did so "because of tiredness and lack of necessary vitality." He noted, "Reaction moderate." Before the injection Hitler had complained of lack of sleep and exhaustion. Afterward, however, he was "instantly alert," and able to survive a two-hour conference with the tedious foreign minister, von Ribbentrop. Over dinner he was "noticeably lively" as compared with lunchtime. He stayed up until one A.M. and was then able to get to sleep without any sedatives. "Führer extremely content," Morell jotted down. And if Hitler was happy that was good enough for him.

But those troublesome tremors would not go away entirely. On May 9, 1944, Morell noticed a pronounced tremble in Hitler's legs and commented in his papers that this was "probably caused by worry (over the invasion that is imminent: where?)" —probably the biggest triumph of the top secret Anglo-American *Fortitude* deception strategy, which was designed to make the Nazi High Command believe that D day was scheduled as early as mid-May. Morell's remedy was to inject Hitler that day with intravenous shots of glucose and iodine, and with intramuscular shots of the male sex hormone Testoviron, and of his multivitamin product and liver extract.

It took the bomb attempt on Hitler's life on July 20 to kill the tremor, even if only for a few weeks. Hitler sensed, incidentally, that something evil was about to happen. He would tell the physician (Diary, November 9) that when he left the Berghof a few days before the bomb blast he had a premonition that he would soon be in grave danger. "He said he also told E[va Braun] this when he said good-bye to her . . . and had made his dispositions accordingly." The most significant consequence, as noted, was that his left leg stopped trembling and even his hand tremor almost completely vanished after that shock. Reflecting on these nervous problems, Morell expressed the conviction that they were the consequence of a "trauma to the convolutions on the right side of the brain, since such symptoms increase in frequency with worry."

To outward appearances, the bomb left Hitler unscathed. But he had suffered considerable damage. In a special memorandum, Morell wrote early in October 1944 Hitler's comments on it. "He says that the weeks since July 20 have been the worst of his life. He has fought and won a heroic struggle the likes of which nobody, no German, can ever imagine. Despite the most agonizing pains, and despite hours of faintness and nausea of which he's never breathed a word to anybody even when they inquire, he has kept a stiff upper lip and fought it all back with iron determination and energy. Often, he says, he has been in danger of crumpling, but by sheer willpower he has always managed to overcome his condition."

Morell's own health was not improving. Early in 1942 he had, as he wrote in one letter, "a big row causing . . . a frontal hemorrhage which however rapidly got better." Since then however his lesser muscles wearied easily, and later in 1942 his heart was causing serious problems, as he wrote two years afterward to Professor Weber: "I had my first serious attack of angina pectoris after a miserable airplane flight, with a T_{II} that stayed strongly negative for some time, and then later regulated again. The QRS opening is gradually getting bigger." Early in May 1944 he fell ill for a few days and had to summon his assistant, Dr. Richard Weber, from Berlin, and in July or August 1944 he had a further minor heart attack.

The escort doctors, Brandt and Hasselbach, heartlessly exploited his indisposition to assail his standing with Hitler. Envy was a powerful motive. Although Hasselbach had been in Hitler's entourage on and off since 1936, he had only been summoned once by the Führer and that was after the bomb emergency of July 20, 1944. Brandt had attended him more often, but their envy of Morell, who visited Hitler almost every day, was understandable. Other doctors willingly backed the growing campaign against Morell. In 1943 a leading Munich doctor visited the Reich health chief, Dr. Leonardo Conti, and urged him to oppose Morell's treatment methods and above all the wholesale use of injections, since clinical experience gathered in Munich hospitals indicated that the prolonged administering of injections was harmful, possibly even fatal.

The notion that Morell was doing pioneer research in theoretical medicine was met with mocking laughter by the experts. How, they asked, could Hitler's doctor find the time necessary to keep up to date with the latest advances, let alone conduct meaningful research? The campaign against him plumbed quite low depths. In January 1944 Morell scribbled down some of the more disrespectful remarks to bring to the attention of the Army's Chief Inspector of Health:

That good ol' house doctor who's just carted around, more out of kindness than anything else, until he can be put out to grass.— They give him this and that for his factories from time to time. Becker—the Squire of Schwanenwerder—B's not a chemist at all. . . . I [Morell] was made a laughingstock both as to my medicine, my business and my family.

But all this whispering and intrigue came to nothing. Captain Assmann would write, "The attempt to get rid of Dr. Morell, by force if by no other means . . . failed because Hitler wanted it to fail. Himmler, Bormann, the entire staff around Hitler—and especially Brandt and Hasselbach—were well aware of the dubious quality of Morell's therapy and tried several times to get him ditched. Hitler wouldn't hear of it." After the other doctors' final intrigue against him backfired—the attempt to have him fired over the so-called anti-gas pills affair—Morell would write on October 26, 1944 to the Reich film chief, SS-Gruppenführer Hans Hinkel, in evident satisfaction: "I think I can boast that my Chief is *always* satisfied with his physician. Because again and again I hear only the highest praise from him."

Small wonder that the escort doctors failed in their last attempt to overthrow Morell. He would later claim they tried seriously to put his head in a noose: Brandt certainly maintained that he had been systematically, perhaps even deliberately, poisoning the Führer with strychnine, in the guise of pills taken against his gastrointestinal problems. In the event, Hasselbach and Brandt were the ones to be dismissed by Hitler.

What was the truth about Hitler's epigastric pains? Hasselbach deduced that they must have been due to some neurosis since otherwise Morell's "unsuitable and useless drugs" would hardly have resulted in an improvement. That they did work wonders is evident, for instance, from the diary on December 8, 1944: "Pains at the earlier spot (right upper abdomen) were so violent after three more hours (around six A.M.) that he had me sent for. Yesterday afternoon he took a lot of aggravation: the air war and military situation—some general who didn't obey his orders . . . Intravenous injection of Eukodal and Eupaverin—spasm at once began to go gradually away.—Just now he claims he's facing the worst burdens of his entire life. His nerves are taking a beating from coming events, and what with the constant terror air raids on German cities. Result is it only takes the tiniest thing to trigger off these spasms. He says he's quite clear in his own mind there's nothing objectively wrong with his gastrointestinal tract because he's never had blood in his stools or vomit."

DESPITE the military collapse that had by now occurred in France, Hitler had begun preparing his forces in late summer of 1944 for a counteroffensive in the Ardennes, a final push that he hoped would "Dunkirk" the British army a second time. After that he would deliver the master stroke against the Red Army. At this crucial moment in planning Germany's military fortunes, he was struck down by jaundice and confined to bed again as he had been in August 1941. His staff found him staring apathetically at the ceiling, all interest gone.

From the jaundice too, Hitler recovered in time. For a while after that his legendary mental faculties remained with him: the all-encompassing memory bank, charged with facts and figures and names and data; the gift to extract instantly the essence of any report, the hypnotic effect on other men. But as the darkness of defeat approached Berlin, and as the burden of decision increased, that ominous tremor in his hands and legs returned.

Hitler's nervous problems had no long-term remedy. On October 30, 1944, after Morell had been summoned urgently at six A.M. to Hitler's bunker, he wrote: "Führer said he'd worked right through the night and had had to face up to a very grave decision over which he had got very worked up inside. This worry had welled up more and more inside him until suddenly, as it always does when he's really worried sick, his stomach knotted up into a cramp again."

Once again the professor rapidly made up a combined Eupaverin and Eukodal injection, but the intravenous injection was not easy because of the many needle scars of these last months. He "again drew attention to the need to give the veins a rest for a while."

On November 3 he noticed that the tremble in Hitler's left leg and hands was getting more pronounced. "When July 20 came," insisted Hitler, "all this shaking suddenly stopped. But now it's crept back again and it's worse than ever." Morell attributed it to the constant burden and irritation.

Hitler asked, "What is to be done against it?"

Morell answered, "Peace and quiet! Keep out of arguments!"

More to the point, he added that Hitler might try electric shock or water treatments. But as usual Hitler wanted quick and easy solutions. "Isn't there some kind of medicine or shot you can give me against it?" he asked.

"Vitamin B_1 and nicotinamide," was Morell's reply, "along with tranquilizing medicines. But if you take them to excess they'll put a damper on *everything*." He privately noted, "What would be very much to the point here would be massages!" But he knew there was not the slightest prospect of getting Hitler into the hands of a masseur.

Hitler's logic must have told him that the war could no longer be won. His loyal secretary Christa Schroeder tackled him one December 1944 day: "Mein Führer," she said, "we have *lost*, haven't we?" Hitler shook his head without explaining why: why else had Providence spared him from that bomb on July 20 if not to lead the German people on to final victory? Where the logic of his eyes no longer supported him, his blind faith continued to inspire him: he just had to live long enough and victory would be theirs. And to live long enough he needed Morell—and his warming and pleasant injections.

Morell, for all his avarice, was no fool. He had laid serious plans to extricate himself from the Führer's headquarters before it became a deathtrap. In his diary of November 14, 1944, we find his sorrow on learning of the death of a Professor Becher six weeks earlier. "Sad, not so much because of the works we published together . . . as that I was counting on him as my replacement here. Fifty plus, vegetarian, nonsmoker and tee-total. Fine scientist, particularly on the gastrointestinal tract and bacterial flora (wrote books about them). Unmarried, just lived for his work." Morell had also been grooming his assistant Dr. Weber for the post, and in order to introduce his former laboratory assistant Ruth Krause to Hitler, he had brought her to Berlin to take blood samples on November 26, 1944.

AS 1945 OPENED, blindness began to close in on Hitler's right eye. His back was bent, his hair had grayed, his vocal chords were fatigued and knotted. Hasselbach would describe during an interrogation: "Hitler's body began to stoop (kyphosis of dorsal spine), which may have been due in part to lack of exercise. . . . A tremor of head and hands was quite noticeable, particularly when [Hitler] brought a cup of tea to the mouth or signed documents."

He seldom appeared in public now, but medical experts who saw him on the newsreels studied his rhythmically trembling hands, his tottering gait and the other symptoms, and deduced that Hitler had contracted *paralysis agitans* (trembling palsy), also known as Parkinsonism. Ear, nose and throat doctor Erwin Giesing recalled noticing in September 1944 how Hitler's right hand shook so uncontrollably when an SS corporal brought him a document to sign that he had to put his hand down on the desk and wait a while before dashing off the signature in one scratchy flourish.

Hasselbach and Brandt, who it must be realized treated Hitler only until their dismissal in October 1944, disputed the Parkinsonism theory. But Giesing, who chanced to see Hitler at close quarters on February 13, 1945, thought he recognized the characteristic "masked facies" of a Parkinsonism victim. Professor Schenck, who was brought in during the last weeks in April to treat civilian casualties in the Reich Chancery bunker, was taken aback by his "fixed, lifeless expression" and could only attribute this to a disease of the mid-brain.[2] On April 2 Morell wrote that Hitler had "a lot of major worries and is sleeping badly." He added the explanation, "Military situation *very* bad! So tremor in left hand very marked." After seeing Hitler on April 11 or 12 the noted Professor Maximilian de Crinis of the Le Charité hospital also suspected Parkinsonism, according to what Conti said under interrogation some months later.

Morell was not sure, but both his desk diary and Hitler's—which have spent the last forty years on opposite sides of the

[2] So Schenck wrote to me recently. Clearly all this opens up possibilities for a serious examination of Hitler's mental health in the final months of the war. See especially the paper by Professor R. Hassler on the Parkinson syndrome in volume V, part III of *Handbuch der Inneren Medizin* (Springer, Berlin, 1953).

Atlantic—prove that even he now reluctantly accepted that it might be Parkinsonism, because he began dosing Hitler regularly during the last two weeks of his life with the appropriate medication—namely, daily increasing amounts of a drug called Homburg 680.

So that was Hitler, viewed under a doctor's microscope. The late ENT specialist Dr. Giesing, who treated him after July 20, 1944, rounded off his assessment in November 1945 with this verdict: "The phenomenon called Adolf Hitler, who regarded himself as elected by Providence as the chief exponent of the Twentieth Century, is no more. We survivors who knew him have a duty to do what we can by our objectivity and judgment to ensure that no false aura arises around his life and death, and that he does not live on in the mind of the German people as some kind of martyr, a man who could have gladdened our lives and liberated us, 'if only the others had so desired and decreed.'"

The Treatment

ACTUALLY," said Morell to escort doctor Karl Brandt as they shared a cell in 1945, "Hitler was never ill." But if that were so, we might well ask, why did Morell need to amass such an arsenal of medicines to treat him?

This author has identified seventy-seven different medicines and preparations administered by Morell to Hitler during the period of the diaries, 1941–1945.[1]

Modern experts find this exceptional. As early as 1945 an American Intelligence summary on Hitler's health problems pointed out the likely consequences: "Constant medication over a period of years may have upset the physiological balance of his body to such an extent that even normally harmless drugs would be relied on. Thus a person may become addicted to such medication even though the substances employed are not drugs of a habit-forming nature."

"Among the objections brought forward by doctors against this method," states another source, "there is a fundamental one saying that such injections certainly are apt to give the patient the transitory feeling of well-being, but that they exhaust the stock of physical and psychical forces a man is supposed to have, at a much faster pace than . . . normal. Such a man shows signs of mental and bodily decline . . . at a much earlier period of life."

After the war Morell tried to dismiss his methods as a kind of harmless supplementary nutrition. We do not know by what criteria he selected the medicines he used. He certainly favored

---

[1] See Appendix II.

60

the products of his own companies, which was harmless enough: but he evidently used new drugs without testing for side effects, which was not. He would prescribe a new medicine for Hitler, usually an underdose to be on the safe side; if unpleasant effects developed he would furtively write to a specialist or institute asking them to conduct tests on animals. Thus in 1944 after suspecting that his use of Homoseran might have caused a dramatic acceleration in Hitler's blood sedimentation rate, he secretly wrote asking for clinical tests on rabbits. (In fact blood sedimentation is not something that can be easily affected.) There is no trace of Morell testing new medicines on himself first, in the way that Dr. Giesing took quantities of Ultraseptyl and the controversial anti-gas pills in 1944.

Morell refused to believe that his medicines might be actually harmful. The objective value of many of them is still disputed. It is unlikely that another doctor would have given glucose injections as he did. "There was a widespread medical practice to give shots of concentrated glucose solutions as a kind of 'osmotherapy,'" writes Schenck, "to detoxicate, to influence organic ailments and to stimulate the heart and blood circulation. A fifty percent solution is useful for dehydrating the brain. In earlier times one or two fifty percent injections were commonly given after strokes. But *twenty* percent glucose—there's no way that could have any effect."[2] Glucose might cause blood sugar to increase from perhaps 80–100 mg to 110–120 mg percent but would then drop very rapidly again. Morell also claimed to be making his twenty percent glucose injections to increase the calorie supply to Hitler's body. It is true that glucose is absorbed rapidly and induces a transitory sense of well-being. (American interrogators surmised, "Hitler might have dealt with situations very differently after a glucose injection.")[3] But the objective increase in calories would have been minimal, as each twenty percent shot would contain only two grams of pure glucose, equivalent to only 8 of the 2,300 to 2,500 calories required daily by a grown man with a sedentary job.

Even then Morell did not use a reputable glucose like Merck's Dextrose, or Osmon or Calorose, but characteristically used his

[2] Schenck's authority is H. Königer, *Krankenbehandlung durch Umstimmung* (Leipzig, 1929).
[3] OI/CIR/4.

own brand—in fact most of the drugs he administered in bulk to Hitler were manufactured by Hamma or its parent company, Nordmark. Morell darkly claimed to have his reasons for not using the Merck product and for not injecting stronger solutions. When Ribbentrop told Morell (Diary, June 3, 1943) that he was used to taking forty percent glucose solutions—earlier because of low blood pressure but more recently because of a slackness in the heart muscle—Morell commented in his notes, "I think such injections are too strong, because of the danger of a thrombosis [a blood clot in the heart]. I referred to the clotting of the withdrawn blood in the Merck glucose solution at Zhitomir. I myself never use solutions of over twenty percent." It is just possible, thought not proven, that Morell may also have known of the belief, now supported by clinical experiments, that massive glucose injections can cause brain damage.

What is certain is that Hitler would not have noticed any lasting benefit from just twenty percent glucose injections. If injected together with Strophantin, or if Coramin or Cardiazol had been used too, it would have been different because they stimulate and revive. Strophantin acts on the heart muscles like digitalis. The effect of Coramin lasts about an hour or two.

In a study written for this author, Professor Schenck shows that Morell proceeded ultracautiously in his usage of drugs supportive of the peripheral circulatory system, like Coramin, Cardiazol and Sympathol: he never administered more than one-third and often less than a quarter of the normal dose, so any effect must have been more imaginary than real. "No way could such minute doses have eliminated a heart insufficiency such as had already resulted in edemas on the feet," he said. As for the glucose injections Schenck concludes that the only indicated usage was that in conjunction with Strophantin. Otherwise, says Schenck, glucose could have only "placebo effects which Morell undoubtedly knew how to reinforce by the spoken word."

IN SCHENCK'S opinion many of the drugs used by Morell—like glucose, Mutaflor, Omnadin, Tonophosphan and some of the hormone treatments—could be classed as "specific or nonspecific tonics."

Omnadin was one such nonspecific tonic. Known to doctors

since 1937 as a vaccine, Omnadin had all the prestige of its manufacturers, I.G. Farben, behind it: it was a mixture of proteins, lipoid substances of gall, and animalic fats. It was credited with antigenic properties (the ability to form antibodies), so it would normally be injected at the onset of an infection like the common cold. Königer's view of it was: "Omnadin is a medicine of very mild effect that is always well taken and can be administered daily even to the seriously ill without hesitation. It is highly praised for its effect on flu and grippe-pneumonia, as well as for other bronchial pneumonias and anginas." The same positive rating was accorded to Tonophosphan, a Bayer product containing an organic phosphorus compound, used as a stimulant for unstriped muscles and also to supply phosphorus; it was listed in the 1937 *Gehe-Codex*, the principal pharmacological handbook, as a "powerful nerve tonic and metabolic stimulant."

Mutaflor has been referred to earlier (page 30). The idea was that strains of coli bacteria characterized by their particular aggressiveness would exploit the displacement principle: some natural bacteria in the intestine could malfunction and cause digestion pains. The job of the coli bacillus supplied by the Mutaflor capsules was to replace these by healthier and more active strains which would overrun them. Schenck says, "This hypothesis . . . had numerous supporters but scarcely any among the leading German clinical experts or bacteriologists, who doubted whether minute quantities of externally introduced bacteria could displace those produced by the body itself." When Mutaflor failed to banish Hitler's epigastric pains permanently Morell turned to injections of Progynon (which consisted of benzoic acid and dihydro-follicle hormone). This increased circulation in the gastric mucosa and tended to prevent the painful spasm of the gastric walls. Morell also injected intramuscularly Progynon B Oleosum forte; both these injections gave some relief.

IT WAS PRIMARILY with his vitamin products that Morell had attracted the attention of specialist journals in prewar years. The vitamin products then available consisted of pure synthetic vitamin C without additives. Morell's chief chemist, Dr. Kurt Mulli, later claimed that Morell's Vitamultin was the first vitamin product to contain combinations of vitamins in therapeutically adequate amounts. Reasoning that Hitler's diet was unbalanced and inadequate, Morell began administering regular injections of Vitamultin-Calcium, one version of which was a blend of vitamin B_1, ascorbic acid, calcium, and nicotinamide. "It was particularly to Morell's credit," claimed Mulli, "that he recognized the broad therapeutic value of nicotinic acid."

Vitamultin-Calcium attracted criticism. Professor Schenck voiced his objections as follows: "The injection solution contained 40,000 international units (or two grams) of vitamin C and 0.012 percent, or 6,000 international units, of aneurin-hydrochloride (equivalent to 18 mg of vitamin B_1) for every 100 cc of the liquid, which was packaged in 2 cc ampoules. Each ampoule would therefore contain only 0.04 g of ascorbic acid–calcium and 0.36 mg of aneurin B_1—minimal quantities which could not remotely meet daily requirements and were thus devoid of any therapeutic significance." Admittedly, the product was not always consistent in its composition. Franck gives the contents of the later Vitamultin ampoules as 0.01 percent, or 0.002 g per ampoule, of nicotinamide, far below man's daily need of 0.012 to 0.02 g; but each ampoule also significantly contained 0.3 percent, or 0.6 g, of p-Amidobenzoyldiethylamino-ethanolhydrochloride, otherwise known as procaine, an anesthetic related to cocaine but substantially less toxic, recommended in the early 1940s as a painkiller for use with intravenous injections. The single intravenous or intracardiac dose was from 0.03 to 0.1 g, or injected subcutaneously 0.5 g. But again each ampoule of Vitamultin-Calcium contained only 0.006 to 0.012 g, so once again it would be far below the recommended effective dose for procaine.

Morell injected ampoules of Vitamultin-Calcium intravenously into Hitler, and he provided it for Mussolini too. From the diaries we see that he usually coupled it with injections of glucose. He also prepared special Vitamultin-Calcium "F" tablets for Hitler to eat—the F standing apparently for *forte*. Thus on February 20, 1943, we find him ordering by telephone "a one-off special order" of ten packets of two hundred Vitamultin tablets for headquarters.

It should be pointed out that the bars of Vitamultin produced by Morell's factories by the million for the German Labor Front were different, usually consisting of unspecified quantities of glucose, glycerine, vitamins B_1, B_2, and C, nicotinamide and sodium phosphate. Among the raw materials supplied to Morell for his Vitamultin manufacture were vanelin, aneurin, cocoa powder and coffee. According to a June 1941 document Vitamultin tablets contained 8 percent rosehip butter, with a vitamin C content of 3.2 percent; 3 percent yeast extract; 3.2 percent dried lemons; 4 percent dried wheat germ; 0.6 percent calcium biphosphate; 4 percent skimmed milk; 2.4 percent dehydrated lemon juice and 74.8 percent sugar. And from a letter from Morell to Speer's representatives at Brünn on January 16, 1945, explaining why he needed higher priority ratings for the product, we see what he claimed for Vitamultin: it was necessary during winter months "to increase resistance to infectious diseases and to get even more work out of the arms workers."

The most controversial of Morell's injections were his hormone products. They attracted even more criticism than the glucose and Vitamultin injections. There was just not enough clinical experience available about possible side effects of repeated hormone injections over a period of years.

By 1939 there were three generations of hormone products: the first were dried endocrine glands processed into tablets; these were virtually worthless. The second generation processed the extracts of these glands, and these did have a vague tonic effect. This second generation along with a third generation, which was just beginning to appear from 1937 onward, of hormones which had been isolated from the organic extracts and whose chemical composition had been completely understood, were the ones used by Morell. (Modern medicine is now progressing from the third to a fourth generation, that is to hormone products which have been chemically restructured to attain specific effects.)

Among those of the second generation which Morell administered both to his faithful Führer and to Mussolini were Orchikrin and Prostakrinum. Both were his patent Hamma products, the former being identified as follows in the 1939 *Gehe Codex*: "Extr. tot. Testis Tauri juven., Prostatae et vesic. semin."—that is, extracts of testes, prostate and seminal vesicles of young bulls. It was indicated for all types and consequences of genital hypoplasia (the excessive smallness of an organ) and for sex hormone deficiency in the male. But according to Professor Schenck, "No specific effect was expected. At best a nonspecific or placebo effect was contemplated."

The same went, says Schenck, for Prostakrinum, which was listed only once, in the 1939 *Gehe Codex*, and defined as "an extract of seminal vesicles and prostata." Morell used it to counter depressive moods. One Orchikrin pill was equivalent to three grams of fresh testes; a Prostakrinum pill was equivalent to one gram of prostate and seminal vesicles. The pills were heavily coated in sugar. We do not know whether we can assume from this that Morell suspected a hypertrophied prostate in Hitler, or just a general insufficiency in sex hormones. According to Schenck there was less probability of any specific effect on Hitler's sex glands than a general tonic effect. "Evidently," he postulates, "Morell used these products with this in mind and mainly when Hitler felt tired or low."

Among the third generation of hormone products administered by Morell to Hitler were Cortiron—a hormone generated by the suprarenal gland—and Progynon B Oleosum, both produced by the reputable Berlin company Schering. He injected Cortiron intramuscularly to combat muscle weakness and to influence the body's carbohydrate metabolism and fat resorption; Cortiron's primary uses were against diseases and insufficiency of the suprarenal gland. Progynon, an ovarian hormone, was the first to be isolated from the female sex gland. In addition to these Morell administered testosterone, the male sex hormone, which had the power of restoring flagging male sexual characteristics. It had already been isolated and was being artificially synthesized with the formula $C_{19}H_{28}O_2$.

As for the iodine products he injected, like Septoiod, Morell was familiar with these from his years as a general practitioner and used them on Hitler correctly, to combat the common cold and against progressive arteriosclerosis. Morell had once published a paper on another iodine called Lipojodin. He sweepingly recommended to Ribbentrop, "Iodine is very suitable for anybody over fifty" (Diary, June 3, 1943).

D URING World War II, the Allies had a virtual monopoly of mass production of penicillin. When the British and Americans invaded northern France in June 1944 they took 600,000 portions of penicillin with them—not much, as it turned out. But in Germany, despite the intensive efforts of the major pharmaceutical concerns, pure pencillin had still not been isolated from the mould culture media. This did not, as it happened, prevent Professor Morell from treating several patients with his own brand of what he prematurely called "penicillin." In August 1944 a Paul Schönfeld wrote to him from Berchtesgaden recalling that after Morell had treated the suppurated bed of his fingernail with pencillin during June the suppuration vanished the next day. And on November 7, 1944, a self-satisfied Morell would write to the sister of a Luftwaffe officer killed in action: "I can still see him standing before me with his boyish smile as I treated his leg injuries with penicillin. . . ." The German press claimed that Morell was the first to succeed in the mass production of penicillin. But the truth was that in Germany only Professor Kilian of Breslau had managed to isolate it, and then only in minute quantities. Rival Hitler doctor Karl Brandt would comment after the war, "Let me just say this: when I drew Hitler's attention years earlier to the vast importance of the work being done on penicillin in America and Britain, Morell had not the foggiest notion what I was talking about and afterward confused it with phenacetin—something completely different."

So even though Morell might claim to have applied "penicillin powder" (Diary, July 20, 1944) at best it must have been some kind of vacuum-dried mould culture medium processed into a powder with talcum. "Obviously it would be a travesty to describe this as penicillin," observes Schenck. "Moreover, as Soviet practice demonstrated, such products are anything but harmless, as the mould impurities can result in violently allergic skin reactions." Morell's own papers show that the attempts of Hamma chief chemist Dr. Mulli to reproduce the Allied successes were unsuccessful and that the Hamma product was weak and frequently toxic. Morell's claim was pure humbug. Schenck comments, "He evidently wanted to show that he was giving Hitler the best treatment available to modern medicine and that he was overtaking the British and Americans."

The history of Hamma's involvement was this: in a circular dated December 6, 1943, the Reich health authorities had called upon the medical community to start intensive research into penicillin and related antibiotics. Researchers from all over the Reich would convene in the spring to compare notes. On January 10, 1944, Hamma's Olmütz laboratory was allocated one such research field—ways of isolating the substances from cultures and media—while Morell's private Berlin laboratory was to investigate the pharmacological applications of penicillins by tests on animals and cultures. In fact, although his letterhead read "The Professor Dr. Theo Morell Private Research Laboratory," it was Professor W. Laves who directed the penicillin research for Morell. And while Laves would write to him on March 4, from the Hamburg office, "We can record major progress in our work on penicillin," Morell's own agenda and daily records leave a different flavor.

On February 14, 1944, when Morell telephoned Olmütz, Dr. Mulli had read out to him an American article about mass production of penicillin in the United States. Morell was envious, and noted down his own needs for his next talk with Hitler, "Research 100,000 Reichsmarks," and later still he added what was presumably the outcome: "Reichsleiter [Martin] Bormann," and, "A research unit must swiftly be set up named after Dr. Morell." In the conversation, Mulli had also told him their current penicillin yield: it was barely twenty portions from twenty liters of medium. That was not much. On February 21 we find Morell talking with Bormann, Hitler's powerful secretary, about his research and the urgent need for laboratory apparatus. Hitler, of course, was proud of the advanced research being conducted by his doctor. He awarded Morell the civil version of the Knight's Cross during February, and on the twenty-first Bormann informed him that the Führer had ruled exceptionally that Hamma Inc. might set off one hundred percent of its research expenses against tax.

Before the war Hitler had promised Morell an electron microscope, one of the rarest and most advanced research tools available to modern science. Only four such microscopes were built by the Berlin company of Siemens during the war. Hitler now ordered that the set earmarked for the Academy of Military Medicine in Berlin should be diverted to Morell instead. Early in 1944 the microscope was ready for delivery. On May 21 and 22 the doctor had the first talks with the specialist who would control the installation for him. On May 24 they drove around

Bavaria looking for suitable locations, and found one at Bayrisch-Gmain, near Reichenhall. There was further proof of Hitler's awe of Morell on June 26, when Bormann wrote to Reichsminister Dr. Hans Lammers, the top civil servant, "The Führer has decided that the costs of the electron microscope and its software and the entire costs of its installation are to be borne by the Führer's purse. The Führer wants to make this donation as a contribution to the scientific research of Professor Morell."[4]

He had his eye on a fine building in Berlin too as emerges from a letter to him from Mussolini's doctor, Zachariae, on December 3, 1944: "For your sake I was extremely sorry that you didn't get that so-called Clinic for Nature Healing in Berlin, the old balneological institute, to set up a model clinic along your own lines. You could have made real headway there, and it would have been a better monument to your career than the gentlemen who are working there now and who were given the institute as a relic of the Hess era."

Literally nothing came of Morell's new tool, the electron microscope, despite his exalted rank. On March 14, 1945, he would write to Hitler's adjutant's office, again pulling rank, protesting that although his Research Institute for Electron Optics was being built under the architectural direction of Professor Hermann Giesler and on the Führer's instructions, two of the forty building workers had been drafted into uniform.

Of course his rivals howled with rage at the blatant favoritism showed toward Morell. Brandt later wrote, "Since not even the most basic requirements could be met, this priceless instrument was never used." Besides, while Morell wanted to use it to investigate his beloved coli bacillus, the scientist attached to the institute, Dr. Siebert, was more interested in aerosols. Whatever the cause, the microscope had not even been switched on by the time the war ended.

D ESPITE the generous infusion of Hitler's personal funds, Morell's penicillin research stagnated. The Hamma product rapidly went bad, as Professor Rostock, a reputable army expert, quickly established with laboratory tests. On April 29, 1944, Mulli

4 National Archives microfilm T-253, roll 36, Bl.486350-1.

warned Morell in a letter: "We have now produced several hundred ampoules of penicillin, with which we are carrying out extensive tests at the local hospital," but difficulties were cropping up: he had now made the unpleasant discovery that frequently one and the same penicillin strain could yield exceptionally toxic substances.

Despite these production snags, from early May 1944 Hamma's Hamburg location was also turning out penicillin products. Morell himself was still ignorant of the product's use. In his notes of August 21, he showed that he intended to ask Dr. Mulli about penicillin: "Is it injected? Intramuscularly?"

The other doctors fumed with annoyance. When it came to treating Hitler's chief Wehrmacht adjutant Rudolf Schmundt— hideously injured in the bomb attempt of July 1944—the ear, nose and throat doctor Giesing wanted to administer captured American penicillin, of which Surgeon General Dr. Handloser had managed to procure a few ampoules. Morell managed to prevent it. Giesing struck back, surreptitiously removed two ampoules of Hamma penicillin from Hitler's living room at the Wolf's Lair, and sent them for analysis by the Institute of Biochemistry at Breslau and by the Institute of Hygiene and Bacteriology at Königsberg. These found that the ampoules had no significant penicillin content. Giesing gleefully passed this information on to Brandt, and Morell had to accept it. It must be said that he was conscientious enough not to conceal his ultimate failure: "A test of ampoules at Olmütz," he would warn his Kosolup Dye factory on March 18, 1945, "has shown that every single ampoule was useless—sterile and therefore toxic."

IN THE ABSENCE of a German penicillin, the Germans used sulphonamides. After Domagk's discovery of the antibiotic powers of the sulphonamides, scores of pharmaceutical companies greedily began researching into ways of synthesizing new sulphonamides that were sufficiently distinctive to be patented. In the space of a few years more than two thousand different sulphonamide compounds were announced, all differing marginally from each other in their outer molecular structures for no real reason other than to make them legally patentable.

Professor Schenck says today, "This phenomenon resulted

in the development of some sulphonamides that were a considerable improvement on the original ones, but also some that were in fact quite toxic." One of the best was Eubasin, manufactured by Nordmark in Hamburg; Morell however testified that he used it only once, injected intragluteally, but never again "since it caused pain." The most poisonous was Uliron. Scarcely less toxic was the sulphonamide marketed as Ultraseptyl. It bore the generic name sulphamethylthiazol, while its chemical composition was an even bigger mouthful: 2-(p-aminobenzolsulphanamido)-4-methylthiazol. Morell swore by it, no doubt because it was manufactured by Chinoin, a Budapest company in which he had an interest. Chinoin had belonged to a family of Hungarian industrialists called Wolf, who escaped the fate of most Hungarian Jews by emigrating to Switzerland under the protecting hand of the Party in return for which the company was transferred to German ownership.

As early as 1940, researchers had discovered that Ultraseptyl had serious side effects, particularly on the kidneys and nervous system. Writing a survey of the sulphonamides in the *German Medical Weekly* of September 28, 1942, the well-known clinical expert Professor J. Vonkennel stated that Ultraseptyl "despite its great efficiency is no longer in use because of its great toxicity"; it tended to crystallize out in the renal tubules. Morell unquestionably knew about these damaging side effects because he insisted on a high liquid intake after each dose of Ultraseptyl. Despite this he continued to use it to the exclusion of others. He would write an unsympathetic letter to his architect Giesler on January 21, 1944: "Sorry to hear you've been flat on your back this last week, but I did warn you not so long ago never to go on journeys without a tube of Ultraseptyl." Morell kept prescribing it until far into 1944. As Schenck says, "This does not indicate that he had addressed his mind very closely to the sulphonamide problem as either a doctor or scientist. Otherwise he would have abandoned it by 1942 at the latest."

He administered Ultraseptyl to Hitler either in his usual trivial injections—probably in doses of one gram dissolved in 5 cc—or in one or two tablets each containing half a gram to be taken after a meal with fruit juice or water, that is, one gram of Ultraseptyl, which could never have helped much against any infection. Schenck says, "Ultraseptyl was used by Morell on every pretext and opportunity, often underdosed and thus ineffectively, but sometimes as a controlled sulphonamide shock treatment, of five or six daily, over three to five days, in line with the then current sulphonamide practice."

Morell prescribed Ultraseptyl for a variety of common complaints including Hitler's persistent catarrhal inflammations of the upper respiratory tract and angina, although even then doctors were warned, "The effect of sulphonamides on acute tonsil infections is doubtful," and "with influenza there is only limited success inasmuch as the accompanying inflammations are dispelled."

"He would give large doses of sulfonamides for slight colds," grumped Dr. Karl Brandt under American interrogation in 1945, "and gave them to everybody around Hitler's headquarters."

As with Morell's "penicillin," Brandt did what he could to discredit Ultraseptyl. He showed to Hitler an opinion of the pharmacological institute of Leipzig University to the effect that Ultraseptyl damaged the nervous system. These warnings did not fall on entirely deaf ears. Hitler noticed that the drug was not good for him, and there was a showdown with Morell: On October 19, 1944, we find Morell noting that he had at three P.M. that day instructed Hitler to take three Ultraseptyl tablets three times a day against a cold. Four hours later, however, there was a little mutiny by Hitler. "Führer telephones," he wrote, "says he can't take any more Ultraseptyl as after three tablets he gets a taut stomach just like recently, and he attributes his recent condition [when he had hepatitis] to the large Ultraseptyl intake. I declared this was absurd, but we'll stop giving further Ultraseptyl. Of course, his cold's going to linger on, I said. I only wanted him to take as much as he did because I thought he wanted to get well again *immediately* whatever the cost." Morell grudgingly gave Hitler some shots of Tibatin, a reputable sulphonamide that was readily absorbed.

Today Ultraseptyl is no longer manufactured or sold.

Morell's Business Empire

A FEW WORDS ought to be spoken about Morell's financial situation and business interests.

For treating Hitler, he was paid 300,000 Reichsmarks altogether from 1937 through 1940. From 1941 onward he was paid 36,000 Reichsmarks plus 24,000 RM expenses, according to Aloys Becker, who handled his affairs. This payment included treatment of the adjutants and escort personnel at Hitler's headquarters. The Reich Chancery transferred to his bank account 5,000 RM each month. As for his other professional income we know something from a statement by his assistant, Dr. Weber, who held the fort in the Kurfürstendamm practice in his absence. On June 5, 1944, Weber advised Morell that the bombing of the capital had affected the takings of the practice and that gross 1943 income would be 86,497 RM; but if the fees due from Party bigwigs like Goebbels and Funk were included, gross income would top 110,000 RM. Weber anticipated that the takings for 1944 would be some twenty-five percent higher.

What about Morell's business ambitions? Without his ready access to Hitler it would not have been half so successful, but even so they earned him far less than his Kurfürstendamm practice. While his factories had a turnover of millions, most of the income went on repaying loans.

One of his biggest moneyspinners was Vitamultin. Even the SS had to swallow the lozenges. On January 12, 1942, SS-Reichsführer Himmler formally instructed Morell: "The Führer has ordained that as of this moment suitable vitamin products are to be conveyed to the units of the Waffen SS fighting on

the eastern front. The firm Hamma Inc. of Hamburg is charged
with the manufacture of these vitamin products." By October
1942 over thirty-eight million bars of Morell's Vitamultin had
been delivered to the Waffen SS. In March 1943 a second order
went to Hamma for forty million bars. Toward the end of 1943
Morell began his own production of Vitamultin, which had until
then been manufactured under license by Nordmark for him:
Hamma Inc. took over the empty and derelict Heikorn factory
building at Olmütz and began production there. From Morell's
papers we see that on June 6, 1944, Hamma Inc. at Olmütz was
employing 930 men and women—in the Vitamultin division
256 employees; Rusla lice powder, fifty-five; Hamma, ninety-
four; other divisions (margarine, vinegar, soap), 425; clerical
staff, 100. Nor was he only producing drugs there. Fighting
constant battles against the drafting of his employees into the
armed services, Morell wrote on January 21, 1943, to Labor
Commissioner Fritz Sauckel, "My Heikorn Factory at Olmütz,
which owns one of the biggest oil refineries in the Protectorate
[Bohemia-Moravia], is receiving daily wagonloads of sunflower
seeds from the Ukraine for the production of oils and margarine."

To finance all this and the Vitamultin production program
for 1944, however, Morell had to raise hefty loans from the
state-owned Bank of German Labor. By the end of 1944 these
loans had still not been cleared, so Morell made no profit from
his venture into the world of capitalism, although he might have
had the war lasted longer.

He dreamed of creating an enormous business processing
animal glands for their secretions and hormones. On November 15, 1943, Morell wrote to a government official boasting
that he had dedicated part of his life's work to researching hormones and putting them into the service of curative medicine.
Hamma Inc. was, he wrote, the realization of his dream. It
was producing high-grade hormone products "that are vital for
our soldiers." For example, his plant was filling ampoules with
liver extract—by the end of July 1943 they had manufactured
eighty to one hundred thousand. A Hamma subsidiary was set
up at Vinnitsa to enable Morell to exploit the immense Ukrainian
slaughterhouses, and the Endocrinological Institute at Kharkov
was taken over by Morell during 1943.

THE QUALITY of Morell's commercial products was hotly debated. The controversy started with his Vitamultin lozenges. The ingredients stated by him differed from those listed in the *Gehe Codex* and again from those stated by Rudolf Franck in his authoritative *Moderne Therapie*.

Billions of the lozenges were manufactured. Thus the German Labor Front's Office of Health and Public Safety issued 390 million of the 2.5 gram lozenges during the first "Vitamultin Operation" of the winter of 1941–42. Morell wanted to get the air force to join in, for obvious commercial reasons: for four months every Luftwaffe soldier should be given one lozenge a day—a substantial business in view of the millions of men involved. The Luftwaffe's experts rebelled: Göring's chief surgeon Dr. Erich Hippke wrote an annihilating report on the value of Vitamultin. But he had underestimated Morell's clout. Hitler's physician complained pompously to Göring. "My product contains," he wrote in a letter dated July 31, 1942, "quite apart from the synthetic vitamins B_1 and C, the vitamins of the B- and K-complexes from natural sources (lemons, wheat germ)." He took the view, he said, that the first duty of medicine was to prevent the onset of illnesses.

Hippke was unimpressed. He was concerned about the quantities as much as the contents. He pointed out that at least seven lozenges a day would be necessary to meet an adult's daily requirements of vitamins B and C; to take just one lozenge was useless. Morell protested to the Labor Front on August 20, furious at Hippke "and his quite extraordinary demeanor toward myself." The Labor Front was convinced that the product had some value, and reassured Morell, "The exact scientists (Professors Stepp, Scheubner, Kollath and Bommer) have all expressed themselves in favor of a vitamin operation." Ultimately, the protest rebounded on Hippke's head, and he was dismissed by Göring.

Morell increased Vitamultin production. In August 1943 Professor Laves wrote to Morell, "I'm going to try to step up Vitamultin output at Olmütz." What was of decided advantage to Morell's business empire was that he was now entitled to scarce raw materials like ascorbic acid from the stocks allocated to the Labor Front.

By 1944 he was churning out billions of the lozenges. On January 23, 1944, his chief chemist, Dr. Mulli, told him, "We have issued invoices for 460 million and are waiting for new orders to roll in." He was going to try to get the product into the Protectorate, which would expand the market by 70 million or more. On January 27, Mulli triumphed, "We now have orders for 480 million. The operation will probably top 560 million. We'll have around four tons of ascorbic acid left over plus the four tons from the Wehrmacht quota." On April 29 Mulli reported that orders had now reached the staggering total of 696,164,616 lozenges of which they had already delivered 657,230,800.

Morell's other promising line was an antilice powder for the troops. Again it ran into criticism, but this time he was less fortunate. During the winter of 1941–42 the troops and civilian population had been plagued by lice. Hitler had mentioned his concern about this over lunch one day, adding that this raised a severe typhus danger. Morell looked into it, and by February 1942 he had developed a lice powder based on the foul-smelling potassium xanthogenate. On March 15, 1942, Hitler had ordered that the margarine factory S. Heikorn at Olmütz be sold to Morell for the purpose of this "Rusla powder" manufacture. For several months the Party blocked the sale, and Morell as usual did not hesitate to mention his boss's name. "As you know," he lectured SS-General Kurt Dalüge, the deputy protector, in a letter, "the S. Heikorn Company was awarded to me on the Führer's orders."

Under the management of Aloys Becker, his protegé and the close personal friend of Johanna Morell, the factory began packing Rusla for the Wehrmacht. Around 250,000 packages were turned out every day. In the summer of 1943, however, manufacture halted as the Army Health Inspection declared its depots were overflowing.

Simultaneously, the first criticism of Rusla was heard. Morell defended his product against the newly appearing rivals in a talk with Hitler that July. "Schreiber wanted to have the impregnation method from the outset," he noted afterward, recording this talk, "and Dr. Bickert wanted a powder. We manufactured the powder, and it is one hundred percent successful—provided it is applied properly. Trouble is, the smell is a bit overpowering. What with that and the troops' general laziness it has not been properly applied everywhere. Now the Inspection wants to go over to impregnation. As soon as I took the first step, big business pricked up its ears and I. G. Farben began manufacturing its own product patented in Switzerland; it's not bad but can't cope with more than about 400,000. Another company had applied to the Inspection with an impregnant, but its basis is the same as mine (potassium xanthogenate); their patent is not open to inspection because everything is kept secret in wartime, but I know their substance is the same as mine. What I want is for the Inspection to give me half of the action, and on this score the Führer came down right on my side. I also pointed out that in Germany only processes can be patented (inventions), but not *discoveries* as in other countries. . . . But as I was the first to manufacture this substance I demanded half the order" (Diary).

The conversation shows the jealousy with which Morell guarded his little empire. Rusla became a gigantic business for him, but short-lived. In 1942 his factory turned out 66,441,545 portions, and in 1943 output rose to 76,562,530. On March 27, 1944, Aloys Becker notified him that the Wehrmacht contract for Rusla was to be renewed at the existing rate of nine million portions per month. And in a further company document dated March 13, 1944, it is stated that 5,000,000 portions were delivered from January until that date, with around 21,600,000 more still to be delivered.[1]

Then the whole business collapsed, leaving behind a smell as obnoxious as the product itself. On March 9, the Labor Front's medical expert, Dr. Schulenburg, sent a company doctor's report on Rusla to Morell's Heikorn Company. Schulenburg reminded Morell's chief chemist, Dr. Mulli, that he had suggested running large-scale trials "using scientific methods." Heikorn had answered only evasively. "As you are aware," Schulenburg's letter continued, "the efficacy of your products is at very least controversial."

In the report drawn up by the Labor Front's division of

[1] National Archives microfilm T-253, roll 36, Bl.6460.

Health and Public Safety the investigators stated: "We conducted the trials: Rusla powder stored in a little box with lice. After twenty-four hours the lice crawled out in rollicking spirits."

Becker would later testify that Morell never made a cent from his business empire. This is largely true. Bank papers among his papers show that in 1944, his best year, he was drawing only 2,000 RM monthly from Olmütz, with a tax deduction of 596.70 RM. Morell would die in poverty.

THE DIARIES OF
THEO MORELL

1941:

Barbarossa and the Leeches

HITLER'S WEHRMACHT fell upon the Soviet Union. On that day, June 22, 1941, his diplomatic liaison officer Walther Hewel noted in a private diary the "calm, mellow mood" in the Reich Chancery building, and the next day he added: "The Führer is in the best possible spirits because of the gigantic successes in Russia (air force)." But that same evening, after tea with the Führer, he added: "Russia: there still are big question marks."

The question marks remained, and the uncertainties of these first months of Hitler's eastern war generated illnesses in him that were to have momentous consequences.

The headquarters to which he traveled on the night of June 24 was called the Wolf's Lair. It had been hastily built on unhealthy swampland outside Rastenburg in East Prussia. "No doubt some government department found the land was cheapest here," sighed Hitler three years later in a conversation with Dr. Giesing. "Or perhaps it was already state-owned so they just set up the Führer's headquarters here." On June 27, German High Command (OKW) war diarist Helmuth Greiner complained in a letter to his wife: "We are being plagued by the most awful mosquitoes. It would be hard to pick on a more senseless site than this—deciduous forest with marshy pools, sandy ground and stagnant lakes, ideal for these loathsome creatures. On top of that we have cold, damp bunkers, in which we freeze to death at night, can't get to sleep because of the humming of the electric air conditioning which makes a terrible draft as well, and then wake up in the morning with a headache. Our underwear and uniforms are always cold and clammy."

As yet Hitler had little ground for worry. The first twelve

special communiqués were broadcast on June 29. In the north, his troops had taken Libau and Dvinsk, in the center 300,000 Russians had been rapidly encircled and Minsk had fallen. By July 4, the Russians had lost 4,600 tanks and countless airplanes. In breezy mood, Hitler often lingered until two or three A.M. talking with his staff about the future—and above all about his plans for colonizing Russia for the Germans. "I will go down in history as the destroyer of bolshevism," he bragged.

Greiner at least had second thoughts. "It was quite interesting at the Führer's again," he wrote on July 4, "but not so much as the last time. He was very quiet and scarcely joined in the conversation." On July 10 Hitler sat up until three A.M. "in a boiling hot bunker" according to Hewel's private diary. And while Greiner reckoned, two days later, that in a few more days they would be better placed to judge the fighting, he added the observation: "We didn't discuss this at all yesterday. At first the Führer just brooded silently to himself. Then he livened up and expatiated for well over an hour about our courageous, daredevil Italian allies, and the headaches they're giving him. I can only marvel at his insight and perception. Apart from this, he's looking good and seems in good health although he hardly ever goes to bed before five or six A.M."

Late in July 1941, Hitler's health collapsed. He had a row with his foreign minister von Ribbentrop, who screamed at him at one stage: "God doesn't let people take a look at the cards he's holding!" Hitler suddenly paled, stopped in mid-retort, slumped into a chair and clutched his heart. Ribbentrop was petrified and promised never to lose his temper again.

WORSE befell Hitler soon after, a "minor affliction" as his grinning generals termed it. He contracted dysentery. For three vital weeks he was weakened by diarrhea, stomach cramps, nausea, aching limbs, shivery feelings and fever. What had caused it? The climate, the insanitary conditions, and his eccentric lifestyle certainly contributed.

The military consequences were serious. Naval adjutant Karl-Jesco von Puttkamer, a tall, cigar-smoking navy captain, observed how the Führer's growing feebleness left him incapable of outarguing the dynamic army generals who came to the war conference each day that summer, determined on scrapping the original encirclement strategy of Hitler's Barbarossa directive, and converting the campaign's main thrust into a traditional frontal assault on the Soviet capital, Moscow. On August 5, Hitler weakly warned the Army's commander in chief, Walther von Brauchitsch, "If this frontal fighting goes on as at present, things are going to seize up solid as they did in World War I."

He managed to get his way this once: "Despite his medical indisposition," General Franz Halder, army chief of staff, entered in his diary three days later, "the Führer has given the Commander in Chief the closest instructions on how he wants the air force squadrons used."

Then the illness worsened and the generals got their way. Field Marshal von Bock's armies would still be struggling outside Moscow when the Russian winter arrived. Reichmarschall Hermann Göring would say under interrogation: "I still believe that had Hitler's original plan of genius not been diluted like that, the eastern campaign would have been decided by early 1942 at the latest."

WORRIED by the onset of this illness, Morell sent a fecal sample to Freiburg for analysis. On August 5 Professor Nissle reported back: "Could not find anything suspicious." But he recommended the use of his own Mutaflor medication. "I need scarcely add that when visiting dysentery areas it is advisable to wear a woollen waistband, to refrain from eating uncooked fruit and salads and drinking unboiled water, and to wash hands thoroughly after every contact with the troops, particularly before meals."

On August 8 Nissle sent to Morell his formal analysis report. The sample was "rich in typical coli bacteria cultures, which approximate however only partly in characteristics those of the original Mutaflor strain, most of them having largely lost their high-grade antagonism; in addition some paracoli bacteria and large quantities of enterococci; neither infectious germs nor worm eggs present."

The sudden illness forced Hitler to bed—now of all times, in the thick of the heaviest fighting on the eastern front. It began with a flying visit to the Ukraine on August 6. Hewel recorded his impressions thus: "Four A.M., took off for Berdichev, flew on three hours across Russia, to Bialystok. At a school there (Rundstedt's army HQ) met with General Antonescu. . . . Strolled through Berdichev. Ruined monastery church. Opened coffins, execution, ghastly town. Many Jews, ancient cottages, fertile soil." The heat wave was still bearing down on them as they flew back to the Wolf's Lair that evening. By the next morning Hitler was ill. It was a little sensation in the Führer's headquarters. Hewel wrote in cryptic language in his diary, using Indonesian, as he had been a rubber planter in his youth in Java: "Führer *sakit* [ill]"—he had not turned up for lunch or the war conference, and was unable to sleep because of his affliction.

Little wonder that his nervous personal physician Morell now began to record the course of this illness in a diary.

August 7, 1941 (Thursday)[1]

At Führer's headquarters. Saw Führer at one-thirty P.M. in map room. Said he'd been sitting down when he suddenly felt dizzy, with attacks of nausea and retching. Had flown to Berdichev yesterday, three hours out and three hours back. Of late he's been looking pretty bad all the time, and pale. I wanted to carry out a +++ but he won't allow it, says he's feeling okay now. This bunker atmosphere has been getting him down for five or six weeks now.

Then Junge suddenly telephoned for me to come *immediately* to the Führer, says he suddenly felt giddy and is over in his bunker.

Hurried over with Junge! [Hitler's] face deathly white. "I feel very bad now," he said, "much worse than I was earlier. Just now I suddenly felt giddy. I don't know what it is. Up here," he said, indicating his left temple, "I feel so strange. Over the last few days it's kept bothering me up there." (Since about a week.) "But a short while ago I had a terrific row, I got immensely worked up and since that time I've been feeling pretty low. And my stomach's been upset for quite a while too."

Pulse normal at 72–76 per minute, regular and full; second

[1] The diary was penciled on small note pages in blue, and proved one of the most difficult to decipher. I am indebted to Mr. George Wagner of the U.S. National Archives, Washington, D.C., for his assistance.

heartbeat accentuated. Forehead above both eyebrows is tender. Tremor in extended hands. No local tenderness of abdomen. Intestinal gases. Tongue furred. Liver of harder consistency and somewhat enlarged.—Injected Vitamultin-Calcium and Glyconorm. Bent the needle on insertion. Gave him a Yatren pill and twenty drops of Dolantin.[2] Fetched blood pressure apparatus. Blood pressure 172–174 mm mercury . . . (as against 136 mm normal). Fetched Septoiod and injected 10 cc intravenously. Applied cold compresses to region of temples and left side of head, and hot poultices. Reflexes of the pupils [to light and convergence] good, eye movements unimpaired. Diagnosis: Vascular spasms with rush of blood to temples caused by various reasons.

[Later:] Can hear a constant buzzing in left ear. Says he's had this before. Professor Eicken did not find anything.[3] He's also planning to get a dental checkup. . . .

Eight P.M. to see the Führer. Pulse now 90, blood pressure still 170 mm. Temperature, armpit 37.2, rectum 37.9. Constant buzzing in his ears over last few days. Left supraorb. much more tender than right. Intestinal gases. Stool these last few days again mushy. Gave him a Yatren pill. Spots where I injected the Glyconorm and Vitamultin-Calcium are now smarting. Eyes, no findings. Heartbeat somewhat accelerated, second heartbeat accentuated. Back of tongue furred.

Eleven P.M. Pulse still 90, blood pressure 170 mm, pulse hard, +++ tense as ever. Temperature, armpit 37, rectum 38, abdomen tense (took altogether three Yatren pills) and intestinal movements. Says the places where I injected the Glyconorm and Vitamultin-Calcium are very painful, but already a bit better than at noon. Checked ears, no findings. I wanted to inject something else, two ampoules of Omnadin, but Führer wouldn't have it. Allowed him a soft-boiled egg, mashed potato and strawberries. But Führer has sent for rice soufflé. Doesn't want me to call in later. Gave him two Phanodorm tablets.

---

[2] Yatren was an iodine product by Chinoin. (One tablet: chinoiforum iodoxychinolinsulfate 0.25 g.) It is really used only against amoebic dysentery, not bacillary dysentery. Certainly Hitler did not have the former, which is a disease almost entirely confined to tropical and subtropical countries.

[3] Professor Carl von Eicken. Director of the university ear, nose and throat clinic at Berlin-Dahlem. See his consultation notes on U.S. National Archives microfilm ML/125.

August 8, 1941 (Friday)[4]

Führer sent word over by valet this morning that he has never had a day in bed since being gassed in the World War, so he thinks he's a rotten patient.

He got up at eleven A.M. I went over, without being sent for. Führer was very irritable, is feeling a lot worse than yesterday, hasn't slept a wink, had no intention of lying in that confined space, he's got to get up and about. Says he's not going to have any more injections for the time being. The places where I injected him yesterday are hurting so badly it puts all else in the shade.

Heartbeat regular, pulse 78, blood pressure lower at 156 mm, armpit temperature 36.6, rectum 37.2, abdomen very tense, still no bowel movement. The buzzing in his left ear is undiminished. I wanted to give him castor oil, but he turned it down flat as well as other laxatives, even stewed prunes, saying they generate too much gas. Would like those Yatren pills more often: it says so on the label, I ought to read it sometime. I told him I'm perfectly familiar with the inscriptions. With many diseases it is possible to take a couple three times a day. We'll have a try with two. If the bowels then work it is bound to be a great relief for him.

"When do you want me to come again?" I asked.

"After lunch."

Führer then got out of bed, dressed and went over to the map room. I sent word over at midday that he should only have tea and a biscuit, with no sweetening in the tea. He ordered spaghetti and strawberries.

I have to comment: I have never before seen the Führer so sour toward me. And on top of this, the catastrophic mix-up of +++ , with the blood pressure already 120 mm, so there was real danger. He says he took two of the Phanodorm tablets to get to sleep but they had no effect. He took altogether six Yatren pills— two on each of three occasions. By one A.M. he had had five watery motions.

August 9, 1941 (Saturday)

Called in on him at one A.M. Blood pressure 149/110 mm, pulse 72, armpit temperature 35.9. Abdomen still tense and murmuring.

[4] Written across a menu dated August 7, 1941. The food was not appetizing: "Fried eggs, turnip, green beans, potatoes, strawberries."

Liver still infiltrated.—He was in good humor. I recommend going for a sail on the lakes perhaps every other day and doing a lot of walking.

Eleven A.M. "I think it's okay again, doctor," he said. "Let's keep the checkup short, shall we? Because I want to go over to the map room." His pulse was 72 (at first that is. Right after the bath it was 96 and then 84), heart inconclusive, except for accentuation of second heartbeat (liver!). Tongue still furred, one watery bowel movement during the night.—One Yatren pill to be taken three times today, and one Intelan and three bars of Vitamultin.

During lunch, after the Führer's war conference in the map room, I was sent for by the Führer. "During the conference," he said, "I suddenly got that buzzing in my ears again." Pulse still 72, armpit temperature 35.8, blood pressure 150/148 mm. Abdomen supple under pressure, liver too. Discussion about leeches. For lunch he had ice cream, boiled potatoes and strawberries. He kept very quiet at the table.

August 10, 1941 (Sunday)
At one last night his pulse was 70 and 68, blood pressure 150+, abdomen full of gas and distended. He said he had eaten an asparagus salad. Ears still buzzing.

Noon to one P.M. Pulse 74, blood pressure 146 mm, temperature 35.8 armpit, 36.7 rectum. Had taken a sedative, there is less buzzing now, his abdomen is less tense but there's a lot of intestinal movement and flatulence. His spirits are pretty [Paper damaged: ?? low. Gave him Yatren?] pills and Calomel to take now and half a powder to take two hours later. Also ~~electric heating pads~~ [deleted]. About five bowel evacuations. (He wanted me to see him before four P.M. but I wasn't there.)

To FIGHT the buzzing in Hitler's ears Morell resorted to one of history's most ancient remedies, leeches. Heinz Linge, Hitler's valet, later described: "Hitler sat in front of a mirror and watched fascinated as the leeches quenched their thirst on his blood." Afterward the Führer of the Greater German Reich breathed a sigh of relief. "Ah, good," he said. "Now my head's as clear as a bell again." Leeches had once been à la mode as a cure for persistent headaches and phlebitis. They secrete a remarkable substance that inhibits blood coagulation; so when they begin to suck, it is like a small bloodletting incision. A Frankfurt doctor called Bottenberg had written several manuals on the treatment. An artificial version of the natural anticoagulant, Heparin, is more commonly used nowadays, although apothecaries in Germany still supply leeches if given a few days' notice.

August 11, 1941 (Monday)

At one A.M. his pulse was 72, blood pressure 150/160 mm, abdomen and gut still tender but supple. Ears still buzzing. I plan to try leeches, injections of Vitamultin-Calcium plus Tonophosphan-forte and electric heating pads.

Forenoon. Pulse still 72, blood pressure 150/155, temperature 36.—Still has those abdominal gases and buzzing in the ears. Left hand shows a tremor. Says he had two bowel movements during the night, not watery any more. Began Mutaflor course, one capsule. Bent my needle injecting Vitamultin-Calcium plus Tonophosphan-forte.

Midday diet: gruel, porridge, strawberries.

Later, from four to eight P.M.: applied two leeches, one on left [warzen (??)] process and one in front of the left ear. First I had made a small prick under the ear, but the skin was like leather, I had to push very hard to draw even the tiniest drops of blood. . . . Führer himself shook the leeches out of the jar. I had to apply them with my fingers, as they slithered out of the forceps. The front one sucked much faster, the rear one only slowly. The front one dropped off first, letting go at the bottom and dangling. The rear one continued sucking another half hour then it too let go at the bottom; I had to rip it off at the top. The subsequent bleeding continued about two hours. I applied a pad of cotton soaked in iron chloride, then a small Band-Aid dressing. On account of the two dressings the Führer did not go to supper.

Afterward the Führer turned up for the war conference and then for the usual tea session. His ears had stopped buzzing!

August 12, 1941 (Tuesday)

At two A.M. his pulse was 72, blood pressure 150/155 +, did not take temperature. Abdomen almost completely supple, though still some gases present.

Noon, pulse 84, blood pressure 150/155. Abdomen supple, some gases. When I removed the iron chloride dressing from the forward bloodletting area, heavy bleeding started again. Dabbed on Suprarinin solution. The bleeding stopped. Otherwise no problems.

Told him not to eat any crisp bread or whole meal bread for three days.

Seven P.M., pulse 72, blood pressure 145 mm. Some throbbing in left head, perhaps caused by the Suprarinin drops? Has had a lot of arguments and tension. But buzzing still not back.

Führer lay down to rest. Against my objections he used the styptic solution when shaving.

August 13, 1941 (Wednesday)

One-thirty A.M. Pulse 78, blood pressure 152/155.

Noon. Pulse 72, blood pressure 144. Had slept very soundly. Ears buzzing a bit. Abdomen and intestine no complaints. Gave him a shot of Vitamultin-Calcium plus Tonophosphan-forte.

August 14, 1941 (Thursday)

One A.M. Führer would not let me give him a checkup, says everything is okay. Still some buzzing in his ears. Talked about doing a white and red blood corpuscle count tomorrow, and that was okay by him. An electrocardiogram too while we're about it. Everything before lunch!

Midday. Carried out the electrocardiogram and blood count. Pulse normal at 72, blood pressure 144 mm. In the evening left for Berlin.

MORELL had this important electrocardiogram of Hitler (see Appendix No. I) assessed by the well-known heart specialist Professor Dr. Weber of Bad Nauheim. Weber's diagnosis was that Hitler had contracted coronary sclerosis. It is confirmed to

Harley Street specialists to whom I have shown the electrocardio-grams. The defect was not abnormal in a man of Hitler's age, 52, but it introduced the danger of a sudden angina pectoris or an embolism with possibly fatal consequences. At first Morell kept this news from Hitler, and implied that the heart and other organs were sound. But he began quietly reading medical text-books on heart diseases.

Meanwhile Hitler's late tea parties continued. For example, on that evening of August 14, Hewel noted that he sat up "from nine P.M. to 3:15 A.M. with the Führer." On the next day, Hewel wrote in part-Indonesian that Ribbentrop was "very con-cerned about the *sakitna kapala*" — the sick chief.

August 15, 1941 (Friday)
Twelve noon arrived at Schwanenwerder [Morell's island villa outside Berlin]. Checked by telephone with [Führer headquarters at] Vinnitsa. Manservant said, "Führer's getting on okay."

August 16, 1941 (Saturday)
Berlin still. Called in, and was told: Nothing much to report. Berlin results: 4.4 mill erythrocytes, 5000 leukocytes. Electro-cardiogram: Lead I, depression of T wave, nervous QRS . . .

August 17, 1941 (Sunday)
One A.M. Arrived back at headquarters. Führer claims to be right as rain. Pulse normal at 72, taking Brom-Nervacit, Mutaflor. —Gave Intelan, Vitamultin, a dessert spoon in the evening. Told him the blood count results. By 1:30 A.M. I was bushed—worn out.

August 18, 1941 (Monday)
Noon to one P.M. Pulse 72, blood pressure 142 mm, Cardiac sounds quiet, tongue furred at rear, no complaints.—Talked about the electrocardiogram (the depressed T_I). Intravenous shot of 10 percent Glyconorm plus Vitamultin-C and intramuscular shot of Tonophosphan.

Yesterday and today we talked over the lack of oxygen and sunshine that he's getting. That's why there's so little hemoglobin and why the red corpuscle count is down. Moreover the bunker is damp and unhealthy, the temperature just right for growing fungi; once my boots were mouldy after being left two days, and my clothes were clammy in the bedroom. New bunker walls always sweat quantities of water at first.

Everybody got rheumatism and aches and pains in every nook and cranny of the human body where anything could go wrong. I myself got sciatica down my left side for two days, and all manner of knee-joint pains and toe aches. Then there are the colds caused by the draft of the extractor fans. I pointed all *that* out after just four days here in the bunker. Everybody contradicted me then, now everybody says I was right. People got chest constrictions, anemia and general bunker psychosis.

Reminded him that I had initially recommended more frequent motor journeys or five days in his special train, a change of scenery to somewhere of greater altitude. At the time the Führer declared that wasn't on because of the centralization of his signals equipment, etc. I also suggested he spend fourteen days at the Berghof.

What I now proposed was this, I said: let's arrange a drive with Hewel and then go for a sail. He said, "I've got conferences tomorrow, so that won't do." I said, "Well then, the day after tomorrow." Take it up with Hewel and Engel.[5]

He said that yesterday evening he took half a spoonful of Brom-Nervacit and slept moderately well. But he doesn't want to get into the sedative habit, so he was going to stop. I urged him to take at least a dessert spoon of an evening. Lunch this midday was pickles without meat, all mashed up, but he doesn't feel like trying it yet, so it was stuffed empanadillos (*Pfannkuchen-Taschen*) with pureed carrots and mashed potatoes, rounded off with strawberries. (We had a talk about Dr. Ley's wife.—I wasn't there, she's at Hochrain near Leipzig for eight to ten days in the clinic for a thorough checkup.— Führer is of same opinion as me. *Gastric.* N[issle]— there found Achylia Gastrica also. In my opinion everything originated with this dysbacteria, with side effects on the liver, gall bladder and intestine. *Hysteria.* And this although I have warned her of the toxic influences that emanate from the intestine. She

---

[5] Lieutenant Colonel Gerhard Engel, born 1906 in Rubenz, had been Hitler's army adjutant since February 1938. His "wartime diaries" were unfortunately recently published by the Munich Institute of Contemporary History although they were written years after the war. Died 1979.

really must make up her mind to take a course of stomach treatment and not just keep meaning to do it.)[6]

August 19, 1941 (Tuesday)

Did not give the Führer a checkup today as he felt fine.[7]

August 20, 1941 (Wednesday)

Pulse 72, blood pressure 138 mm, back of tongue still a bit furred, no problems in gastrointestinal tract. After working a lot yesterday his head was a bit dizzy again, but only minimal buzzing in his ears. Intravenous shot of 20 percent Glycovarin plus Vitamultin-Calcium, and intramuscular Tonophosphan-forte.—After working a lot yesterday he was a bit jumpy (his hands were shaking and his head swimming), so he took Brom-Nervacit, a level dessert spoonful. His sleep after that was good, without any sleeping tablets.

August 21, 1941 (Thursday)

Everything fine, no checkup.

ON AUGUST 20, Professor Weber sent to Morell a written report on Hitler's recent electrocardiogram. "The electrocardiogram you submitted showed: sinus rhythm, left type. Transition to left retardation. Beginning depression of $S—T_I$ and $S—T_{II}$.

"Considerable flattening of $S—T_I$ and $S—T_{II}$. If these are not the consequence of digitalis or an infection, we must assume primarily that the cause is coronary sclerosis. I recommend making further electrocardiograms at fourteen-day intervals."

[6] Frau Renate Ley was one of Morell's patients, and a favorite of Hitler's. The doctor once wrote to her in these terms: "I was very sorry to hear you've got so many worries again and aggravations as well. This is of course very unfortunate for your mental state." He recommended injections of Prävison and Progynon, and Leptormon pills (to be taken only under medical supervision, he warned, "so you won't go taking an overdose again"). She killed herself a year later.

[7] But see Joseph Goebbels' unpublished diary, August 19, 1941: "He [Hitler] unfortunately looks rather weak and sickly. That's probably attributable to his attack of dysentery and to the fact that the last few weeks have taken their toll on his health."

August 22, 1941 (Friday)

He slept very well from four A.M. to eleven A.M. Yesterday afternoon took a dessert spoon of Brom-Nervacit because of nervous symptoms. For a while still some relatively minor buzzing in his ears. Felt well. In fact wanted to do without any further injections; nonetheless gave him a 10 cc shot of 20 percent glucose intravenously (two jabs, injected left) and Vitamultin-Calcium and an intramuscular shot of Tonophosphan. (Bent the needle.) No unpleasant aftereffects.

The discussion of the electrocardiogram by Professor Weber has arrived: either a previous infection, or *coronary sclerosis*. Outburst last night: "Meal repertoire is very limited." Trouble is, he turns down so many things we suggest, and it's getting very difficult to make suggestions what with his being a vegetarian, because carbohydrates lead to the building up of gases. I've proposed he take Enzynorm with his meals, but now he's turned that down.

Of the Mark II leeches, only one is still alive, and I was hoping to apply leeches once more before Mussolini gets here so that his head will be completely clear. "But I can't find the time yet," says Führer. "Right now I'm up to my eyes in work. Of course I want it too."

"But," I say, "I must know in advance, because I want to make a point of using fresh animals."

Gave him a shot of 20 percent glucose solution intravenously with Vitamultin-C, and an intramuscular of Tonophosphan-forte.

August 23, 1941 (Saturday)

Pulse 72, blood pressure 142+ (prior to application of the leeches). Set three leeches (two behind the ear, one in front). The latter sucked well and strong. Head clearer and lighter. Says he found the suction not at all unpleasant. Applied a dressing.

August 24, 1941 (Sunday)

Pulse 72, blood pressure 136 mm. Injected 20 percent glucose solution and Vitamultin-C intravenously, and gave him a shot of Tonophosphan intramuscularly right. Didn't feel a thing of the intramuscular injection (I used a platinum needle). His head is free. Using sedatives because of excitement and worry. Won't be able to get down to the Berghof before December. Ate well. Told

be taking Enzynorm at mealtimes until the coli are settled into his intestinal tract. Talked about how the capillaries begin to calcify in people around fifty.

O N AUGUST 25, 1941, Mussolini arrived at the Wolf's Lair. After a joint war conference and a meal in the mess bunker, the two dictators drove off the next morning to Brest-Litvosk to inspect their troops. That evening they returned, only to depart at eight P.M. by special train to the alternative Führer's Headquarters South at Vinnitsa, in the Ukraine.

August 27, 1941

Journey to the headquarters in the foothills of the eastern Beskides. Train halted en route so I could give the Führer an intravenous shot of 20 percent glucose plus Tonophosphan-forte and Vitamultin-Calcium intramuscular. Took just eight minutes from start to finish, so although the train was running an hour late it made up all the lost time. Mussolini went in the train ahead of ours. We were traveling one whole day, i.e., we left at eight P.M. on the twenty-sixth, and arrived at eight P.M. on August 27.

T HAT DAY, August 27, they dined with the Italian troops. On the following day the journey continued, this time in four-engined Condors that flew for three hours onward to Uman, affording a fine view of Mother Russia and her fertile acreage. In Uman the ground and air commanders, Gerd von Rundstedt and Alexander Löhr, briefed the Axis leaders on the triumphant Wehrmacht advances. Then they drove on through the endless expanses and the still unharvested fields, before flying back to Vinnitsa in magnificent weather. Here Hitler took leave of Mussolini.

August 28, 1941

From seven A.M. to five P.M. the Führer was with the Duce at the front visiting the Italians. His face was sunburnt to a brilliant red and his forehead was very painful with big burned patches, so he was very grumpy. In the evening around eight P.M. we drove off again.

August 29, 1941

In the afternoon (at Deutsch-Eylau) gave him both injections again. He's feeling good. Supper at eight P.M. in the train, then returned to the old headquarters. Tea until 1:30 A.M. with the Führer.

August 30, 1941

Nothing to report.

September 6, 1941

Führer's headquarters. Patient A [Hitler]. Morning, urinalysis. Specific gravity 1020. Reaction: alkali. Albumen: ——— , sugar: ——— , urobilinogen: ——— , blood: ——— , sediment: very sporadic leukocytes and epithalia, coli bacilli.

WITH THIS EPISODE Morell's surviving diaries for 1941 close.

By the fall of 1941 the German forces had thrust deep into the Soviet Union. "Offensive in the east making wonderful progress," rejoiced Hewel in his private diary on October 5. Two days later the Wehrmacht closed its ring around Vyazma, and an entire Soviet army went into brutal captivity. General Alfred Jodl spoke of "the most decisive day of the Russian war," and compared it with the battle of Königgrätz.

But Hitler again succumbed to a mysterious, plaguelike illness. Hewel noted it in his secret language, Indonesian. The Führer was ill, he had "not appeared for either midday or evening meals, although it was Reichsführer's [Himmler's] birthday and he had been invited specially for lunch." Alfred Rosenberg's liaison officer Werner Koeppen also remarked upon Hitler's absence. "The Führer did not put in an appearance for lunch," he wrote, and then: "Nor for supper either." Again the fat physician waddled over. He was at a loss for an explanation, but by October 10 this renewed affliction had fortunately for him passed over. "Spent evening with F.," Hewel wrote. "Wonderfully relaxed and in best of spirits. Completely carefree." On the thirteenth he added, "Führer in best of possible spirits, very relaxed."

What had happened? A letter from the Berlin pharmaceutical company Hageda to Morell, dated November 3, 1941, indicates that Hitler had been attacked by severe nausea and heartburn [*übles Aufstossen*]. Morell suspected that the Mutaflor batch he had been administering might not have been fresh, perhaps even toxic. Hageda indignantly lectured him:

"The Engel Pharmacy has functioned perfectly properly." They calmed Morell with the explanation, "We regularly, though not often, get such reports after our Mutaflor capsules dissolve prematurely in the patient's stomach. Obviously it is undesirable, and the patient finds it most unpleasant, even though the therapeutic efficiency of the coli bacteria is not significantly affected by this. This premature dissolving of the capsules in the stomach might be caused by three things:

1. The patient does not swallow the capsules properly and then does not drink enough liquids, so that the capsules linger on in the gullet and then in the stomach;
2. or the stomach acidity is deficient;
3. or (very rarely) a back-peristalsis of the intestine occurs, so that the contents already in the intestine are forced back into the stomach."

IN THE EAST, the Nazi offensive bogged down in the autumn rains, then froze solid in the Russian winter. While Japan's entry into the war in December 1941 evoked something like euphoria in Hitler—"Now there's no way we can lose this war!" —a few days later he began to brood on Germany's darkening future. "Strange," he said, "that we are destroying the positions of the white race in East Asia with the help of Japan, while Britain has joined the bolshevik swine in the fight against Europe!" (Hewel diary.)

As the seemingly invincible Nazi war machine slowed to a halt, Hitler cast around for scapegoats. He found them: The commander in chief of the army and a number of army-group and army commanders were dismissed. His own responsibilities thus expanded still further. With them, the aggravations and associated health problems multiplied too.

Brain Fever

HITLER was aging. Dr. Hasselbach would say under interrogation in 1945, "Prior to 1940 Hitler appeared to be much younger than he actually was. After that date, however, he aged quite rapidly. From 1940 to 1943 he actually looked his age, while after that time he gave the appearance of having grown old." Goebbels also noticed the aging process in his chief. "The Führer's looks belie his health," he wrote on March 20, 1942. "From just a fleeting look at him one might get the impression of a man in the best of health. But that is not the case. In an intimate conversation he told me that of late he has felt somewhat ill. Now and again he has to struggle with the most violent dizzy spells. He says the long winter upset his spirit so much that it has taken its toll on his health."

On March 28, 1942, Hitler had issued secret directives for the summer offensive in Russia, Operation Blue. But that was just one worry: almost at once the British bombing offensive began. Lübeck was firebombed, and three hundred people lost their lives in the ancient Hanseatic port.

Many other cities would suffer the same fate. Hitler adopted the habit of never going to bed until he was sure the last enemy plane had left German airspace.

He hated the winter and loathed snow. To Goebbels he described the winter fighting in all its cruelty. "It was really quite touching," wrote Goebbels, "to hear him complain about how this last winter inundated him with worries and difficulties. I couldn't help noticing that he's gone quite gray. And as he started talking about the winter's problems he seemed even older."

A few weeks later, on April 26, Hitler told Goebbels that he had to take off three months some time. That was out of the question, but at least he might travel to Berchtesgaden on the pretext of talks with Mussolini. "The Obersalzberg has such a soothing effect on him," Goebbels observed.

Within a few weeks of his arrival there, however, Hitler's general health plummeted even lower. His spirits sank. Morell tried to combat this with injections of Prostakrinum. Operation Blue had to be postponed. And while Hitler had originally planned to stay only a few weeks at the Berghof, he finally remained two months.

Morell's records are missing from September 1941 until mid-1942. During the early summer Morell appears in fact to have spent a month in Munich, treating the ailing Minister Wagner. So he wrote in a letter of August 6, anyway.

After Blue began, Hitler flew on July 16 to Vinnitsa where he had established a field headquarters code-named Werewolf.

Here he was taken ill. In 1945 Morell would say, "Hitler had a brain fever when we were in Vinnitsa . . . in 1942." This was not dangerous, he added. "It lasted a week." There was a lot of this grippe-type of brain fever about until 1943; it was termed "Russian headache," and was not unlike meningitis but less deadly. In most cases it was over in five days or a week.

July 22, 1942

Two P.M. Summoned to the Führer. Says he has a terrible headache, and later stated that the vision in his right eye is somewhat impaired. Heart 66 beats per minute, heart sounds pure and regular, but blood pressure right up to 170 mm! Checked abdominal organs, result inconclusive. His tongue is furred. Injected twenty-five percent glucose solution and 10 cc of Septoiod intravenously, and gave him an intramuscular shot of Vitamultin-Calcium.

Führer then went off to lunch. Told him to lie down afterward and apply cold compresses. Ought to run a blood check.—When asked he admitted he's been working a lot these last few days and couldn't sleep last night. [Diagnosis:] *Arteriospasm.*

At seven-thirty this evening saw him again: he's had a sleep and since getting the injections and two Thrombovetren tablets the pain behind his right forehead has gone away. The impairment of vision right has also gone. Blood pressure: digitally, 150; auscultation, 155/110 (as against 170 earlier in the middle of the day.)— Gave two Thrombovetren tablets.

I'll have to draw off a little blood, around 150 cc, soon. The climate here is too hot for the Führer. For people with translucent, fine, hypersensitive skin and particularly those prone to sunburn, a fresh wind and a cool climate are always more wholesome. That's why the climate in East Prussia and particularly mountain air are so good for the Führer.

July 23, 1942

Forenoon. Blood pressure digitally 145, by auscultation 150/100 mm. Slept well and somewhat longer. No eye pain any more. Wants an eye checkup soon, particularly for focus, as in his opinion one eye sees worse than the other; he presumes it's the right one. In the evening, blood pressure digitally 145, by auscultation 145/100 again. In a very good mood.

July 24, 1942

Took blood pressure at eleven A.M. 150 digitally, 145 mm auscultation. Disturbed sleep. (Five hours all told.)

July 26, 1942

Three-thirty P.M. Blood pressure was 138 mm digitally, 138/95 mm by auscultation. I applied two leeches but they wouldn't suck.

July 27, 1942

Eleven A.M. Intravenous shot of 10 cc of twenty percent glucose solution and 10 cc of Septoiod, and an intramuscular injection of Tonophosphan-forte and Vitamultin-Calcium.

July 28, 1942

Set one leech to his right temple.

July 29, 1942

———[sic]

HITLER had evidently recovered.

The climate at Werewolf was particularly unpleasant. At the end of August the OKW's war diarist *Ministerialrat* Helmuth Greiner wrote to his wife, "Since the day we arrived here at Vinnitsa . . . we have had uninterrupted fine weather and a heat wave. . . . But though we long for rain we dread it too because . . . the humidity here is said to be particularly grim. . . . The Führer can't take the climate and heat, and pines to get back to his bunker [at Rastenburg]. These barracks haven't been built with winter in mind. But by winter the operations in the Caucasus will have been largely wound up."

That proved overoptimistic. The summer offensive slithered to a halt in the Caucasian highlands. On September 9, 1942, Greiner entered in his pocket diary: "Serious crisis of confidence. Field Marshal List sacked, Führer takes over command of Army Group A himself." A few days later he unceremoniously dismissed General Franz Halder as chief of the general staff and began snubbing General Alfred Jodl, chief of the OKW operations staff. Then he brought in verbatim shorthand writers to record every word spoken at his war conferences, to ensure that his orders were actually carried out.

"For two weeks, lunch with the Führer has been dropped," wrote Greiner to his wife, describing the crisis, adding disrespectfully: "And for the time being it probably won't be resumed as Mr. Big has withdrawn into his own solitary fastness."

Morell was temporarily preoccupied with his business empire. To Johanna the doctor wrote on October 22, 1942: "I'm often pretty tired after the many journeys to Zhitomir. I drive two hundred miles every other day, and sometimes every day, and on the badly made Russian roads at that. Today my kidneys are hurting badly. It must be the albumen again (my Patient has got the same trouble too)." He added, "If I get back to Berlin for a few days I'll give Lammers and . . . the Prince of Hesse their checkups."

His high level patients were doing their bit for him. In an act of rare concurrence with Alfred Rosenberg, the minister for the Occupied Eastern Territories, Gauleiter Koch decreed that Morell's factories should enjoy a total monopoly in exploiting byproducts from the Ukrainian slaughterhouses. And Morell's lofty niche shielded him from a lot of unpleasantness. When the Pancreatic Company initiated a lawsuit against him claiming one million Reichsmarks damages because he had now blocked their access to the animal organs of the Ukraine, Morell triumphed in a letter: "They can't touch me." He had only to run to Hitler of course and any lawsuit would be stopped.

"Meanwhile," he continued, "the desiccating of the glands is making great progress. Tomorrow I'm going out there again to check. I hope the vacuum-drying plant and the extraction gear come quickly, because then we can really go into big business. If I get enough equipment I want to start up in Kiev and Poltava. Koch has promised me the Endocrinological Institute at Kharkov too, but I don't want a word of that breathed anywhere yet."

Morell's routine consultation notes on Patient Adolf Hitler for the period after October 1942 are in the files. He scribbled them on quarto-size data cards with printed headings. At the head of Patient A's October 1942 card he noted the general diagnosis: "Variable blood pressure through arterio-spasms. Insomnia." They are reproduced below with repetitive or inconclusive matter omitted (***).

October 1, 1942 (Berlin)

Visited and injected him as usual. Gr. Pros.[1] and intravenous injection of glucose plus Tonophosphan-forte and intramuscular injection of Vitamultin-C.

October 6, 1942 (Vinnitsa)

Injection as usual, blood pressure 145.

As PLANNED, Hitler returned on November 1 to his winter quarters at Rastenburg. Greiner found it as unpleasant as Vinnitsa, and wrote privately at the end of November, "It's horrid here in this dirty green, gloomy, airless forest encampment. It's permanently swathed in fog, and it has an exceptionally nasty dining room that couldn't compete with even the ugliest village pub and frightful bunkers and barrack huts that are either over-

[1] Prostrophanta. This was always injected with glucose.

heated or freezing. . . . What's worse is, the way things are turning out there are a lot of differences of opinion."

Stalingrad still caused the fewest headaches, Greiner would comment in the letter, because headquarters was confident that the situation could be repaired. The real crisis was perceived in North Africa, where the British Eighth Army had broken through Rommel's minefields at El Alamein.

On November 7 Hitler had left in his special train for Munich. On the thirteenth he went on to Berchtesgaden. "It began to snow," recorded shorthand writer Karl Thöt in his hieroglyphic diary, "and after a few days everything had turned into the most magic scenery." Hitler was not enthusiastic about snowscapes. And on November 21 the Soviet offensive tore open the Stalingrad front. On the next day he ordered an immediate return to Rastenburg. By the time he arrived, on the night of November 24–25, the Sixth Army had been encircled and cut off.

Data Card: Patient A [that is, Hitler].   *Year:* 1942.
Address: At present Wolf's Lair near Rastenburg.
Illness: Coronary sclerosis and arterio-spasms (head and intestine), dysbacteria of intestine.

November 23, 1942

Intravenous injection of Gr. Pros. plus twenty percent glucose plus Tonophosphan and intramuscular injection of Vitamultin-Calc. Getting scarcely any sleep because of huge responsibility and overwork.

December 9, 1942

Intestinal gases, bad breath, malaise. 0.2 Calomel twice.

December 11, 1942

Effect almost nil. Gave him 0.2 Calomel again and Mitilax in the evening.

December 11, 1942

Not much effect.—Diet; in the evening, one ampoule of Entero-fagos.

THE EPIGASTRIC DISTURBANCES were certainly a product of his growing frustration. On December 9 Greiner had noted in his diary: "Führer utters strong criticism of the navy—the uselessness of our battleships. I stuck up for them. Führer wants to get down to the Berghof for a lengthy period to clear his head for new decisions. High time too." But Halder's successor, General Kurt Zeitzler persuaded him to stay on at Rastenburg. The weeks dragged by in the Wolf's Lair, cold, dank, and clammy. The transfer to the sunnier south was postponed from one day to the next.

December 12, 1942
Enterofagos twice, light diet.—Continued Hammavit and Vitamultin.—Yatren and Luizym pills permitted.

December 13, 1942
Continuation of Enterofagos for a week, then Mutaflor.

December 14, 1942
General condition good, belly now free of gas (deeply worried by situation).

December 15, 1942 (Data card).
Slept poorly, took Profundol (because of the military situation). —Intravenous injection of twenty percent glucose and Gr. Pr. plus Tonophosphan-forte plus intramuscular injection of Vitamultin-C. —Blood pressure 130 mm, an aftereffect of the Profundol. In a sour mood because of the war situation. Issued him with enough Enterofagos for four more days yet!

THE SITUATION did not improve. Hitler took important decisions which Greiner noted tersely on December 19: "Resolve to hold on to Tunis and Stalingrad too."

December 17, 1942
Blood pressure 134 mm. Gave him two intravenous injections of twenty percent Merck glucose solutions plus Tonophosphan-forte

plus intramuscular injection of Vitamultin-Calcium (I made the injection in the left arm—he experienced a dull pain after the injection). He slept badly, took Brom-Nervacit in the morning.

Data card: Patient A.   *Year:* 1942
Address: At present Wolf's Lair, near Rastenburg.
Illness: Coronary sclerosis and arterio-spasms (head right lower and intestine), intestinal dysbacteria with slight liver complaint.

December 17, 1942

Sent for during the evening by the Führer to ask me about Cardiazol [a heart drug manufactured by Knoll of Ludwigshafen]. Said that Göring had told him he took a tablet of Cardiazol whenever he felt weak or dizzy. Wouldn't it do him, the Führer, good too if he suddenly felt funny during some vital affair?

I advised against it because what Göring has is *low* blood pressure (that is, his head gets too little blood supply) while he, the Führer, is suffering from too much blood when his temper rises, that is from high blood pressure. This being so, if one took a Cardiazol tablet and the blood pressure then went up one might burst a blood vessel. I referred to the episode a year ago (when his blood press was right up to 200 mm), and once in Vinnitsa when he had a brain edema with impairment of vision in his right eye accompanied by high blood pressure (over 170 mm).[2]

The Führer asked me to tell him if things should ever look really black for him, as there are some vital decisions he has to take on Germany's account. He says he has no fear of death; that will just be a relief for him. All he has now is just one worry after another and no time that he can call his own. He says he lives only for the fatherland, for Germany. There is no cure for death, that he knows. But if he should ever fall terminally ill, then I must tell him.

I reminded him of that day last December [1941] and of how I had called in nobody else because I said to myself: nobody can do better than I anyway and somebody else might make a botch-up over it. I preferred to take the entire responsibility even though it might be tough at the time. I also reminded him of that brain edema

[2] See Morell's records for August 7, 1941 and July 22, 1942.

condition at V., and said that—if some improvement had not occurred within twenty-four hours—I would have had to resort to some pretty intensive methods.

He said he trusted me implicitly and in such cases I should continue to treat him just as calmly as I could on my own.

Since I was on the subject of always giving him the most accurate picture of his condition, I referred to the existence of a coronary sclerosis and said this is why I've been giving him iodine for some time now. Subsequent electrocardiograms have confirmed my suspicion, I said. In many people this calcification occurs somewhat faster as a result of intensive hard work, but it usually starts at around forty-five. I added that as the blood vessels of the coronary artery narrow, he may get attacks of angina pectoris. I always have medicine for that at hand, but so must he—in case I am not available—and I left him some nitroglycerine tablets and Esdesan cum Nitro. By injecting glucose, I said, I'm doing what I can to strengthen his heart and also to dehydrate the system.

December 18, 1942

Visit by the Italians—*** *Very* strenuous day! Ciano, Italian generals, Ribbentrop, Göring and the rest.—At ten-thirty P.M. blood pressure was up to 144 mm.

December 19, 1942

Many conferences!!! (Ciano, Laval.)—In the morning injected intravenous twenty percent glucose plus Gr. Pr. and intramuscular Tonophosphan-forte and Vitamultin-C.

In the evening blood pressure up to 154 mm. Gave him two tablespoons of Brom-Nervacit and one Phanodorm.

December 21, 1942

He slept well. Blood pressure 137 (127)/90 mm.—The usual injections. Beginning of Mutaflor course. Evening before that two spoons of Brom-Nervacit and one Phanodorm.

December 23, 1942

Blood pressure is 137 mm, gave usual injections. Slept well, five hours, after Brom-Nervacit and a Phanodorm tablet.

December 25, 1942

Christmas Day.—Usual injections. Sleep as before.

December 27, 1942

*** In a good mood.

BY DECEMBER 28, 1942, the thermometer had fallen to minus ten in East Prussia. The situation on the shattered eastern front was critical. That night Hitler took for the first time in his life the decision to fall back before enemy pressure and give up valuable territory; he ordered Army Groups A and Don to retreat. But still he refused to give up hope for the Sixth Army in Stalingrad. The Luftwaffe began flying round the clock to airlift supplies to the 250,000 besieged troops, but to no avail.

December 31, 1942

*** Grim. (The day before yesterday Frau Dr. L. ✠ during the evening.)[3]

---

[3] Dr. Robert Ley's wife had committed suicide. Hitler was particularly attached to her.

1943:

"I Give Him What He Needs"

THE FEARSOME struggle for control of Stalingrad continued until the end of January 1943. On the twenty-second General Zeitzler asked if Paulus might now honorably surrender. Hitler refused. Paulus, promoted by him to field marshal, radioed Hitler a final message: "Long live Germany," and went into Soviet captivity with the shreds of his defeated Sixth Army. The General Staff called for the evacuation of the Donets basin, but Munitions Minister Albert Speer appeared at headquarters on February 4 and protested. Hitler agreed: to abandon the Donets basin would make it impossible to continue the war. On February 17 he flew down to Manstein's headquarters at Zaporozhye to beef him up for the battles to come. Morell's scrappy notes on the data cards picture Hitler's health during these weeks:

January 3, 1943
In the afternoon blood pressure 152/110. By evening a headache after tiring negotiations (with Speer and others).

January 4, 1943
Injections as before. Blood pressure 132 (after Brom-Nervacit and one Optalidon). On January 4–5 major conferences with Speer, Bulgarians, et cetera.

January 6, 1943
Injection as before.

January 10, 1943
*** ([Romanian leaders:] Antonescu, Roziu, Dr. Stojeson), Funk, v. Ribbentrop. Strenuous day.

Blood pressure 137/97 mm. Injections as always, slept badly as usual.

Double glucose [injection].

Double glucose [injection]. ([Führer conference with Japanese ambassador] Oshima.)

MORELL had begun injecting Hitler every two or three days with double shots of glucose, noted in his records only by "injections as usual" or simply a large X. These recurring entries have been largely omitted.

During the night, stomach pains and violent flatulence after eating green beans. Double glucose.

Injections as usual. Double glucose.

DESPITE his own problems the dictator found time to worry about the little band of stenographers endlessly scribbling at his conference table—Thöt, Reynitz, Dörr, Haagen and the rest. On February 4, Thöt entered in his shorthand diary: "While we were briefly alone with the Führer, he spoke to us. It was very cold in the room, and in his kindly way he said we were probably freezing and he was going to get us an electric bowl fire to warm our places at the table. He said he couldn't stand heat himself while bending over the map table because he got headaches. When Dr. Reynitz commented, 'If the soldiers out there can stand the cold and snow and ice then we too will manage somehow,' that set the Führer talking about the front in a manner we certainly had not been accustomed to here before."

The strain on these civil servants was overwhelming. Along

the eastern front the situation seemed desperate. They wilted under the endless barrage of crisis reports, particularly the stenographers who were privy to every word. On February 16, Thöt secretly recorded: "Dr. Dörr has had a nervous breakdown after displaying a remarkable indifference bordering on downright apathy yesterday. In the afternoon Dr. Haagen ordered a medical checkup by Professor Brandt." Dörr was sent packing to Berlin.

How much greater was the strain on Hitler. But he soldiered on, aided by Morell.

February 4, 1943

Injections as usual.

February 6, 1943

Injections as usual.

February 7, 1943

One typhus vaccination. Double glucose.

February 10, 1943

Double glucose.[1]

February 14, 1943

Second typhus shot and injections as usual.

February 16, 1943

Injections as usual. Double glucose.

O N FEBRUARY 17 Hitler flew to Zaporozhye to see Manstein, then drove on to his old headquarters at Vinnitsa. It was bitterly cold at Werewolf, which had only been designed for summer use. Thöt recorded on the twentieth, "Midday war conference was short—only fifty-seven minutes—but freezing. The Führer

[1] In Morell's papers is a menu from the Vienna Stadtkrug restaurant, dated January 30, 1943; evidently its owner had persuaded him to use his influence against decrees closing down luxury restaurants in preparation for total war. It bears Morell's handwritten note on it: "Feb 10, 43: 11 A.M., discussed this with Führer. The Stadtkrug is to stay open! Prof. Morell."

must have noticed us shivering because he spoke to us afterward. I said if you have to sit still for a long time you do get cold. The Führer confirmed that and mentioned that at least the other gentlemen could move around from time to time." Hitler promised to get a stove installed, and Thöt replied, "Jawohl, that would be fine, mein Führer!" By the time of the next midday conference a small tiled stove had indeed been provided. Hitler asked the stenographer whether it was good enough, and laughed "a great belly laugh" as Thöt nodded. Almost every day Morell recorded giving "injections as usual"; sometimes he jotted just "as usual." On February 22 the dictator flew back to the Wolf's Lair at Rastenburg, only to fly back down to the chilling Werewolf encampment three days later.

February 24, 1943

Injections as usual. Vinnitsa.

WITH the coming of spring, the military crisis passed. On March 16, the panzer forces of SS General Sepp Dietrich recaptured Kharkov, and three days later Hitler felt able to leave headquarters and fly back to Berlin. Thöt wrote, "The flight over German territories was wonderful, and I was entranced. The Reich capital unfolded beneath us magnificently in the blue sunshine. . . . True, we could also see the swathe of destruction left by the air raid on the night of March 1–2."

Two days later Hitler attended the Memorial Day service, and left Berlin in his special train for Munich. On March 22 his car drove him up the winding lanes to his mountainside villa, Berghof. Morell followed two days later. On a data card he entered this brief note:

March 24, 1943

It's *ten* P.M.[2] Arrived at the Obersalzberg. There are Föhn

[2] Times in *italics* are those corrected by the author using a precise log kept by Hitler's valets, Heinz Linge and Hans Junge. This shows that Morell regularly visited Hitler immediately he woke up and stayed between five and twenty-five minutes. It also shows that Morell did not religiously enter *all* his consultations in his own data cards.

[warm mountain wind] conditions and a sudden heat wave. Says his head's aching and thumping. Blood pressure right up, 170–180 mm. Gave him two intravenous 10 cc shots of Septoiod, two table-spoons of Brom-Nervacit and an Optalidon tablet. Rapid recovery!

He's been living in low-pressure areas since mid-November 1942, and now this sudden change; moreover up to a week or ten days ago he's been worrying constantly about the consolidating of the eastern front.

T HEN Professor Morell turned the data card over and wrote down a more leisurely account of the consultation with Hitler.

On March 24, 1943, I arrived at the Berghof from Munich at eight P.M. At nine-thirty, after the war conference, I was called to the Führer. Complained of violent headache and a throbbing head. Temporal artery badly swollen. Looking generally tired and languid. Föhn! He's been up here since the evening of the twenty-second.

Took his blood pressure. It's 170–180 mm! Gave him two intra-venous shots of 10 cc Septoiod, and two tablespoons of Brom-Nervacit and an Optalidon tablet. During the actual injections his head began to clear, and a short time later the throbbing stopped.

Sat up in animated conversation until two-thirty A.M. at the fireside (but no fire!), and I made sure he got fresh air. Führer told me repeatedly he feels much better now.

March 25, 1943

Eleven-thirty A.M. Blood pressure 156 mm/110 mm, pulse regu-lar, no complaints. Injections as usual. Intravenous of glucose and Septoiod and intramuscular of Tonophosphan and Vitamultin-Calcium.[3]

At nine-thirty P.M. the Führer sent for me to take his blood pressure again as the violent headache is back: 156–158 mm/110 mm by auscultation, digitally 156 mm. Pulse regular. Gave him an Optalidon tablet and a tablespoon of Brom-Nervacit. Ought to

[3] There is no record of Morell injecting Vitamultin-Calcium since Decem-ber 19. He continued giving Vitamultin tablets, because on February 20, 1943, he ordered ten packets of 200 to be sent express "as a one-off special manufacture" to Morell c/o the Reich Chancery.

go to bed earlier and not overdo the liquid intake. Föhn! (I myself having heart trouble since afternoon and ill at ease because of the Föhn.)

March 26, 1943

Eleven-thirty A.M. Pulse 72, blood pressure by auscultation 154–156 mm, digitally 150 mm! Feeling generally better. Again rejected a masseur, says that when the worries are gone he will get better anyway.

DURING MARCH Morell had a fecal analysis made. The result was sent to him on the twenty-second. "This was," reported Professor Laves, "a fecal sample after evidently vegetarian nutrition, displaying mainly normal bacterial flora. The individual coli strains that were examined in detail behaved normally in the reactions carried out. The stool contained individual coli mutabile strains (variations) and also strains that were somewhat inhibited in acid formation in maltose and lactose. No traces of paracoli bacilli or degeneration coli." Early in April, Morell had the analysis repeated by the laboratory at his factory at Olmütz. They confirmed: "The fecal sample contains no anaerobe bacteria departing from the norm."

March 27, 1943

Eleven-thirty. Blood pressure 152/156 mm auscultation, 110 mm digitally. Feeling good. Injections as usual! Told him the results of fecal examination by Professor Laves.

March 28, 1943

Eleven-forty A.M. Pulse 72, blood pressure 152–156 mm, digitally 150 mm. (Said the pressure was lower in the Wolf's Lair.)

March 29, 1943

Twelve-thirty-five P.M. Blood pressure 154–156/110.

March 30, 1943

Twelve-fifteen P.M. Blood pressure 156 mm, injections as usual.

March 31, 1943
Twelve noon. Blood pressure 154–156, had slept badly.

April 1, 1943
Eleven-forty-five A.M. Blood pressure by auscultation 140–150 mm, feeling better. At 146 really heavy pressure.

Firstly, should go to bed earlier! Secondly, should take four to six egg yolks with some cream and sugar daily. Thirdly, urged massages (two or three times a week for the present).

April 2, 1943
Twelve noon. Blood pressure 142–147, took strong sleeping dose last night. Began today with No. 2. Injections as usual. Deep snow and snowdrifts. Got permission for aircraft for Olmütz.

April 7, 1943
Eleven-fifteen A.M. Blood pressure 154 (–157). Injections as usual. Duce here.

April 8, 1943
Blood pressure 152–153 mm.

April 9, 1943
Blood pressure 143–150 mm. Injections as usual.

April 10, 1943
In good health, perky. In the evening Duce left. Was here or at Klessheim four days.

April 14, 1943
At *one-ten* P.M. Blood pressure 153 mm and up/110 mm. Injections as on April 7. Had a talk with him about priority ratings [presumably for Morell's manufactures in the raw material allocations of the Ministry of Munitions].

April 16, 1943
Injections as on April 7. Visit of Horthy.

Eleven A.M. Blood pressure 140 mm (took a Tempidorm at three A.M.). Injections as on April 7. (Quisling is here.)

April 20, 1943

His birthday! Began course of Enterofagos in the evening (epigastric gases). (Eva Braun likewise.)

TO OUTSIDERS Hitler seemed to be well again. Sepp Dietrich told Goebbels on April 20 how glad he was that Hitler had repaired his health on the Obersalzberg. "He looks fresh and active," he said. "He is full of pep again, and we can expect the same brilliant feats from him as of old."

April 21, 1943

Eleven-forty-five A.M. Injections as usual.

April 26, 1943

Blood pressure 142 mm, injections as usual.

April 28, 1943

Two 0.2 Calomels, and one of 0.1.

April 29, 1943

Twelve-forty P.M. Injections as usual.

May 2, 1943

Injections as usual.

FROM MAY 2–6, Hitler spent a few days in Munich.

May 4, 1943

Twelve-ten P.M. Injections as usual.

May 7, 1943

Ten-fifteen P.M. Injections as usual. Berlin (Lutze).

VICTOR LUTZE, the chief of staff of the SA, had been killed in an automobile accident. The Party funeral service was held in the Reich Chancery. Hitler had arrived in Berlin on the evening before with Morell.

While in Berlin, Morell took the opportunity to carry out further blood and urine analyses on Hitler. The results were largely normal, although a blood test on May 14 indicated, "All pituitary and both suprarenal gland values are perceptibly high. The blood albumen content is somewhat (six percent) high."

The problem was still Hitler's heart. On May 11, 1943, Morell took a further electrocardiogram before flying back to Rastenburg with Hitler on the next day.

On May 13, Morell took a letterhead from the Führer's headquarters, and wrote by hand to the cardiologist Professor Weber asking for advice. "About two years ago," he reminded Weber, "I sent you one of the enclosed electrocardiograms for an opinion, informing you that it was a gentleman in the Foreign Ministry. You expressed the opinion that this was an incipient coronary sclerosis. Meanwhile I have treated the patient concerned—a man who is subjected to huge burdens and can hardly ever take a respite—from time to time with repeated glucose and iodine injections (frequently giving courses of these injections), in that two or three times a day I inject 10 cc of twenty percent glucose solution and after that 10 cc of Septoiod, which always went down very well. I also applied leeches from time to time. There are no heart or angina pains, but a tendency to arterio-spasms with rapid increase in blood pressure (when worked up) and a serious general insomnia. The intramuscular injections of Vitamultin-Calcium have done a lot of good and I add Tonophosphan-forte on account of the nervous system.

"Recently," continued Morell, "when I gave him a thorough checkup the pulse was 72 and blood pressure 146–154/100 mm, with pure sounds and otherwise completely normal findings, and I made the second attached electrocardiogram. As far as I can see a very minor deterioration has occurred. Would you please be so good as to tell me your opinion on (1) the present result, (2) how it compares with the earlier one, and (3) the proper therapy. If possible in two separate letters, one I can show the patient and one for me. I have been holding back with Strophantin and nitroglycerine for the time being."

Weber's report was not favorable. In a detailed letter of May 17 the cardiologist confirmed, "The two takes of May 11 show: sinus rhythm, left type, possibly also incipient left retardation, slight depression of ST_I and ST_{II}. T_I beginning negative, T_{II} on the base line. Compared with the 1941 take, an unquestionable deterioration has taken place inasmuch as the ST depression has become clearer and the T_I, which was at that time still clearly positive, is now negative. The T_{II} which was still clearly positive then now virtually coincides with the base line. The electrocardiogram of May 11 this year reinforces my earlier diagnosis: coronary sclerosis, and this is evidently a progressive case."

Professor Weber allowed himself the following suggestions as to how Morell's anonymous VIP patient should be treated: "I would urgently recommend three or four weeks' complete rest. In cases like this you can never make a definite prognosis, but in all probability things will not take a turn for the better while it is not possible to be specific about how much time is left. I recommend treatment either with Teominal or Deriphyllin or Iodine-Calcium-Diuretin, administered for three weeks, then a pause of three weeks and so on repeatedly. Any smoking to be stopped completely, there must be liquid intake and a low-salt diet, and one day per week confined to fruit juices (one liter) provided this does not conflict with his job, and there must be no other eating or drinking during those twenty-four hours and actual work must be cut back to an absolute minimum.

"Regular midday rest of at least one hour and as much sleep at night as possible."

Probably recognizing that he was talking about Adolf Hitler himself, Weber added in resignation: "I realize that these measures which are absolutely indicated are nowadays hardly possible or completely impossible for a man in a responsible position, but as many of these points as possible should be heeded if his strength is to be maintained."

Morell ignored the specialist's advice. There is no evidence of his applying any of the drugs or treatments recommended by

Weber. He stuck to his own remedies and to "injections as usual" of his own brands of drugs.

May 11, 1943

Eleven-forty-five A.M. Injections as usual and double glucose.

May 14, 1943

Eleven A.M. Twenty percent glucose plus 20 cc of Septoiod intravenously and intramuscular shots of Vitamultin-Calcium and Tonophosphan-forte.—He got no sleep at all last night because of loss of Tunis and [RAF attack on] Pilsen.

A SERIOUS CONSTIPATION seized up Hitler's bowels for several days, causing him agonies. Morell tried laxatives of increasing savagery: Relaxin, cod-liver oil, Leo pills, Mitilax and Calomel.

May 17, 1943

Eleven-forty A.M. Injections as usual. Gave him two 0.2 Calomels and four Leo pills. ([RAF bombing of] Eder and Möhne dams!)

May 18, 1943

Began a new course of Enterofagos ampoules: one ampoule twice a day. Relaxin too first.

May 19, 1943

Relaxin but no bowel movement of significance.

May 20, 1943

Noon. Injections as before. Still suffering from gas!

HITLER had planned to go to Vinnitsa but suddenly decided to return south to the Obersalzberg. On May 21 he flew down there from Rastenburg. "He wants to have a thorough rest there first," wrote Goebbels, "to get back into shape for the next weeks and

desired."

We also have a frank description by Lieutenant-General Count von Schwerin who had to report to Hitler late in May at the Berghof. "I reported in the prescribed manner," he testified on November 12, 1945, "and Hitler came over to me—a man stooping as though under a heavy burden, with slow and even tired steps. At that moment a bottomless sympathy for this man flooded over me, more powerful than any feeling I have sensed before or since. This instinctive welling up of human compassion was so huge that it dominated me throughout the time I was with this man. . . . I felt almost as though a voice inside me was whispering, Just look at this poor man, how bowed down he is! . . . He just cannot carry the burden that he has assumed. Hitler was completely down, and in bewilderment I looked into his lusterless, weary eyes with their unnaturally blue color. . . . There could be no doubt at all that those were a sick man's eyes. It may be that he had rehearsed this scene."

Marshal Antonescu told Hitler that he had also had stomach problems, but that his Viennese-born dietician had got rid of them for him. Morell arranged for this girl, Marlene von Exner, to come. It would be September 1943 before she assumed her duties. Meanwhile, on June 8 a typical Berghof menu would read: "Orange juice with linseed gruel, rice pudding with herbal sauce, crisp bread with butter and nut paste."

May 25, 1943

Twelve-thirty P.M. Injections as before! Blood pressure 154 mm, diet! *** Last night he took five Leo pills without effect.

May 26, 1943

Twelve-fifteen P.M. Three tablespoons of cod-liver oil. By evening still no effect worth talking about.

May 27, 1943

Twelve-forty P.M. Two Luizym tablets, one tablespoon of Belladonna Obstinol and one tablespoon of Obstinol. Gruel and porridge for lunch. Still gases in the evening. Two tablespoons of Obstinol, one of Belladonna Obstinol, two Luizym tablets.

May 28, 1943

Wakened at noon. Twelve-thirty P.M. abdomen still tense, but far less. Injections as before. *Very* irritable, easily aroused. Calomel twice 0.3. Perhaps I should try warm compresses. Suggested massage, shortwave treatment, enemas, et cetera—all turned down. I showed him the book but he still refused!

Afternoon and evening, considerable bowel movements! Abdomen more supple. Only a little gas left. Allegedly has lost nine pounds in the last four days. Took three tablespoons of olive oil before the war conference, an intravenous injection of 0.015 Eupaverin after the war conference, immediate relief from the spasms.

Was at supper. Stayed very lively long after, and was up until 2:30 A.M.

[Contact] Professor Zabel (Reichsleiter Bormann).
Strictest diet! Strictest diet!

May 31, 1943

Twelve-thirty P.M. Injections as always (10 cc twenty percent Glycovarin and 10 cc Septoiod intravenously, plus intramuscular injections of Vitamultin-Calcium and Tonophosphan-forte).

DURING these last May days of 1943, Hitler was battling with his generals over his plans for Operation Citadel, a major counter-offensive at Kursk on the eastern front. The rows may have contributed to his epigastric pains. Morell suspected other causes. On May 30, he sent a fecal sample to Olmütz and asked for an immediate investigation whether there had been fermentation or decomposition. "After eating a vegetable platter," thus Morell depicted the origins, "constipation and colossal flatulence occurred on a scale I have seldom encountered before. These were followed by intestinal spasms. Cod-liver oil had no worthwhile effect, Belladonna-Obstinol had slight effect and only two 0.3 Calomels had complete success against this constipation, while the spasms did not subside until I had made an intravenous Eupaverin injection. Unfortunately the fecal sample was delivered to me only today, while since yesterday lunchtime the patient has been getting a low carbohydrate diet with few potatoes (eating rice instead) and little fruit, et cetera, juices. His condition is now good again. Send me your findings as soon as possibe and also have a quick look round for the vari-ous bacteria."

The fecal samples were submitted to both Nissle and Laves for analysis. Laves reported the sample had "a bright brownish color and showed a rich dash of gall-colored, partly emulsified oil (laxative)." He remarked upon the presence of coli aerogenes bacilli and a few coli bacteria that weakly fermented in lactose. He summarized his report in the words, "There is evidently a slight dybacteria of alimentary origin, probably only transitory in nature."

Professor Nissle also spotted the aerogenes bacteria. On June 5 he wrote a detailed letter to Morell reproving the physi-cian for the unhygienic food preparation at headquarters. "Importance must be attached to staff washing their hands thoroughly with soap and water before handling raw food, and to rinsing each individual salad leaf and the like in running water; the same goes for fruit—apples and pears should always be peeled first, as our examination here shows their peel is invariably filthy with bacteria. No doubt," continued Nissle anxiously, "you will in addition to your dietary measures rec-ommend that he continue the Mutaflor cure, and I hope that the masses of aerogenes bacilli, which must have got in with particularly heavily infected material, will soon be displaced from the intestinal flora again; that's why I would ask you to send me a further fecal sample for investigation after eight or ten days and perhaps a second sample some while after, in case our analysis of the first is not satisfactory."

Nissle did make one suggestion. "Chinese medical practice suggests that raw food should always be individually plunged for a few seconds into boiling water; they do it mainly on ac-count of helminthous [worm] eggs and dysentery that are wide-spread there." Nissle admitted that this was quite a radical method.

Certainly Dr. Zabel, director of a nature clinic in Berchtes-gaden, was not enthusiastic about it. On June 28, Morell spoke with him about Hitler's diet. Zabel flatly refused to lay down what or how much Hitler should eat without being advised as to Hitler's health, appetite, weight and other factors. "I particu-larly want to avoid the Führer getting the impression that because he is being served separately these amounts have been specified by me," wrote Zabel to Morell.

Morell proposed to Zabel that the salads should be briefly boiled. Zabel was horrified. "Just for the record," wrote Zabel, "let me repeat that this adds to the burden on the gastrointestinal tract while not definitely getting rid of the bacteria, and simultaneously destroys virtually all the water-soluble vitamins, ferments and enzymes."

June 1, 1943

Twelve-thirty P.M. Two injections of Glycavarin intravenously, and intramuscular shot of Vitamultin-Calcium and Tonophosphan-forte. Still a bit constipated.

June 2, 1943

Telephone call from Nissle: found masses of aerogenes bacilli (from the salad?).

June 3, 1943

Twelve noon. Injections as always. Still some gas.

June 5, 1943

Twelve-thirty P.M. Injections as always. Feels okay! Telephone call from Professor Laves: also found masses of aerogenes and paracoli-like bacteria.

June 6, 1943[4]

The Reich foreign minister von Ribbentrop had invited me to lunch at Fuschl at one P.M., but only arrived around two-thirty P.M. or even later after his wife had called him several times.

First I chatted with Frau von Ribbentrop about population policies. Wants marriage limited to twenty years, state subsidies for illegitimate children so that the mothers don't just have one, et cetera. Says [Reich Women's Leader] Frau [Gertrud] Scholtze-Klink is apparently not suited for her job—says that all this standing in line by women is a useless waste of time, et cetera.

[4] Note by Morell, on several sheets of his notepaper and headed "Memorandum written on Monday morning in Munich, Hotel Regina."

After lunch he invited me upstairs to talk something over. Now it came out why he had asked me to lunch—to speak to me about the Führer's health and my treatment of him.

Was it a good thing, he asked, for the Führer to get so many injections?—Ribbentrop's army medic Dr. Conrad is in fact primarily a sports doctor and hostile to all injection treatments, from what I've been told (by Limpert).—And, was he getting anything other than glucose?

I replied: Iodine is very appropriate for anybody over fifty.

But isn't he perhaps getting too much?

I said: I would have been permitted to administer in one injection as much iodine as I have so far included in forty shots (that is, with no more for one or two weeks).

Was I giving him anything else?

I replied: "I give him what he needs."

He said he also has glucose given to him (which I used to give him earlier and later recommended strongly because of his low blood pressure). Now because of a slackness in the heart muscle he gets a forty percent glucose solution.

I comment: I think such injections are too strong, because of the danger of a thrombosis. I referred to the clotting of the withdrawn blood in the Merck glucose solution at Zhitomir. I myself never use solutions of over twenty percent.

Then he went on about the need for strong abdominal massages for the Führer (no doubt he is thinking of his own Kersten,[5] whom he's been trying for years to get in with the Führer; both

---

[5] Felix Kersten, a Swedish nature healer practicing in Berlin, was masseur to Himmler and Ribbentrop. See his *The Kersten Memoirs, 1940–1945*, and particularly chap. xxiii, Report on Hitler's Illness, pp. 165–171, with its "diary" entry of December 12, 1942. According to this bogus source a paralysis of syphilitic origin that had first shown in Hitler in 1937 recurred in 1942. The blood tests published in this book disprove this completely. As Hitler's adjutant Julius Schaub states (in his papers deposited in this author's collection in Munich), there was never any such "Black Dossier" as Kersten alleges, nor any such progressive paralysis. Kersten's unpublished but genuine diaries are with his family in Stockholm. Schaub tells us that Hitler refused to have anything to do with this masseur, commenting: "There's not an ounce of surplus fat on my body and my brain has got enough to do as it is. So why should I let such a Nature's Apostle get his hands on me? My name's not Rudolf Hess—he gets a fresh nature cure prescription every other week. If this man is so fantastic, it puzzles me that the lot of you are always so ill."

Wolff[6] and Himmler have tried to get me to send Kersten into action on the Führer). This man once massaged me in Zhitomir in 1942 and left me aching all over for two weeks. The diagnoses that he waffled on about as he did so—left larynx, pylorus and/or a malfunctioning nerve leading in that direction(??) [sic]—completely overlooked the chronic nephritis and the chronic damage to the heart muscle with coronary calcification.

I said: I refuse to subject the Führer to these violent stomach massages, but I would be in favor of gentle body massage to stimulate his circulation.

You mean on account of the spasms?

Yes, in general, I am much in favor of massage and particularly as one gets older. Anyway I've been nagging the Führer about it for years and even ordered a masseur up from Munich who massaged a whole row of acquaintances like Hoffmann, the Schönmanns,[7] Minister Wagner, et cetera and whom I also got to massage me so I could see what kind of massage he did. But right up to this day the Führer has flatly refused it.

Why don't you say then that in that case you can't accept responsibility?

Then he turned to the subject of breathing exercises [*Atemgymnastik*]. This was no doubt at the instigation of Hewel, who when he was hospitalized under Professor Koch of Berlin got friendly with a pretty little "gymnastics assistant" who instructed him and whom he actually wanted after his return to introduce to the Führer; he approached me several times with the suggestion that the Führer really ought to start doing such exercises with the young lady concerned.

I indicated that the Führer probably wouldn't make much time available for *that*. I thought it more to the point to stand still occasionally during walks and take deep breaths with a walking stick held across one's back and under one's arms in order to keep an upright posture.

That started him off on the whole business of going for walks.

[6] Karl Wolff, born May 13, 1900, in Darmstadt, was Himmler's personal chief of staff since November 1936 and his representative at Hitler's headquarters until 1943. Still alive.

[7] Probably the family of Marion Schönmann, an elegant young lady in Hitler's Munich circle of friends.

The Führer, he said, must go for walks several hours a day. (Oh, happy foreign minister, that you can spare so much time!) The Führer, he continued, must climb hills and do strenuous exercises to train his body. (That's the whispering of the sports doctor again!)

I retorted, I have to reject that utterly as it would be quite unsuitable for the Führer. He should go for lots of walks but on level ground and without overexertion.

He said, Why, he's got nothing wrong with his heart, has he? Or are you thinking of the spasms and circulatory problems?

I answered, Yes. (Of course I have no right to discuss the cardiological findings with others.)

But the Führer should not always drive to the teahouse and back. He ought at least to make the return trip, with its hills, on foot.

You'll have to tell the Führer that, I replied.

He said, There's got to be a total change in the Führer's entire body to make him capable of greater resistance. He's always been plagued by these stomach ailments, some time back he had that constant diarrhea and now these last weeks all over again.

I pointed out that this latest episode was not diarrhea but constipation and the illness had come about because of suspect raw foods.

He said he knew that, but that if the Führer had been more robust the bacteria would not have been able to gain a foothold or only to a small extent. He said he had wanted to tell me all this and that was why he had invited me over. So, he summarized, what I must attach importance to were

1. massage;
2. breathing exercises;
3. going for walks.

I remarked that there was nothing new in all this, and I was already paying heed to this and stimulating such ideas.

Walking down the steps he began all over again, whereupon I pointed out that he was already a difficult enough patient, but the Führer was even more so as he turned down most things right from the start. As we said our good-byes (in the meantime his wife had also come) he referred again to his three points and still seemed convinced that he was dishing up something new to me. How unencumbered and naïve laymen often are in their medical opinions!

The Credit Goes to Morell

PREPARATIONS continued for Citadel, a two-pronged attack on the Russian salient at Kursk. Hitler vested much hope in this offensive. But there were difficulties in amassing all the men and equipment in time. Meanwhile he remained at the Berghof. Morell continued to treat him, guarding his privileged position in Hitler's entourage with as much jealousy and cunning as before.

June 9, 1943

Twelve-forty P.M. Injections as always. Talked with Führer about Nissle's letter.

June 11, 1943

Pulse 72–78, blood pressure digitally 144 mm, by auscultation 144–153 mm. Complains about stomach gas.

June 12, 1943

Injections as always, belly free of gas, frail.

HITLER went to Munich on June 15, where Morell saw him at twelve-thirty, and returned to the Obersalzberg the next day.

June 16, 1943

Injections as always, in good health.

June 17, 1943

Began Mutaflor course.

June 20, 1943

Twelve-forty-five P.M. Injections as always. No complaints at all except he didn't sleep. Is looking very good. Complains of worry caused by responsibilities.

GOEBBELS however wrote on June 21 after seeing Hitler, "Unfortunately he does not look at all healthy. One can see how the last few months have gnawed away at him. There is only a vestige of the physical fitness we all used to admire so much in him."

June 25, 1943

Injections as always. ***

ON JULY 1 Hitler returned to the Wolf's Lair, and before he spoke to several hundred assembled officers about Citadel, Morell gave him the usual pick-me-up:

July 1, 1943

Intravenous injections of glucose, plus intramuscular of Vitamultin-Calcium and Tonophosphan.

July 3, 1943

Injections as before. Has a bit of a throbbing head after major conference yesterday and this morning. Slept only two hours last night—and badly this afternoon!
(Raise matter of Zabel's cooking, lice powder, et cetera.)

July 3, 1943 (memo.)

Two P.M. to see the Führer. While I was treating him I discussed the dietary arrangements with him. Führer asked me how this diet kitchen was going to work. I indicated that I have reached with Professor Eppinger[1] of Vienna a (written!) agreement that until

---

[1] Professor Hans Eppinger was senior physician in a famous school of Viennese internists. He had been summoned to Moscow when Lenin had his heart attack. When the pro-Nazi King Boris of Bulgaria fell suddenly ill in August 1943 it was Eppinger whom Hitler sent to Sofia—he arrived too late except to confirm that Boris had died a typical "Balkan death," poisoned by a

the lady who is at this moment still directing the dietary department for Marshal Antonescu is free the best assistant after her is to come up here, and make herself available at all hours.—The kitchen itself will be ready in eight to ten days.

I then turned to the subject of Dr. Z[abel], who was previously different (humble) but has now begun behaving rather oddly toward me. Only recently he insisted on making his own inquiries before issuing the diet, although I stated precisely what was lacking. And in doing so he made the most detailed notes on the analyses and findings I had commissioned, which was unpleasant insofar as they did not only concern the Führer's epigastric problems, because I have always been careful to arrange everything under strictest secrecy, using different names, et cetera. That is why I have also made no statements about the cardiological and circulatory findings; the Führer said I am quite right, and that this is no concern of Z's—*I* alone am his doctor. I also remarked that Dr. Z had sent word up to me at the Berghof on account of the salad, saying that he had heard it reported from the Berghof that I provide specially prepared salads. I told the Führer that I am always glad to be able to add in new things, and don't want to take away anything. The Führer mentioned how much he would like pea and bean soups and suchlike, but he doesn't dare because of flatulence. I reassured him with the hope that we may make so much headway that eventually he can be given everything. I also mentioned that when Dr. Z telephoned to inquire after his health I said it was good, and Dr. Z had thereupon sent me a detailed confirmation of the telephone conversation in which he again reverted to the leaf vegetables.

In the course of the conversation I also said to the Führer that if anybody ever had to be called in I would certainly do so. I was also going to have to mention something that I would not normally mention—at this point the Führer interrupted, I should tell him after the injection, whereupon he then reminded me—I told him that Benno von Arent was absolutely right to curse as Dr. Z had made a totally false diagnosis in his case.

If only Dr. Z had given him glucose injections he would have made an equally enthusiastic supporter and propagandist of him.

---

still unknown hand. Eppinger would take his own life after 1945 upon finding out that one of his senior doctors, Weigelböck, was involved in concentration camp experiments. He felt that a director should take some responsibility for his junior's actions.

I would also have diagnosed dysbacteria, quite apart from the faulty heart and circulatory system. Within one and a half or two months of his leaving Dr. Zabel I would have had him cured. Dr. Z had earlier been an optician, I said, and evidently hadn't the vaguest notion of heart and circulatory problems, and that was why I would not tolerate him interfering in the treatment of the Führer.

I had packed my things and was walking out through the room in which the Führer was sitting eating, quite alone, when he invited me to join him.

I mentioned that I am going without breakfast to lose weight. I have to lose twenty pounds. The Führer was very concerned and insisted I shouldn't overdo the diet or I might do myself serious harm. I explained that I am doing it bit by bit and not the way they did it in that Berlin clinic with Hewel, using mercury injections (Salyrgan) which are quite dangerous up to a point. In Berlin they had two very worrying days with Hewel. In sanatoriums, I said, it was common practice at the end of a cure if other methods had already attained the desired weight reduction. But in three or four weeks the weight loss of thirteen to eighteen pounds would be restored simply by quenching one's thirst. Field Marshal von Brauchitsch told me the same after taking the cure at the White Hart.[2]

I then reverted to the subject of lice powder. In two months I would stop deliveries as the Inspectorate has declared its depots full. When he asked me how much I am turning out daily I said one million minipackets, equivalent to 250,000 daily rations. The Führer was astonished and asked how I managed. I replied, we have six or seven hundred girls doing the filling, as it is difficult to package this powder by machines. There are four machines on hand, but they need three or four people to man them and often break down.—Schreiber[3] wanted to have the impregnation method from the outset, and Dr. Bickert wanted a powder. We manufactured the powder, and it is 100 percent successful—provided it is applied properly. Trouble is, the smell is a bit overpowering. What with that and the troops' general laziness it has not been

[2] Field Marshal Walther von Brauchitsch, commander in chief of the German Army from 1938 until retired by Hitler in December 1941. The White Hart is a famous Dresden sanatorium.

[3] Colonel (Med.) W. Schreiber, department head and hygienist at the Academy of Military Medicine in Berlin.

properly applied everywhere. Now the Inspectorate wants to go over to impregnation. As soon as I took the first step, big business pricked up its ears and I. G. Farben began manufacturing its own product patented in Switzerland; it's not bad but can't cope with more than about 400,000. Another company had applied to the Inspectorate with an impregnant, but its basis is the same as mine (potassium xanthogenate); their patent is not open to inspection because everything is kept secret in wartime, but I know their substance is the same as mine. What I want is for the Inspectorate to give me half of the action, and on this score the Führer came down right on my side. I also pointed out that in Germany only processes can be patented (inventions), but not *discoveries* as in other countries. We had also manufactured the oxidation product over a long period and in that connection hit upon ignition, for which I had applied for a patent as this had not yet been publicized anywhere. We had not offered this to the Inspectorate on account of the ignition. But now the Delizia[4] company had begun manufacturing tablets which did not call for ignition, and the Inspectorate was going to authorize these instead. As I was the first to manufacture the *chemical*, however, I was demanding to be given half the order.

As the Führer still wanted to rest a bit, I took leave of him. (Signed) Dr. M.

July 6, 1943

Injection as usual. Blood pressure 130–132 mm, pulse regular, couldn't sleep more than three hours because of worry (our big attack in the east began yesterday morning). I said he should sleep this afternoon as long as possible. Claims he has an edema on exterior aspect of left tibia from time to time. Not at this moment. Location lies above the former eczema location (indicates permanent changes in cellular tissue of hypodermis!).

July 11, 1943

Injections as always. Blood pressure 135/95.

[4] Delizia was a company in Saxony which hit upon the same chemical, potassium xanthogenate, and solved the technical problem of impregnating it into linen. But the Boehringen Company developed a lice powder of far greater potency, and Morell's Rusla dropped out of the race in 1943–44. Morell then attempted to dump it in Romania and Italy.

THE GERMAN OFFENSIVE Citadel stalled in immense minefields. By now the Allies had also landed on Sicily, putting around 160,000 troops on shore within three days. Three days later Stalin unleashed his counterattack at Kursk. It was enough to make any dictator sick. Then came rumors that Mussolini was plotting to defect the Axis cause. On July 18, as Hitler prepared to fly down to meet him in northern Italy, he was seized by what Morell would later describe as one of the worst attacks yet.

July 18, 1943

Journey from Führer's headquarters to the Berghof. Injected Eupaverin intravenously and Eukodal subcutaneously. Gave him Euflat and Luizym.—Stomach massage and diet. Spastic constipation with violent pain and a lot of intestinal gas (gastrocardiac symptom complex[5]).

ON THE OBVERSE of the data card Morell wrote a more lengthy note on this worrying episode:

Führer had me sent for at ten-thirty A.M., said he has had the most violent stomach pains since three A.M. and hasn't slept a wink. His abdomen is as taut as a board, full of gas, with no palpation pains anywhere. Looking *very* pale and exceptionally jumpy: facing a vital conference with the Duce in Italy tomorrow. Diagnosis: *Spastic constipation* caused by overwork over the last few days— three days with virtually no sleep, one conference after another and working far into the night.—Last night he ate white cheese and roll-ups [*Rolladen*] with spinach and peas.

As he can't duck out of some important conferences and decisions before his departure at three-thirty P.M., no narcotics can be given him; I can only give him an intravenous injection of one ampoule of Eupaverin, some gentle stomach massage, two Euflat pills and three spoons of olive oil. Last night he took five Leo pills.

Before leaving for the airfield I gave him an intramuscular

[5] This was what German doctors called the "Roemheld Complex." Because the stomach is distended upward it interferes with the heart and causes heartburn.

injection of an ampoule of Eukodal. He was looking very bad and rather faint.

In the Condor airplane Reichsmarschall Göring wanted to give me a few final tips (Ondarza was standing just behind him): "You must give him Euflat. That once helped me a lot."

"Yes, two tablets three times a day. I'm doing it already."

"But you've got to keep doing it over a long period. I took them for eighteen months. And then you must give him Luizym too!"

"We're already doing that too!" (He got the name wrong at first, but Ondarza corrected him.)

During the actual flight Hitler let off wind, which resulted in some improvement. Upon reaching the Berghof I gave him another body massage, with more Euflat followed by the Luizym I have been giving him now repeatedly for some time.

In the evening he had some quite easily digestible nutrition and went to bed around twelve-thirty, after taking a Phanodorm-Calc and half a Quadronox tablet.

July 19, 1943

From the Berghof to Treviso and back! Duce!!!
In the morning injections as always.

At six-thirty A.M. his abdomen is supple; he has slept well and let off a lot of wind. Injections as always. I recommend that he take some bars of Vitamultin with him for the talks. At six-forty-five A.M. he drives off, takes off at seven-thirty from Salzburg (with Baur at the controls) via Rosenb., Kufstein, Innsbruck, and Brenner to Treviso (just before Venice). From there onward by rail and car. Führer is in good form. No complaints at all on return flight either. Back on the Obersalzberg this evening he declares that the credit for the day's success goes to me. He feels, he says, completely well again.

July 26, 1943

At two A.M. we get the news: the Duce has resigned.
Injections as always, nine-thirty A.M.

July 27–28, 1943

Destruction of Hamburg.

July 28, 1943

Blood pressure 143/95 mm. Injections as always.

July 30, 1943

Injections as always.

August 1, 1943

Saw him in the afternoon. He has worked right through the night with many conferences. Pulse 72 per minute, regular but weak. Set up oxygen gear [in Hitler's study] for occasional use.[6] Blood pressure 127/85 mm. His upper right forehead is throbbing.

August 5, 1943

Injections as always, blood pressure 136 mm.

August 9, 1943

Injections as always.—Meal and oxygen bottle *very* good. I had the oxygen bottle set up in the Führer's bunker a few days ago for him to inhale and possibly even to blow off into the sleeping quarters. The Führer is *very* content with it, one might even say delighted.

August 13, 1943

Injections as always.

August 19, 1943

Eleven A.M. Injections as always.

ON AUGUST 19 Professor Nissle sent in a further fecal analysis report. "I think I can assume from this," he wrote, "that your patient's condition has largely or completely improved." In detail he reported, "Masses of typical cultures of coli bacteria, of which about half are now in complete accordance with the Mutaflor strain, with only a few scattered aerogenes bacilli among them, no other germs, and no helminthous eggs. Thus the mixture of intestinal flora is considerably less than at the time of the previous analysis; above all, the disruptive aerogenes bacilli which were previously present in great quantity have

[6] In his daily notes Morell noted on August 18 and 20, 1943: "Dr. Conradt about small army oxygen apparatus."

been eliminated except for a minute remnant." The fecal sample sent to Professor Laves was checked with the same result.

One episode at this time illuminates the atmosphere at Hitler's headquarters, and Morell wrote a detailed memorandum on it—after all, one never knew. "On August 20, 1943," he minuted after a visit from Hitler's new dietician, "Frau Exner came to see me and complained that the people from whom we get the vegetables for the Führer's kitchen all know whom it is for. . . . That would make it easy for toxic substances to be added. There are many foreign—French, Polish and Russian—laborers on the farms. She cannot accept the responsibility under these circumstances. It is proposed to deal with this by picking the vegetables ourselves at first, and then setting up our own market garden which would be the best solution." Morell took it up with the chief of Hitler's security branch, SS-Brigadier General Rattenhuber. He evidently did nothing because on September 1 Morell sent for him and "again read out the protocol to him at six P.M. and advised him to put it on file." Again Morell cautiously made a file note on this. Again, one never knew.

He wanted urgently to go to Berlin for a few days where his practice in Kurfürstendamm now seemed likely to be right in the heart of the RAF's next air raid series. Fearing a Hamburg firestorm catastrophe in Berlin, Goebbels ordered the capital largely evacuated, and Morell noted on August 19 that he must talk with Hitler about "journey to Berlin to get everything safely outside." He had added a handwritten memo to this, "Postponed, after discussing this with the Führer this morning," but when the massive British air raids on Berlin began on the twenty-third Morell insisted on permission to build a bunker at his dwelling out at Schwanenwerder. On August 31, he noted: "Führer, permission for bunker construction project."

August 25, 1943

Eleven-twenty A.M. Injections as always.

IN HIS AGENDA for that day Morell jotted down: "Eleven or eleven-thirty P.M., take tea with the Führer." He was approaching the zenith of his modest power as Hitler's doctor. Over the next months he was often invited to join Hitler for tea at night, as the valet's logs show. Hitler's guests on August 30 at midnight were, "foreign minister and Ambassador Hewel, joined at two-twenty A.M. by Professor Morell. Finished four A.M." Morell was exhausted and longing for sleep, but he was not going to miss a chance like this. The other participants took turns to duck the tedious parties—the brothers Bormann, the secretaries, the adjutants and orderlies. Sometimes Albert Speer or his righthand man Karl-Otto Saur came in, or Speer's rival architect Hermann Giesler, but seldom one of the other doctors like Brandt or Hasselbach. Evidently the old Morell friendship with Heinrich Hoffmann was briefly restored, because the photographer was also to be seen there until three, four and even five A.M., sipping tea and jabbing at the pastries as Hitler's voice rasped on. Goebbels occasionally came but had better things to do and avoided the sessions in later months. Morell would not have been Morell if he had not always accepted.

August 27, 1943
Morning, six-fifteen A.M. Injections as always. *Seven* A.M. Flight to Vinnitsa.

HITLER had gone there for urgent talks with Field Marshal von Manstein and the army commanders. He flew back that afternoon to Rastenburg.

August 31, 1943
Eleven-fifteen A.M. Injections as always.

September 4, 1943
Eleven-fifteen A.M. Injections as always.

September 8, 1943
Six-fifteen A.M. Injections as always. [6:40 A.M.] flight [with Hitler to confer with Manstein and the commanders in chief] at Zaporozhye.

September 15, 1943
Ten-fifty A.M. Injections as always. Looking very good indeed!

September 18, 1943
Order juices for chief [that is, Hitler] but not raspberry.

September 19, 1943 (agenda)
Electrocardiogram of chief [evidently not performed].

September 20, 1943
Eleven A.M. Injections as always. [He again went to see Hitler at four-twenty P.M. for ten minutes.]

September 23, 1943
Eight-fifteen P.M. In the evening, gave him a check up after supper: strong flatulence, spasms caused by mental worry. His belly is showing a more fatty disposition. Gave him Eupaverin plus half an Eukodal intramuscularly. After a few hours everything was okay. Ordered a diet. The injection location bleeding slightly.

September 27, 1943
Monday, *eleven-ten* A.M. The last intramuscular injection site is hurting, it began to do so yesterday evening and disrupted his sleep.—Infiltrated without a surface inflammation. Ordered electric warming pads for his sleep this afternoon. Plan to administer Rubefat this evening.

September 29, 1943
Eleven A.M. Injections as always.

October 2, 1943
I'm at Distelhausen and in Berlin.

October 3, 1943
Two-thirty P.M. [Lunched with Hitler.] His right forearm is painful and a swelling is beginning in the upper arm. Rheuma medicine has not helped.

October 7, 1943
Eleven A.M. Injections as always. Right forearm badly swollen. Applied Franzbranntwein lotion. Gauleiter conference today. Is looking very good.

October 14, 1943

Ten-fifty A.M. Injections as always.—Has slept badly, too many worries!

October 16, 1943

Eleven A.M. Injections as always.—Ditto.

October 17, 1943

Sent for me at six A.M. because of stomach pains and intestinal spasms. (Has had a lot of worry in the last few days.) Gave him intravenous shots of Eupaverin plus intramuscular of Eukodal. By midday almost pain free.

October 18, 1943

At ten in the morning injections as always (visited later by Cyrill[7]).

October 19, 1943 (agenda)

[Handwritten note:] Vitam. Führer.

October 20, 1943

Eleven A.M. Injections as always. ([Display of tanks and flak equipment at] Arys.)

October 23, 1943 (agenda)

Führer electrocardiogram [this was evidently not made] plus Prog. ol. plus liver extract. Speak to F. about professorial appointments. *** At three A.M.: discussion with Führer, approves my suggestion! Put it in writing tomorrow!

October 26, 1943

Eleven A.M. Blood pressure 150 digit., by auscultation 160/100 mm. Injections as always.—Sleeping badly because of major worries.

October 27, 1943

Eleven-forty-five A.M. Blood pressure 150/100 mm by ausculta-

---

[7] A Bulgarian delegation consisting of Prince Cyrill and the Regent Filoff, appointed after the assassination of King Boris, arrived to see Hitler at eleven A.M.

tion, says he's suffering from transitory flatulence again (a whole host of worries!).

November 5, 1943
Ten-fifteen A.M. Injections as always. Transitory gases. Took two Luizym tablets and an Acidol-Pepsin at lunch.

AT FOUR P.M. on November 7 Hitler left Rastenburg by special train for Munich where he was to hold a traditional speech in the Löwenbräu beerhall on the next day. On the ninth he returned to the Wolf's Lair.

November 8, 1943
At Nürnberg railroad station: injections as always.

November 11, 1943
Eleven-ten A.M. Injections as always.

November 16, 1943 (agenda)
Electrocardiogram of Chief!! *Disçuss.*

November 18, 1943 (agenda)
Electrocardiogram of Chief.

IT IS almost as though Hitler feared having the electrocardiogram. Still without having had it performed, he left on the nineteenth for Breslau, was treated by Morell as usual at 9:50 A.M. the next day, delivered a major speech in the Century Hall in that city at noon and returned to Rastenburg.

November 21, 1943
Injections as always, outside Breslau.

MORELL HIMSELF then went on a business trip, inspecting his little pharmaceutical empire. On November 20 we find him in he went on to Pilsen and Kosolup on the twenty-fourth. His Breslau and Prague, on the twenty-first in Olmütz, from where vacant place at Hitler's nocturnal tea parties was taken by escort doctor Hasselbach. On November 25 Morell returned to the Wolf's Lair, was invited to dinner with Hitler at nine P.M. and stayed on until 3:40 A.M. with him. By then Hitler had climbed aboard his special train "Brandenburg" for the short trip to Insterburg air force base in East Prussia, for the next day's display of the latest equipment including secret jet planes.

November 26, 1943

Ten-thirty-five A.M. Injections as always.—Mutaflor. Gases. [Eleven A.M. arrival at] Insterburg. In the evening he says he hasn't been able to sleep a wink.

November 27, 1943 (agenda)

Patient A Glyconorm prescription, Blondi [Handwritten:] Peru Balsam.

November 28, 1943 (agenda)

Talked it[8] over with Führer this evening, November 28. Says my adjutant Pfeil is to get in touch immediately with Reichsleiter Bormannn tomorrow in Berlin, and the latter is to do everything necessary.—Dr. M.

December 1, 1943

Three A.M. Flatulence, gave him intramuscular shot of half ampoule of Eukodal and half of Eupaverin and more Euflat pills.

December 10, 1943

Looking very good. Excellent appetite.—At lunch and dinnertime I give him two Glyconorm capsules as well as the Luizym (as I have done these last two weeks).

APPARENTLY Morell was hardly called upon during the last weeks of 1943. He sat in on the tea parties almost every night, but his earlier custom of visiting Hitler every day just before breakfast stopped. Evidently Hitler was going through a rare relatively calm period. Militarily the front lines seemed stabilized. No

----

[8] Evidently the supply of scarce raw materials for Morell's Hamma company.

Allied invasion was anticipated before the spring of 1944, while on the eastern front the onset of winter was slowing down the Russian offensives. In the air war too Göring's defences were increasingly successful against the RAF night bomber offensive.

By this time Morell had a second VIP patient, Mussolini, brought to Hitler's headquarters in September 1943 after his dramatic release from a mountain prison by SS and paratroops. His health was poor, and Morell took him under his ample wing. He wrote on December 17 to acquaintances, "My lofty patient is in good health, and I can say the same for a second patient that I now have in the south too. Unfortunately it seems that for the next few weeks we are not going to swap our eastern location for one further south, as I had so very much hoped. . . . Despite excellent health my chief won't let me out of his sight for fear something happens to my plane on the journey. And by rail it all takes too long."

Morell also touched upon the scene at headquarters. Much had changed. Schaub was seldom there after being slightly hurt in an air raid on Munich. Bormann was often away on business in Berlin and Munich. "Heini Hoffmann does not often put in an appearance and only pays a flying visit for a few days at a time every month or so. There's scarcely anybody left of the old clique. The headquarters has got too big, and everybody's wrapped up in himself. I've pulled back into my own shell a bit, and do scientific research and work on my business projects as far as I can find time for them."[9]

[9] Letter from Theo Morell to Helmut and Anneliese Schreiber, December 17, 1943, on National Archives microfilm, T-253, roll R-45, frames 1498332–3.

1944:

"Vitamultin-Forte"

MORELL'S papers for 1944 exist in several forms, quite apart from the laboratory reports and correspondence relating to Patient A. They include a small pocket diary, and data cards and detailed dietary records on Hitler. After the bomb plot in July with its ensuing medical complications, the files become voluminous. Morell wrote several parallel accounts, with several pages of handwriting for each day, no doubt to protect himself should there be subsequent investigations and intrigues. We see from these entries the scope of his medical activities, and we note that even when Morell himself was afflicted by heart disorders (April 19) he was reluctant to step aside and allow another to make the injections of Hitler. Later in 1944, we cannot help remarking that when Morell was incapacitated, his patient's health seemed to improve quite rapidly. The unfortunate role of the sulphonamide drug Ultraseptyl on Hitler's health becomes apparent from these diaries. A mysterious special version of Morell's patent Vitamultin product appears, denoted only as "Vitamultin-forte"—evidently it contained a special additive not used in the others. He administered it to Hitler for the first time on March 14, 1944, and carefully recorded its effect, and then started using it on Ribbentrop, Frau Göring and Himmler too.

The excerpts that fcllow are from the diaries, unless otherwise stated, with less relevant material, like normal blood pressure and temperature readings, edited out (***).

January 2, 1944
At Wolf's Lair. Visited Lieutenant-Colonel (med.) Dr. Bickert, of the War Department. Handed him [reports on] flu treatment with Gr. Prostrophanta, Hamma liver extract, odorless Rusla powder and impregnation techniques. Discussion on penicillin. Called on Ribbentrop at Gross-Steinort for supper. From twelve-thirty onward with Führer for tea. Turned in at five-thirty A.M.

January 4, 1944
Dr. Makkus returned from leave. *** My weight down to 225¾ pounds, am doing without lunch. *** Visited Linge, fully recovered. Evening with the Führer, gave him Eupaverin and Eukodal injections on account of spasms. Talked with [Press Chief] Dr. [Otto] Dietrich over dinner.

January 5, 1944
Midday. Invited to lunch with the Führer (alone).

January 6, 1944
Discussion with Ambassador Rahn[1] (Italy) and electrocardiographic examination. SS-Obergruppenführer Wolff called on me briefly. Gave him drugs to take back to Italy [that is, for Mussolini]. Evening: went for tea [with Hitler].

January 6, 1944 (agenda)
Evening with the Führer. Bro-Valoton bath. Analyze Slibovicz for methyl alcohol.

HITLER had become concerned about samples of hard liquor, Slibovicz, sent him by the Croatian leader Ante Pavelic and by the city of Linz. He asked Morell whether they might contain the toxic methyl alcohol. In the winter of 1931–2 four hundred people had died in the United States from drinking bootlegged liquor, which contained up to 75 percent methyl alcohol and other impurities. Morell had the two samples analyzed by war department laboratories in nearby Lötzen, quoting a "Führer order" for added urgency. Dr. Bickert—who would be killed in

[1] Rudolf Rahn, Hitler's special ambassador attached to Mussolini's puppet government.

action during the Ardennes offensive at the end of the year—
sent Morell his results on the next day: they were negative.

January 7, 1944

Checkup on Reich foreign minister von Ribbentrop (weak
heartbeat—Glyconorm plus injection of Vitamultin-Calcium). ***
Supper, invited by the Führer: talked over a lot of things (alone).
Late evening invited to tea.

January 8, 1944

Weighed in this morning at 230 pounds! Had a massage and
a day's fasting and thirsting; two tablespoons of cod-liver oil and
four Boxberg pills. At noon Miss Eva [Braun] telephoned, says she's
had the sniffles and a runny nose for three weeks now, and now an
inflammation of the maxillary sinus. Was seen six months ago by
Professor Heymann of the university. Ultraseptyl on the right did
not help. Further X ray necessary, also heat treatment, facial vapor
baths, vitamins, et cetera. The toxins must be eliminated. I sent her
the medicines (Vitamultin-Calcium, liver extract, Omnadin and
Intelan). *** Baur called on me. He had left Vinnitsa airfield
posthaste at five P.M. because of a Russian tank alarm, and brought
foodstuffs with him, although the paymaster in charge didn't want
to issue anything from the depot! *** Joined Führer for tea. At
three A.M. I weighed myself again: 224 pounds. Seen it through well.

January 9, 1944

Professor Reiter of Reich Health Agency. My liver product
authorized. *** Weather mild, light snowfall, windy. In the afternoon I drove over to Rastenburg for an hour's fresh air. *** Went
over for tea with the Führer at nightfall. [*Data card:*] At two-thirty
A.M. gave him an intramuscular shot of Eukodal and Eupaverin
because of flatulence (caused by worry).

January 10, 1944

Weighed 222 pounds after massage.—Telephoned Dr. Mulli: a
letter has come from the General Commissioner for Health signed
[Professor] Rostock about a joint research effort on penicillin.[2] ***
In Italy Ciano has been sentenced to death. Spent the evening with

[2] On Morell's penicillin research efforts, see pp. 67–70.

the Führer. [*Data card:* gave Frau Exner[3] instructions on different diet (against gas formation).]

MORELL'S AGENDA shows that he attempted throughout January 1944 to persuade his "Chief" to agree to an electrocardiogram and a typhus vaccination. Again throughout February the word "typhus shot" was typed on the daily agenda sheet, but Hitler would not find the time.

January 14, 1944

Heini Hoffmann came.

January 15, 1944

* * * In the evening tea with the Führer.

January 17, 1944

* * * Gloomy day. Spent the evening with the Führer (and Heini Hoffmann, et cetera). * * *

January 18, 1944

Seven P.M. Supper with General Model [commander in chief, Army Group North] in the special train "Braunschweig."

January 20, 1944

Wolf's Lair. Telephone conversations with Königsberg, [Gauleiter] Koch—Flu * * * Vitamultin, liver extract, Intelan * * * Was telephoned by Speer[4] from the Hohenlychen Clinic.—I then telephoned Professor Gebhardt at Hohenlychen, and on Führer's instructions telephoned [Reichsminister Dr. Karl] Frank in Prague about Hacha. In the evening I discussed Speer and Hacha with the Führer.

---

[3] Marlene von Exner, Hitler's expert dietician, born in 1919. Later in 1944 she would be dismissed from Hitler's service on Bormann's insistence that she had non-Aryan blood which made her a security risk. She now lives at St. Veit an der Glan in Austria.

[4] Albert Speer, Hitler's architect, had been Minister of Munitions since the death of Fritz Todt in February 1942. From the autumn of 1943 his office was called Minister of Armaments. One of Morell's clients, he survived twenty years in Spandau and died in 1981.

January 21, 1944

Phoned Minister Frank in Prague about Hacha. Called the Führer back about this. Spent the evening with the Führer.

January 22, 1944

In the afternoon I was sent for by [Japanese ambassador] His Excellency Oshima. Hewel[5] was present. Evening with the Führer.

January 23, 1944

Lengthy discussion with General Model about his daughter, evening with the Führer.

January 24, 1944

In the evening at nine-thirty P.M. a major discussion with Reichs-leiter Bormann (about professorial appointments, Dr. B.!!!). ***

January 25, 1944

Drove over to Königsberg to see Gauleiter Koch. Gelatine capsule laboratory. *** In the evening (or rather at night) went for tea with the Führer (Sepp Dietrich there too).

January 27, 1944

Twelve-thirty P.M. The usual shots before a major speech, this time to a generals' meeting (approximately 105 generals).

MORELL had entered in his agenda that day: "Two-forty-five P.M. Spa House, Chief's speech." At Schmundt's suggestion Hitler had summoned his principal generals for a two-hour pep talk. The shorthand record shows that Hitler painted a grim picture of the future and rhetorically declared that he expected every field marshal, indeed his entire officer corps, to muster around him with daggers drawn if the worse came to the worst. Field Marshal von Manstein interrupted him and declaimed, "And so

---

[5] Walther Hewel, ambassador and one of Morell's few friends at head-quarters; born March 23, 1904, he was Ribbentrop's liaison officer on Hitler's staff. He became engaged to Blanda-Elisabeth Ludwig, who had nursed him after he was badly burned in a plane crash at Salzburg. He committed suicide in the same manner as Hitler—swallowing cyanide and shooting himself in one temple on May 1, 1945, in Berlin. His widow still has his diaries.

it will be, Mein Führer!" For this ambiguous declaration, he was dismissed from his position as commander of an army group.[6]

January 29, 1944 (data card)

Wolf's Lair. Afternoon, five-forty P.M.: injections as always before a major speech (tomorrow's broadcast).—Says he didn't sleep last night because of the big air raid on Berlin.

January 30, 1944

At ten P.M. I received news of grave damage by an air mine to Schwanenwerder. ***

January 31, 1944

In the morning I called Miss Besslich, who said eight phosphorus bombs fell there. Hanni's birthday *** telephone her in Olmütz with birthday greetings. At midday Dr. Weber telephones—bomb damage in the apartment at our practice too.

February 1, 1944

Wolf's Lair. Last night I again asked the Führer about going to Berlin. Said I should ask again tomorrow. When he asked me how long I'd be away I said two days. If need be I can fly back. Führer sent for me this morning for treatment. Says he wants to bear all the bomb damage costs himself. I shouldn't get bogged down in negotiations with the authorities, that would take too long. Departure for Berlin. [*Data card:* Injections as always.]

February 2, 1944

In Berlin. After arriving there I briefly inspected the bomb damage at the practice, then the damage caused by the air mine at Schwanenwerder. The house next door was destroyed. ***

February 5, 1944

At nine A.M. I drove off through the devastated Berlin to see Speer (and Professor Gebhardt) at Hohenlychen. Returned at three-thirty to the Kurfürstendamm practice. ***

[6] David Irving, *Hitler's War* (New York and London, 1977), p. 598.

February 6, 1944

Returned this morning to the Führer's headquarters. * * * Dr. Ley is here, *has stopped drinking.* *** Spent the evening with the Führer (and discussed Speer and hospital).

February 8, 1944

Discussion with Dr. Müller [personal assistant] in Reichsleiter Bormann's office about Vitamultin and equipment.

February 10, 1944

General Schmundt's got flu, particularly nose and maxillary sinus. This evening he had a fever of 39 and then 39.6, so I injected Gr. Prostrophanta and Ultraseptyl intravenously, with intramuscular shots of Hamma liver extract, Vitamultin-C and Omnadin ***.

February 11, 1944

*** Saw Führer at noon. He now has catarrh in upper respiratory tracts, particularly the left tonsil *** and bronchitis (caught it from General Schmundt?)—Gave him Vitamultin-Calcium plus Omnadin plus Hamma liver extract intramuscularly. This evening at nine P.M. his pulse was up to 84, temperature 36.7, his left leg kept trembling. Gave him a Tussamag against the coughing.

Professor Gebhardt telephoned from Hohenlychen about Speer: his temperature is 37.4 and 37, but rust-colored sputum and liquid bloody exudate [an effusion of blood] as far as fourth rib while lying down.—Professor Koch. Reichsführer SS Himmler: packet of two Ultraseptyl—six Vitamultin, two Boxberger pills, four Intelans, two Kalzan.

THE RUSSIANS were now on Polish soil. An American corps had established a fragile beachhead in Northern Italy at Anzio, and German attempts to eliminate the beachhead were failing. The Anglo-American bomber offensive had dealt great devastation to the German munitions factories and particularly the aircraft industries. Hitler began suspecting traitors everywhere. On February 12 he wound up the Abwehr Intelligence Service under Vice Admiral Wilhelm Canaris: it had done him no good.

February 12, 1944 (data card)

Führer well again, but very tired (has a load of worries). Gave him some Tussamag. In the evening violent colic. At two A.M. injected Eukodal plus Eupaverin intravenously.

February 13, 1944 (data card)

Saw him at two-thirty in the afternoon. After taking the Tussamag he suffered colic again and spasms! Intramuscular shots of Eupaverin and Eukodal. Later in the afternoon: two 0.3 Calomels at five P.M., and at ten P.M. he began vomiting, though still no bowel movements.

February 14, 1944 (data card)

From midnight to two A.M. frequent bowel movements. At two P.M. he still had a lot of wind. The powders had not worked, he said, and certainly not as well as in the past; said he must have the most thorough evacuation and absorption of the gases. I gave him some Kajovit, a teaspoonful. Two tablespoons of cod-liver oil plus four Boxberger pills. Weak!

February 15, 1944 (special note)

Saw Patient A at ten this evening. Blood pressure was 146/95 mm *** pulse varying around 90. Terrific pains in the transverse colon (winds).

Ate porridge and stewed apples (same as lunchtime).—Gave him Mitilax.

I propose chamomile tea with a little cognac.—With the porridge as always two Glyconorms and six to eight anti-gas pills, with two Euflat pills.—Warm compresses or electric heating pads. He got no sleep either last night or this afternoon.—I recommended massage and a warm enema of chamomile tea, but he refused them (yesterday too).—For the flu he took altogether eight Ultraseptyls (and took one and a half Luizyms, six to eight anti-gas pills and two Euflat pills without being told to).

February 16, 1944 (data card)

*** Winds. Glucose intravenously, plus intramuscular shots of Tonophosphan-forte, liver extract and Vitamultin-Calcium.

February 17, 1944

Wolf's Lair. Went with Professor Hoffmann to get X rays at Lötzen. Evening with the Führer. [*Data card*: Everything fine.]

February 18, 1944

Wolf's Lair. Evening with the Führer. [*Data card*: Glucose intravenously plus liver, Vitamultin-Calcium, Tonophosphan-forte intramuscularly. Blood pressure 151 mm ***]

February 19, 1944

Went to Lötzen with Heini Hoffmann to pick up the [X-ray] films. *** Evening with the Führer.

February 20, 1944

Wolf's Lair. Double glucose as always. Evening with the Führer. [*Data card*: Intravenous glucose plus intramuscular Vitamultin-Calcium, Hamma liver, Tonophosphan-forte. Blood pressure 151 mm, feels on top of the world again.]

February 21, 1944

Wolf's Lair. Evening with the Führer.

February 22, 1944

Wolf's Lair. Saw Führer as always. In the evening took the train to Munich. [*Data card:* Blood pressure 140 mm, feels okay and the tremor in left leg and shaking of the hands has gone.]

February 23, 1944

In the train to Munich.

February 24, 1944

Arrived three P.M. Went to Führer building, treated Patient A [Hitler]. In the presence of his immediate entourage the Führer then handed to me the Knights Cross of the War Merit Cross. Finally we went to the Bürgerbräu beerhall for the Führer's speech. Party Foundation Day. The Führer left, and I went to the Regina. *** Found myself in the air raid shelter there, cold and damp, with many generals and Dr. Goebbels, et cetera.

HITLER had come to Munich to speak in the Führer Building to Party veterans on Party Foundation Day; afterward he drove on to Berchtesgaden, where he would stay until mid-July 1944.

Eva Braun was shaken at the change in him. He had become old and grim. He had a permanent stoop, as though ducking beneath a low arch. "How is the Führer, Frau Junge?" she asked one of the secretaries, according to the girl's notes. "I don't want to ask Morell, I don't trust him and detest him."

For security reasons the Berghof had been camouflaged with netting, and its huge windows were covered. Only a dim twilight filtered through into the Great Hall inside. The work went on inside by electric light. During the last months Bormann had also supervised the tunneling of air raid shelters into the Obersalzberg itself.

February 25, 1944

Munich: Spent three hours at noon down in the air raid shelter again, everybody was coughing, a lot of colds around. Breakfast in the hotel. *** Drove to Reichenhall with Gretl Braun [sister of Eva] and visited Minister Wagner in hospital. (Bronchial pneumonia with exudate.) Arrived at the Berghof around eleven P.M.

February 26, 1944

Berghof: Had a fit of the shivers during the night with pain on my left side *** and temperature rising rapidly to 39. For hours I was tormented by a throat irritation but couldn't cough it away. *** In the morning had an injection four times in my right thigh. At first there was no more Ultraseptyl, it got to me at eleven A.M. Two tablets to be taken four times a day. In the afternoon because of a lot of cardiac difficulty I was injected intravenously by Colonel (med.) Dr. Siewers with Prostrophanta and an intramuscular shot of Ultraseptyl.

[Hitler] at Klessheim castle ([meeting Romanian head of state] Antonescu).

SINCE MID-FEBRUARY 1944 Hitler had complained that his right eye was seeing everything as though through an opaque veil. Dr. Erwin Giesing would write in November 1945 that Hitler had several times told him about a turbidity he had had in the vitreous humor of his right eye for the last eight years or so. According to the opinion of his then ophthalmologist it was uncurable. Giesing speculated briefly that this might be a turbidity typical of those caused by syphilis, but there were no other signs of a congenital syphilis, for example, Hutchinson's Teeth (narrowed and notched permanent incisor teeth).

On March 3, 1944, Professor Löhlein came to the Berghof and performed a detailed eye examination on Hitler. His report was afterward found in his files. "On closer questioning," Löhlein had written after seeing Hitler, "he mentioned that he had experienced a light stabbing pain, of transitory nature, in his right eye recently. He reads, of course, a good deal—especially before falling asleep—and the presbyopic glasses prescribed in 1935 are hardly enough for this purpose now." He noticed incidentally that Hitler's eyes displayed no strong defensive reaction to instilling of drops or to tonometry. He also described, "After determination of normal inner pressure by palpation, mydriasis of pupils was induced, right with Homatropin, left (currently the eye with better vision) only with Veritol."

After half an hour, ophthalmoscopy by Löhlein showed the refractive media of Hitler's left eye to be clear. But the background of the right eye was obscured by a delicate veil. "With the use of a magnifying mirror," explained Löhlein, "a very delicate, faintly mobile, diffuse turbidity of the vitreous humor could be observed, obviously composed of infinitesimal particles." Löhlein's diagnosis attributed this to "minute hemorrhages into the vitreous humor. These hemorrhages do not seem to originate with the blood vessels of the retina. *** Probably a transitory variation in pressure possibly caused by a vessel spasm is the explanation of the presence of blood."

Löhlein recommended local application of heat—perhaps twice a day with electro-thermopor or Sollux lamp. "A discussion with Professor Morell was held in the presence of the Führer, during which means of preventing the recurrence of such hemorrhages were discussed. Everything contributing to the avoidance of unnecessary excitement, particularly during the period immediately before the night's rest, such as diversion in light reading, was recommended."

March 3, 1944

Down to Salzburg station to collect Professor Löhlein, the ophthalmologist of Berlin University, arriving from Giessen. He saw Patient A and prescribed new glasses; a slight turbidity of vitreous humor in right eye (perhaps in consequence of capillary hemorrhage.—Potassium iodide!) *** [*Data card*: Professor Löhlein went in twice, I later went in alone.]

March 7, 1944

To Fuschl to see Reichsminister von Ribbentrop. *** Visited Leni Riefenstahl, Österreichischer Hof at Salzburg, for a checkup.

March 8, 1944

Berghof. At midday reported to the Führer on Leni Riefenstahl, the Duce and Zachariae. Gave him Brom-Nervacit. *** In the evening I was called up by the Führer on account of violent flatulence (had a lot of anxiety these last two days).—Spastic constipation.—Injected Eukodal and Eupaverin intravenously, and gave two Calomels. Application of warmth in the evening. Führer telephoned for Eva [Braun]. Ambassador Rahn and SS-Obergruppenführer Wolff are here. ***

March 9, 1944

Berghof. Big row between Ribbentrop and the military about striking Italians. Gave Ribbentrop a checkup yesterday. Spoke with Führer about promotion of Dr. Z[achariae] to colonel (med.) and award of War Merit Cross first class, also with Wolff. Gave Führer his injections at noon as always [10 cc twenty percent glucose solution intravenously]. In the evening he had a lot of trouble again, and no stool!—At midnight gave him five Boxberger pills, two tablespoons of cod-liver oil. ***

March 14, 1944

Berghof. Gave Patient A a shot of Vitamultin-forte for the first time. *** Before the injection he was very limp and tired, had spent a sleepless night. After it he came to life at once. Had two hours of talks with the foreign minister, was noticeably fresher over lunch than at noon, kept up a very lively conversation. Stayed wide awake a long time tonight.

He slept well after that without sleeping tablets, so it was a very refreshing sleep. Führer very pleased!

March 15, 1944

Berghof. Patient A, injections as always. Visit of the Prague regime to Schloss Klessheim. [*Data card*: double glucose.]

March 16, 1944

Berghof. Schloss Klessheim. Visit of the Bulgarians, and conference. Gave Patient A an injection of Vitamultin-forte.

March 17, 1944

Berghof. Visit of the Bulgarians (Prince Cyrill, Michoff, Filoff, Dr. Zankoff, chef du cabinet Syroff, ambassador Tagaroff) and talks with the Führer. Patient A as always. [*Data card*: *** double glucose and Vitamultin-forte.]

March 18, 1944

Berghof. Visit of Horthy and major conference with Führer at Schloss Klessheim until ten P.M. this evening.

HITLER issued a crude ultimatum to the Hungarian regent Admiral Miklos Horthy, and on the following morning German troops marched into Hungary.

March 19, 1944

Hanni left Salzburg at ten A.M. for Vienna (staying at the Bristol). Birthday greetings to Minister Speer at Schloss Klessheim. (Left knee trouble, with pleurisy.)

HITLER needed every ounce of strength, as he prepared his commanders for the coming Anglo-American invasion of northwest Europe. Shorthand writer Thöt described in his diary on March 20, "Two-thirty P.M. Set off from the big flight of steps in altogether four automobiles: the Führer in the first car, the security unit in the second, personal physician Professor Morell in the third and Major (med.) Dr. von Hasselbach, Lieutenant-

Colonel [Walter] Frentz, [Ludwig] Krieger and I in the third. Drove over to Schloss Klessheim in a blizzard. Shortly after three P.M. a speech there by the Führer to the generals and fortress commanders in the West. After that he conferred with field marshals von Rundstedt and Rommel, and with Grand Admiral Dönitz and the other commanders." Hitler told them he expected the Allies to land in Brittany or Normandy—their moves toward the Calais area were a feint. So he still had his wits about him.

March 21, 1944

Berghof. Patient A telephones about his eyes. [*Data card*: Saw him about eyes. Inconclusive.] Back down to Berchtesgadener Hof.

March 23, 1944

Berghof. Injected Patient A as always. Feeling good, slept well. Headache, some wind. Antonescu (Romanian) visiting at Schloss Klessheim. Spoke with Professor Löhlein; he demands Hitler take a complete rest for two months; impossible.

March 24, 1944

Berghof. Went to Schloss Klessheim, for second day of the Antonescu visit; there with Dr. Zilisteanu, Davidescu, Zachariae, von Killinger.[7] Antonescu wants Vitamultin too!—Saw von Ribbentrop: blood pressure 103, pulse 120. Gave him intravenous glucose, intramuscular liver, Vitamultin-forte, Glyconorm, Tonophosphan.

March 25, 1944

Berghof. Hewel's birthday.—Patient A as always. [*Data card*: double glucose.]

March 26, 1944

Berghof, saw Patient A, intramuscular injection of Vitamultin-forte. Then von Ribbentrop.

[7] Manfred von Killinger, born July 14, 1886, was consul general in San Francisco until 1939, then German minister in Pressburg, and from 1941, in Bucharest. He committed suicide on September 2, 1944, as the Russians invaded the Romanian capital.

March 28, 1944

Berghof. Injected Patient A as always. Treated Reich foreign minister von Ribbentrop at the Berghof too: pulse 96, intramuscular injections of Vitamultin-forte, Glyconorm, liver and intravenous shots of glucose and Prostrophanta (stabbing headache). Said hello to Reichsmarschall Göring.

FOR THE FIRST few days in April Morell appears to have tended Ribbentrop and Frau Emmy Göring more intensively than Hitler, about whom there are no entries in his papers.

April 6, 1944

Berghof. At one-thirty A.M. I had to visit Frau Göring. Gave Patient A his injections as usual. Drew the Führer's attention to the fact that the monotonous Zabel nutrition will result in the stomach becoming unaccustomed to richer diets, and that I am therefore against it.—At twelve-thirty P.M. Professor Morell [sic] telephoned Professor Haase,[8] authorization of the products (only applied for). At one-thirty A.M. again visited Frau Göring.

April 7, 1944

Berghof. Visited Frau Göring, injected Vitamultin-forte. Visited Reich foreign minister Ribbentrop at Fuschl, injected intramuscular glucose, Tonophosphan-forte, liver.—Himmler as usual.

April 9, 1944

Berghof. Treated Patient A as always. [*Data card*: double glucose.] * * *

April 10, 1944

Berghof. * * * Injected Patient A with Vitamultin-forte.

April 12, 1944

Berghof. Gave Patient A the usual injections. [*Data card*: Double glucose.] * * * Minister Wagner ✠ [*died*].

[8] Professor Werner Haase, born August 2, 1900, one of Hitler's earlier escort doctors (and also his last). His widow informs this author that he was beaten to death in Soviet captivity after the war.

April 13, 1944

Berghof. Injected Patient A with Vitamultin-forte. Visited Frau Göring. Injected Vitamultin-forte.

April 20, 1944

Slept very badly last night, only two hours, injected [myself with] *** camphor. Colonel Dr. Siwert: injection of camphor plus Gr. Prostrophanta plus Vitamultin-Calcium plus Strophantin intramuscularly.—Impossible to move my arm.

CAMPHOR dissolved in oil was used as a hypodermic injection in the treatment of serious conditions in which a heart failure is feared. This practice has now largely been abandoned.

April 20, 1944

I took twenty drops of Esdesan, later eleven more drops. Last night I slept from one to six A.M.

During the morning saw Patient A at Schloss Klessheim, and injected Prostrophanta and glucose, Vitamultin, liver. *** Midday [Hitler's birthday] tank display at Klessheim. Esser, Heini [Hoffmann], Giesler, et cetera, there. Gave Patient A an intramuscular shot of Vitamultin-forte.

Anxiety about the Invasion

BY THIS TIME Morell himself was ill. His Berlin assistant Dr. Richard Weber would later describe this as "the dear old doctor" taking refuge in his illness. "At any rate," insisted Weber, "he was not as ill as he maintained. Saying he was sick, he sent for me to look after him, but once I was down there he took the opportunity to 'give me a buildup,' as one would now say. I was introduced to Hitler's staff and was introduced to Hitler himself on one occasion. In this way my name became familiar. I think Morell's idea was to boost me like this so that when the time was ripe he could make himself dispensable and slip out of Hitler's entourage. Then I would have had to take over his job."

Morell did what he could to foster the sick image. Dr. Mulli, convinced, wrote to Professor Morell on May 3, 1944: "I was sorry to hear from your wife that you are not in good health." And in Morell's papers is a letter from him to economics minister Walter Funk dated May 12, 1944, giving a graphic account of his malady: "Since my lung inflammation a few months ago," he apologized, "after which I had to go straight back to my job, the heart problems created by the constant living in bunkers and barracks have been aggravated by having to attend many state visits I had to attend when I had to stand on my feet half the time. A further unfortunate influence is the altitude of the Obersalzberg, with its days and nights of endless snowfalls or rain showers and the weeks of constant Föhn winds.

"I also found," explained Morell, "that the chemical vapors emitted by the smokescreen generators had a very unpleasant effect on the respiratory tracts, and in addition they were bad for the heart. For weeks on end this mountainside was smoke-screened, often several times a day, and the Berghof of course most of all. The effect of all this was that I found myself increasingly short of breath, when climbing stairs I had to pause after only a few steps, and finally because of anginal conditions I had to spend more time at night out of bed than in it. An electrocardiogram I took of myself came up with a very unsatisfactory trace, and I really had to fear the worst. Only for the Führer's sake did I hold off getting treatment so long, and even this was illusory inasmuch as the dozen doctors I called in over the last six months, half of them professors, couldn't get into my veins at all or only managed after countless probes. As Strophantin injections are the only shots that can help me at such an advanced stage, and these can only be made intravenously, I had to fetch my Dr. Weber who's the handiest of them all with the needle and who's the only one able to find my veins every time. I also got the Führer's permission to move down to the Berchtesgadener Hof immediately as it suits me a lot better 1,500 feet lower down."

This was the first time that Weber had stood in for Morell. Weber later (1967) related, "When I saw Hitler at that time, that was in May 1944, he looked fresh and healthy to me. I noticed none of the symptoms that we hear so much about today. His facial expression was neither masked nor fixed, his face color was not unnatural, his hands did not tremble, he was not dragging one leg." (However, Hitler himself would say at the end of July 1944 that at this time, early in May, his left leg used to shake uncontrollably even when he was lying in bed at night.)

One thing seems clear: in May 1944, the doctor was often less robust than his patient. "At present I drive up to see the Führer every day at noon," he wrote on May 12. "I give him his treatments, and I get back down here to the hotel almost always around two P.M., and I lie in bed here almost all day to give the old ticker a bit of a rest cure so that I will be fit enough again to go on journeys with the Führer."[1]

Professor Laves wrote to Morell on May 15 expressing his best wishes for a rapid recovery. And we find that on June 5 Weber himself wrote from Berlin suggesting that Morell stay in

[1] Letter, Morell to Funk, May 12, 1944, National Archives microfilm T-253, roll 40, pp. 1913–15.

bed at least eighteen hours a day and take Digilamid for a while rather than Strophantin, "and try for a while with vessel-widening drugs." Weber conceded, "With your bad veins you also have to take into account that it may be impossible to make injections into you for a while."

Morell continued his almost daily injection treatments of Hitler as his papers show:

April 22, 1944

Visit by the Duce. Klessheim castle.—Berghof: Double glucose.

April 24, 1944

Gave Patient A injections as usual, Vitamultin-forte, and left in the evening for Berlin.

April 27, 1944

[Back at] Berghof. Patient A.

April 30, 1944

Berghof. Patient A has a slight cold; I injected glucose plus Ultraseptyl and intramuscular shots of Vitamultin-Calcium, Hamma liver and Omnadin. *** Slight cough. Ribbentrop's birthday.

May 3, 1944 (data card)

[Dr. Weber] left for Berlin.

May 4, 1944

Berghof. Patient A, I made an electrocardiogram! I and II lead: isoelectric T—strong muscle current.

Subsequently a series of injections of twenty percent glucose occasionally with added iodine (Septoiod 10 cc) intravenously and Vitamultin-Calcium and Tonophosphan intramuscularly and various quantities of Glyconorm or liver extract. Per Os: Vitamultin tablets, 4–6 a day, at meals. Also Luizym and Glyconorm and Euflat or anti-gas pills from time to time.

Recommended but not adopted: Massage, early retiring, prolonged stays in open air, restrict fluid intake. Further necessary: inhaling free oxygen two or three times a day. Intravenous injections of glucose with added Strophantin and possibly also with heart muscle extract in phosphoric acid. At first three times daily, then every second day. Restrict fluid intake to 1200 cc daily. Testoviron intramuscularly. If not feeling well don't hesitate to take a swallow of coffee or 10 to 15 drops of Cardiazol. Make sure of regular bowel movements. Since neither anginal syndromes nor obstructions appear, the immediate prognosis is favorable. Smoking and drinking fortunately not involved. Necessary: electrocardiogram after a day's work [and] heart X ray.

May 5, 1944

Gave Patient A intravenous injections of glucose and Prostophanta, and intramuscular of Vitamultin-Calcium, Testoviron and Omnadin. *** Massage flatly rejected in spite of my pleading. Total daily rest ten hours as required. An earlier retirement is impossible because of air raids. Consented to reduction of fluid intake to 1200 cc daily. Presence of slight edema formations on shin bone could be noted under finger pressure.

May 6, 1944

Injected Patient A with glucose, Vitamultin-Calcium and Testoviron.

May 7, 1944

Patient A still has a head cold. Ultraseptyl doesn't help him any more. Blood pressure 140/108 mm, injected glucose intravenously plus Vitamultin-forte plus Testoviron plus Glyconorm intramuscularly. ***

May 8, 1944

Stayed down here at hotel. Telephoned with Dr. Goebbels and Dr. Ley (who has blood pressure of 200).

May 9, 1944

Up to the Berghof. Patient A has a headache on the left side. His legs are trembling (invasion imminent, but where?).—Intravenous shots of Glucad. plus Septoid and intramuscular of Testoviron, Vitamultin-forte and liver extract.—Must drop Pyr. and Cardiazol, and use Chineurin only prophylactically.—Ley's blood pressure down to 140 (bloodletting of 120 cc). Dr. Goebbels fine.

May 11, 1944

Berghof to see Patient A, injections of glucose, Testoviron, liver, Vitamultin-forte!

May 12, 1944

Patient A, injected glucose, Testoviron, Vitamultin-Calcium, Tonophosphan-forte. State visit by the Slovaks at Schloss Klessheim.

May 13, 1944

Hanni departed via Salzburg. Paid a visit on Hewel in hospital.

May 14, 1944

Berghof, Patient A, injected glucose intravenously, plus Testoviron, liver, Vitamultin-C intramuscularly. Oxygen inhalation! Went up there midday.

May 15, 1944

Stayed down at the Berchtesgadener Hof.

May 16, 1944

Patient A as usual at the Berghof. Intravenous shots of glucose, Septoiod, and intramuscular of Testoviron, Tonophosphan, Glyconorm; he states gastrointestinal tract and respiratory passages are all okay.

May 17, 1944

Stayed down at the Berchtesgadener Hof.

May 18, 1944

Patient A, intravenous of glucose, Testoviron, and intramuscular of Glyconorm.

May 20, 1944

Patient A. Glucose intravenous, plus Testoviron and Glyconorm intramuscularly. Frau von Ribbentrop operated on by Professor Gebhardt in Salzburg (appendix ***). Holzmutter, Jr., here with Schnepf and two other gentlemen for negotiations on the release of endocrine glands to Olmütz. First talks with Dr. Riedel on the electron microscope.

May 21, 1944

Went up for lunch at the Berghof. In the afternnon to Reichen-hall, Café Flora. *** Called on Dr. Riedel for conference on the electron microscope.

May 22, 1944

Injected Patient A with glucose intravenously and Testoviron, liver and Glyconorm intramuscularly. Electrocardiogram inconclu-sive (great improvement).—Spoke about electron microscope (Dr. Riedel).—Visited Hewel, introduced to his fiancée.

May 23, 1944 (data card)

Discussion of electrocardiogram.

May 24, 1944

Visited Patient A, then to Reichenhall with Dr. Riedel, looked over real estate in Bayrisch- and Gross-Gmain [for housing the electron microscope].

May 26, 1944

Gave Patient A an intravenous shot of glucose, plus intramus-cular of Testoviron, Glyconorm, and after defecation two intra-muscular shots of Vitamultin-forte.

May 27, 1944

Minister Lammers's [sixty-fifth] birthday.[2]—Visited Hewel.

May 28, 1944

Injected Patient A with intravenous glucose, plus intramuscular liver, Glyconorm, Tonophosphan-forte.

May 30, 1944 (data card)

Double glucose.

[2] Dr. Hans Lammers, lawyer and Reichsminister, was chief of the Reich Chancery and head of the civil service. Born May 27, 1879. On this birthday Hitler gave him his rented Schorfheide hunting lodge with a large estate and 600,000 Reichsmarks from his own purse. (Letter Bormann to Lammers, May 17.) His wife and daughter committed suicide in May 1945 after being raped by French troops at Berchtesgaden. Sentenced to twenty years by the Americans at Nuremberg.

Marriage of Gretl Braun to SS-Brigadeführer Fegelein.[3]

THE ALLIED INVASION of Normandy began soon after midnight on June 5–6, 1944. It was the decisive Allied thrust, but Hitler had stopped worrying about it, and it was not taken seriously at the Berghof. Certainly, it found no mention in Morell's diary. Hitler was not wakened until lunchtime, as usual, and got his regular double-glucose injection.

Thus the routine remained unchanged: Morell lingered in his hotel, gasping for air down in the valley, while Hitler ruled his shrinking empire from his mountainside villa 1,500 feet higher up; occasionally the doctor arrived with his black bag and syringes to give the dictator the injections that each man now believed indispensable.

Soon a million British and American troops stood on French soil. On the night of June 15–16 the German secret weapon attack began on London. Until the late winter, thousands of pilotless V-1 bombs would rain down on southern England. In the last week of June the biggest German army group, Center, collapsed on the eastern front, and an avalanche of Russian forces poured through Poland toward the German frontier.

Hitler remained at the Berghof, his health still not good. When his veteran housekeeper Anni Winter saw him she was dismayed by the change in him. He was emaciated and weak, she said, with only "scarecrow arms" that shook uncontrollably. For lunch he might eat a plate of white bean soup with a spoon of oil, followed by a little plate of lettuce. "Look," he appealed to her, "they won't let me eat anything. Have them show you what you can cook for me and how." She made him a couple of thin apple pastries that afternoon, and he gobbled them down as though half starved. Frau Winter would later recall, "Morell was collaborating in his treatment of Hitler with a homeopath

[3] Hermann Fegelein, born October 30, 1906, at Ansbach; had been SS liaison officer on Hitler's staff since January 1. Margarete (Gretl) Braun, born August 31, 1915, in Munich, was Eva Braun's younger sister. Fegelein was shot by firing squad in Berlin on April 28, 1945, for desertion. Morell was on conspicuously good terms with Fegelein, and is rumored to have given the couple a wedding gift costing 50,000 Reichsmarks.

Professor Zabel of Berchtesgaden. Morell had installed a special cook on the Obersalzberg just to cook the menu for Hitler—this bean soup and lettuce salad!"

June 6, 1944

Went up to see Patient A. [*Data card*: Double glucose.]—Afterward visit by Hungarians, [Prime Minister Count Döme] Sztójay.

June 8, 1944

I was awarded the Grand Officer's Cross of the Royal Bulgarian Alexander Order. Gave Patient A his injections of glucose and Tonophosphan-forte, Vitamultin-forte. Visited Frau Göring.

EARLY in June 1944 Morell had a fecal sample routinely analyzed by Nissle and Laves. Laves reported on June 5, "Practically speaking, result of examination is normal." Nissle completed his analysis by the eighth. "Though the bacteria content of the specimen was conspicuously small," he stated, "the composition of the intestinal flora was most satisfactory since no pathological elements were to be found."

June 10, 1944

Berchtesgaden. Went to see Patient A, injected glucose intravenously, Tonophosphan, Vitamultin-forte, Glyconorm. [*Data card*: Double glucose, blood pressure 150/108, received fecal analysis report.] *** Treated Eva Braun: intravenous Strophantin, blood pressure 110; treated Miss Schneider,[4] intravenous Strophantin, plus liver and Vitamultin-Calcium intramuscular.

June 11, 1944

Berchtesgaden. Up to the Berghof at midday, Giesler there. Dictated letters all afternoon. In the evening at the Berghof, a discussion with the Führer and Bormann about the electron microscope.

[4] Herta Schneider was a close friend of Eva Braun who now lives at Garmisch-Partenkirchen.

June 12, 1944

Berchtesgaden. *** Gave Patient A intravenous injections of glucose, and intramuscular of Vitamultin-forte, Tonophosphan-forte, liver; intravenous injections Miss Schneider of Strophantin. Telephoned Berlin three times about damage from air mines.

ON JUNE 16 Morell flew to his factory at Olmütz, had a conference there with Dr. Leonardo Conti, the Reich health chief, and returned to his Berchtesgaden hotel on the nineteenth.

June 19, 1944

Olmütz, flight to Munich, then to Berchtesgaden. Patient A, then hotel.

June 21, 1944

Berchestgaden. Patient A.

EVIDENTLY Hitler's health ceased giving trouble. Morell stayed down in the valley for the next week and did not see him. His mind was full of his new electron microscope.

June 27, 1944

Berchtesgaden. Dr. Mulli arrives from Graz. In the afternoon to Hochrain Castle with Dr. Riedel, conference in the evening about instrumentation for the electron microscope with him.

June 28, 1944

Berchtesgaden. Telephoned Siemens about the microscope. Gave Patient A a Testoviron shot. With Mulli and Riedel to Reichenhall. ***

July 2, 1944

Patient A as always. [*Data card*: Double glucose.]

July 3, 1944

Hotel. Patient A sent for me, as always. Blood pressure 157/117.

July 5, 1944

Berchtesgaden. Patient A as always. [*Data card*: Double glucose.]—Conversation with General Zeitzler.[5]

July 6, 1944

Berchtesgaden. Patient A, nothing new.—Called on Zeitzler.

July 7, 1944

Berchtesgaden. *** Four-thirty P.M. Inspection [of war equipment] at Schloss Klessheim and war conference there.

July 8, 1944

Berchtesgaden, injected Patient A with glucose, iodine, Testoviron, Tonophosphan, Vitamultin-forte. ***

July 9, 1944

Berchtesgaden. Heini [Hoffmann] at the Berghof. Treated Erna [Hoffmann].

July 11, 1944

Berchtesgaden. Patient A. [*Data card*: Visit, no change.]

July 13, 1944

Patient A as always. [*Data card*: double glucose.] Supper at the Berghof. Esser there.

July 14, 1944

Flight from Berchtesgaden, that is, from Salzburg, to the Wolf's Lair. Patient A has flu and conjunctivitis in both eyes. Some hair shampoo got into his left eye, and it smarted badly. Gave him some cocaine-adrenaline solution—Targesin solution.

[5] Kurt Zeitzler, Colonel-General. Born June 9, 1895, Zeitzler had been chief of the General Staff since September 1942. He had become disenchanted with Hitler's strategies in what the General Staff regarded as its own theater, the eastern front, and on June 30 withdrew, pleading a nervous breakdown. Hitler paid no attention, but after the bomb plot replaced him by Heinz Guderian. Died September 25, 1963.

ON THIS DAY Hitler left the Berghof—forever, as it would turn out—and flew back to his Rastenburg headquarters. There was no other way to halt the threat to the Center. The passenger cabin's curtains were drawn. He saw nothing, and had no desire to look. Perhaps he could not stand the light, what doctors call photophobia. "The year before," Dr. Giesing would reflect in November 1945, "he had stopped making industrial inspection trips although before the war he had really enjoyed going on journeys. He lived in his bunker and learned all he needed to know, the successes and failures, by wire and radio, but never by seeing things for himself. This self-inflicted isolation in his bunker was not by any means a security measure . . . he developed something of a bunker mentality. It was the only place he felt at home: the only place where he got the kind of climate he liked (thanks to an air-conditioning system) and the only place he could work and think. He often used to proclaim that he could really only work at an altitude of 1,300 feet above sea level, because his native town of Braunau am Inn was at that elevation."

The Führer staff were already waiting at the Wolf's Lair for him. Stenographer Karl Thöt described in his diary, "How beautiful it is out here. The whole site is resplendent with luscious greenery. The woods breathe a magnificent tranquility. The wooden hutments, including ours, have meantime been heavily bricked-in to afford protection against bomb splinters. We all feel well at ease here. It's become a second home to us."

July 15, 1944
Führer's headquarters, Wolf's Lair. Called up Hanni and Mulli at Olmütz. Dr. Conti telephoned me.

July 16, 1944
Wolf's Lair. Patient A as usual. [*Data card*: Eye well again.]

July 18, 1944
Wolf's Lair. Patient A here as always. Slept well, feels good.

The Assassination Attempt

A T ABOUT ONE P.M. on July 20, 1944, something incredible happened. "All of a sudden there was a frightful crash," as Theo Morell described it to his wife afterward, "and I shouted to an orderly: 'That's it! Now they've found us. That was a bomb!' But the orderly said, 'Oh, no, sir, I know that sound from World War I—this was something else.' And at that moment Hitler's valet burst in and said, 'Quick, Herr Professor, quick! You must come to the Führer at once!' "

A bomb attempt had been made on Hitler's life. The hut in which he had been standing was now wrecked, and his mangled and maimed officers were bleeding on the collapsed floorboards. "In the conference room," stenographer Thöt recorded that day, "before the conference began, Colonel Count von Stauffenberg, who had been ordered here for a briefing, had placed a briefcase containing a bomb with a timefuse under the map table; in fact it must have rested just in front of poor Berger's feet." Heinrich Berger was one of Thöt's fellow shorthand reporters.

Their colleague Heinz Buchholz later wrote, "I remember it as a clap of thunder coupled with a bright yellow flash and clouds of thick smoke. Glass and wood splintered through the air. The large table on which all the situation maps had been spread out and around which the participants were standing—only we stenographers were sitting—collapsed. After a few seconds of silence I heard a voice, probably Field Marshal Keitel, shouting: 'Where is the Führer?' Then further shouts and screams of pain arose."

From this moment on Hitler's real health problems, as opposed to his purely neurotic ones, began.

July 20, 1944 (Thursday)

Wolf's Lair. Went over to Patient A at eleven-fifteen A.M. and gave him injections as always. [*Data card*: double glucose.]

Then an *Attentat* with an explosive charge! on the Führer! [*Data card*: Pulse afterward 72. Treated him. Injury.] Visit from the Duce.

FOR THOSE of us," navy Captain Heinz Assmann would write afterward, "who bore the brunt of the explosion standing right next to Hitler, his escape unscathed will always seem a miracle." And Thöt echoed him. "In the conference room," his diary records, "the devastation was frightful, but it must be regarded as an immense stroke of good fortune that the Attentat did not happen in one of the bunkers but in a barrack hut—in a room with four windows which were all in fact wide open, so that the blast was able to get out. . . . Worst injured was unfortunately our colleague Berger, who was on shorthand duty with Buchholz. . . . He was rushed to hospital and operated on, in fact both legs were amputated. The operation was performed by Colonel (med.) Dr. von Hasselbach."

The men who had a few seconds earlier been listening to Hitler's words now tumbled out of the wrecked hut, injured, bleeding, their hands and faces blackened and burned, their hair singed and stained yellow, their uniforms ragged and dirty. "The Führer's physicians arrived immediately," recalled Buchholz. They removed over one hundred oak splinters from the Führer's legs—mainly the right one. He hardly noticed the pain. He too was baffled by his escape. As Morell galloped into the bunker's sleeping quarters, Hitler greeted him with a disdainful remark: "It's nothing really," he said with a grimace. Then he actually grinned. "I'm invulnerable," he shouted. "I'm immortal!" Morell dressed his wounds. Hitler changed out of his tattered and singed uniform and said, "Morell, let's get a move on, Mussolini will be here any moment."

A few days later he would pay his respects on the surviving officers in the Karlshof army hospital at Rastenburg. The

Hitler in 1939

Professor Theo Morell

Hitler and Morell

Morell writing in his diary

Part of the Morell diaries at the National Archives

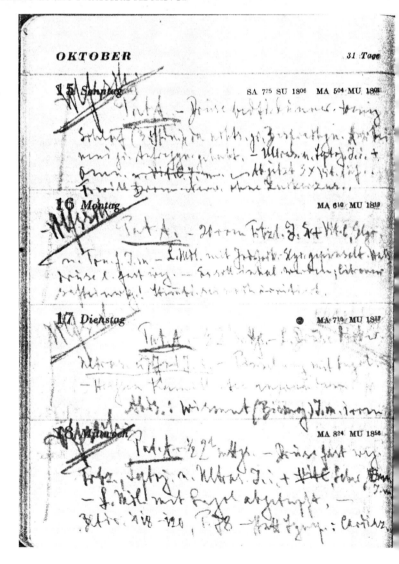

Typical diary page

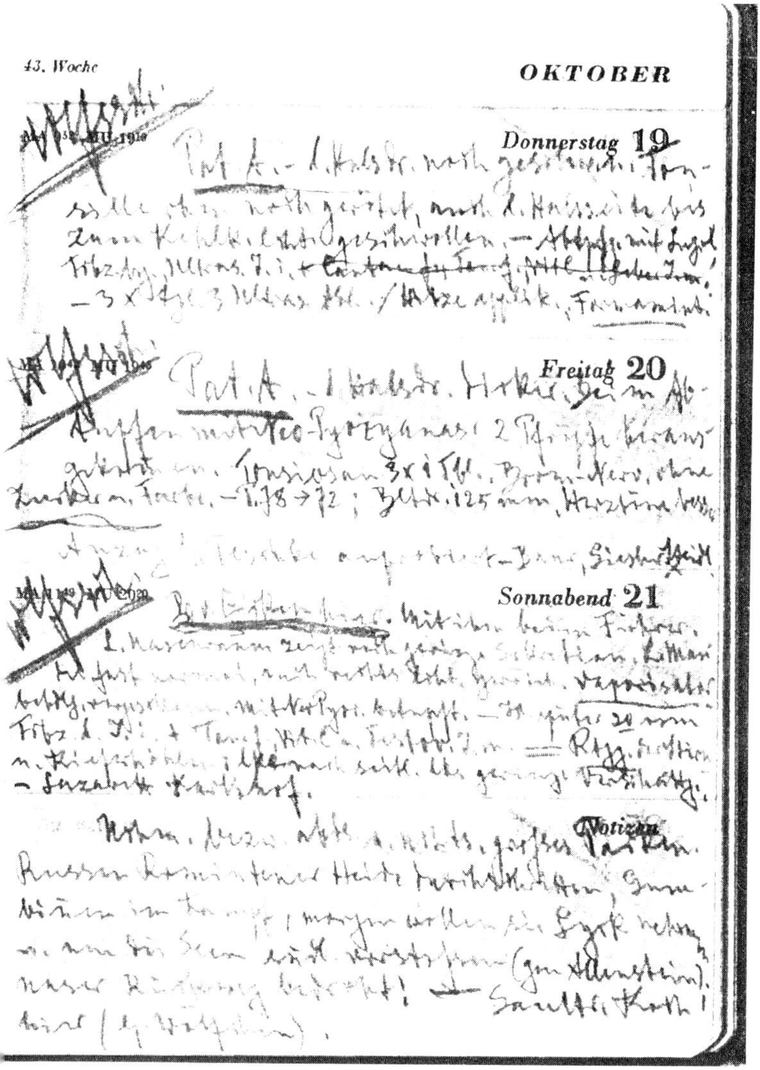

43. Woche

OKTOBER

Donnerstag 19

Freitag 20

Sonnabend 21

Notizen

Morell receiving the Knight's Cross

Typical Hitler/vegetarian menu

7. Juni 1943

============

Orangensaft
mit Leinsamenschleim

--

Reispudding
mit Kräutertunke

--

Knäckebrot D mit Butter
Nuxo - Paste

Electrocardiogram of "Patient A"

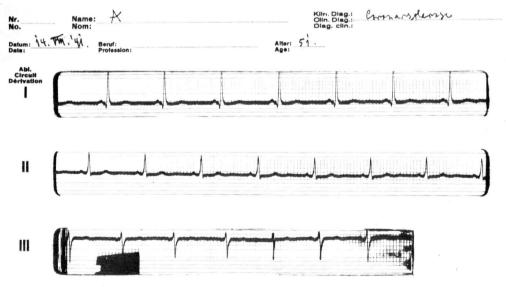

| Nr. No. | Name: A Nom: | | Klin. Diag.: Clin. Diag.: Diag. clin.: | Coronarsklerose |
| Datum: 14. FM. '41 Date: | Beruf: Profession: | | Alter: 51. Age: | |

Abl. Circuit Dérivation

I

II

III

Imprimé en Allemagne — Printed in Germany

Prof. Dr. Th. Morell.

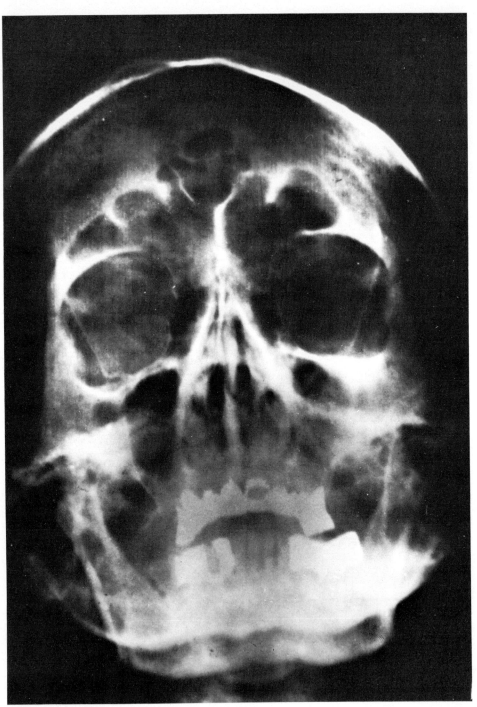

X-ray of Hitler's skull

photographs show the blinded Rudolf Schmundt, his face terribly burned, gripping Hitler's hand in both of his. When Hitler reached Assmann's cot, he said, "There you are, seriously injured—yet you were not the ones marked down for assassination. These gentlemen were after me and only me: yet I escaped completely unscathed. Four times in this war my enemies have tried to do away with me like this, once and for all. Yet not once have they succeeded."

The immediate medical result of the blast was unexpected. The tremor in Hitler's left leg vanished. "The miracle is," he said eleven days later to General Jodl, "that the shock got rid of my nerve complaint almost entirely. My left leg still trembles somewhat if conferences go on too long, but previously this leg used to shake in bed. With this shock, that's vanished almost completely—not that I would recommend this kind of remedy." (The surviving shorthand reporters recorded his words.) The inevitable conclusion is that this tremor must have been neurotic in origin.

But a severe gash on his head had clearly affected Hitler's inner ear. His eyes flicked constantly to the right—"nystagmus." He kept imagining that he was falling over to the right. Twice that evening as he went for a stroll he found himself wandering in the darkness off the path—again to the right.

July 20, 1944 (a typed memorandum)
Patient A: eye drops administered, conjunctivitis in right eye. One-fifteen P.M. Pulse 72.
Eight P.M. Pulse 100, regular, strong, blood pressure 165–170. Treated injuries with penicillin powder.[1]
Right forearm badly swollen, prescribed acid aluminium acetate compresses.[2] Effusion of blood on right shinbone has subsided. On back of third or fourth finger of left hand there is a large burn blister. Bandage. Occiput partly and hair completely burned, a palm-size second degree skin burn on the middle of the calf and a

[1] For Morell's "penicillin" see page 67.
[2] Interrogated on September 10, 1945, Hasselbach would comment in this connection: "Dr. Morell applied a bandage soaked in acid aluminium acetate on the elbow. This resulted in dermatitis with pruritis which lasted about two weeks." (OI/CIR/2)

number of contusions and open flesh wounds. Left forearm has effusion of blood on interior aspect and is badly swollen, can move it only with difficulty.—He is to take two Optalidons at once, and two tablespoons of Brom-Nervacit before going to sleep.

THE LONG-TERM psychological effects of the murder attempt were interesting. Major Cortez F. Enloe, Jr., who interrogated nearly all the doctors from Hitler's headquarters on behalf of the medical branch of the U.S. Strategic Bombing Survey, later wrote, "The group of old-school Prussians who tried to murder Hitler contributed largely to Germany's defeat. Their attempt set in motion in the mind of that evil and uncertain man a chain of psychological reactions that separated the Führer from his advisers and friends and gradually undermined his psyche. In the end, these reactions trapped Hitler in the maze of his own obsessions and left him with self-destruction as the only escape."[3]

Goebbels confirmed this assessment in a conversation with finance minister Schwerin von Krosigk, who noted in his diary in April 1945: "The 20th of July did leave its mark on him, both physically—he can still not use one hand because it trembles so much—and mentally: the blow to his trust has been serious, and he has become increasingly distrustful and solitary."

July 21, 1944

Wolf's Lair. He slept only two hours last night.—Invited to tea this evening. Before the nighttime tea session the Führer gave me a [birthday] present, a gold watch.

July 22, 1944

Wolf's Lair. Patient A. Slept only an hour last night. Gave him the usual injections and treatment. [*Data card*: *** double glucose.] My birthday—I'm fifty-eight. This morning [General] Korten✠[4] and Colonel (GS) Brandt✠.[5] [*Data card*: *** Double glucose.]

---

[3] *Collier's* magazine, May 1946.

[4] Günther Korten, General der Flieger, born July 26, 1898, was the Luftwaffe's chief of staff; his death was a critical loss for Germany.

[5] Heinz Brandt, Colonel, chief of the Operations Division of the General

HITLER'S ESCORT DOCTOR Karl Brandt had hurried back to Rastenburg from Berlin as soon as the bomb blast was announced. He was disturbed by the blood seeping steadily from Hitler's ears. Morell shared his concern, and telephoned the ENT specialist Professor von Eicken in Berlin. But Eicken was in southern Germany attending his daughter's wedding. So on July 22 Brandt fetched in Dr. Erwin Giesing, a major (med.) at the army field hospital at nearby Lötzen. Giesing was blond, scarfaced and, like Eicken, an ear, nose and throat specialist. He wrote very full records of the weeks that he spent treating Hitler.

Interrogated on August 30, 1945, Giesing would say this of his first consultation with Hitler: "Facial expression at the time of examination (July 1944): fatigued, exhausted, with appearance of senility." On October 18, 1944, a week after his dismissal, Giesing wrote a summary of his treatment of the injured victims. He said that his ear treatment had established the following about Hitler's ear injuries:

Ears: Right—large, kidney-shaped central rupture lower front and rear. Bleeding badly. Whispering perceived only immediately into ear. Pronounced combined deafness of middle and inner ear. Indications of nystagmus to right.

Left: Slit-shaped central rupture 3 mm long lower rear. Whispered speech perceived at 4 meters. Slight combined deafness.

After Giesing's first visit on July 22 he treated Hitler almost every day. Before his first such treatment he called on the severely injured General Schmundt. The adjutant warned him that Hitler was a "mighty, but mystic superman." Shortly after that, Giesing was standing in this superman's bunker, but his first impression was different.

"He looked to me like an aging man—almost burned out and exhausted," Giesing would write in November 1945, "like somebody husbanding every last ounce of his strength." Hitler was stooped; he was limping on his right leg and carrying his arm tucked into his tunic Napoleon-fashion. The face was ashen, the eyes bloodshot, the lips swollen.

Staff. He had been involved in the plot against Hitler and from his hospital deathbed bewailed the fact that his accomplices had not at least warned him to make himself scarce. The stenographer Berger and General Schmundt were the two other fatalities caused by the bomb.

"Doctor," he said in the slightly awed tone he used when talking to experts, "I hear you are taking care of my friends. I was reluctant to bother you. For the past two days—since the explosion—I have had a sharp pain in my right ear and have trouble in hearing. My valet tells me it's because I shout too much. But enough of myself. Tell me, truthfully, how are the others?"

Over the next weeks Giesing would twice get the opportunity of giving Hitler a complete physical and neurological checkup (late in August and early in October 1944). His findings largely confirmed those of Morell. Hitler was about as tall as Giesing (174 cm). He weighed about 160 pounds. His hair was thin, his body skin remarkably white; there was an outsize gold bridge in his right lower jaw, and his genital organs apparently normal—so Giesing claims to have observed.

"Outsiders often suspected a hypertrophy of the right arm or the shoulder muscles," he continued, "but there was no sign of this. . . . Nevertheless his physical endurance was astounding, particularly at big Party events like parades and marches, where he stood for hours on end with his right arm outstretched." Giesing found no clinical abnormalities in Hitler's heart or lungs; the pulse was full, regular and quite strong, he said. The increases in blood pressure reported by Morell were attributed by Giesing to the susceptibility of Hitler's autonomic nervous system to anger and worry.

As for Hitler's neurological and psychiatric condition, Giesing stated that these two examinations in August and October 1944 revealed no abnormality. "The commotio labyrinthi on the right side, which I described in my report of June 12, 1945, was originated by the shockwave, which caused a major rupture of the right tympanic membrane, and by blast damage to the semicircular canals and cochlea of the inner ear. From what he himself said, Hitler was hurled by the force of the explosion from his original position at the middle of the map table to the vicinity of the left doorpost of the exit." Hitler's behavior during Giesing's frequent consultations showed not the slightest signs of a commotio cerebri let alone a contusio cerebri.

It would be the late autmn 1944 before Hitler partially recovered from the assassins' attack. Then the trembling returned. He joked about the growing debilities, but this only highlighted his concern about them. "Before the bomb went off I had this tremor in my left leg," he said to his secretaries. "Now it's moved over to my right hand. I'm glad I don't have it in my head. If I just kept shaking my head things would look pretty bleak."

Some doctors believed that the growing lameness of Hitler's right arm was a "conversion hysteria"—a reaction in which some real or imagined physical phenomenon became the token of an unpleasant memory. Cortez Enloe would write: "This shaking of Hitler's right arm indeed became the symbol of the gradual breaking up of his personality following the attack on his life. The impact of this betrayal upon the ruler's psyche consumed his mind in the end."

July 23, 1944

Wolf's Lair. Patient A. *** Professor von Eicken here.[6] [*Data card*: Because of serious bleeding from the ear.]

July 24, 1944

Wolf's Lair. At two A.M. sent for by Patient A, who complained about the burns on his arm, the thick alcohol bandage, inflammation and swellings. He hadn't sent for me at once as I was asleep, so von Hasselbach applied a lotion and dressing.

In the morning saw Patient A [*Data card*: double glucose] as always. ***

July 26, 1944

Wolf's Lair, gave Patient A his injections as always [*Data card*: double glucose].

[6] Professor Carl von Eicken of the ENT clinic of Berlin University. In his consultation notes Eicken wrote on July 23: "Consultation at Führer's headquarters with Professor Morell. July 20, bomb attempt. Contusions to right upper and forearm. Burns on left and right shinbones. Both tympanic membranes ruptured. A lot of blood in right auditory canal." After sketching the two eardrums, Eicken entered his findings: "Some blood in nasopharyngeal canal. Whispered figures: 10 cms on the right, over five meters on the left. The A-1 fork: +6 on the right, +35 on the left. Lateralization to the right. The Weber test was lateralized to the right. Heard o6 on the right but greatly truncated. No nystagmus, no dizziness."

July 27, 1944

Wolf's Lair. Saw Patient A at midday. The ENT doctor [Giesing] was there. Ear still bleeding at times. Führer talked about letting some blood, but his blood pressure was 140, which was normal, so it is not necessary.—Must take a tablespoon of Sangostop three times, and two Koagovit tablets three times; if his ear still bleeding tomorrow than we will inject some Koagovit.

GIESING was intensively attending to the problems developing in Hitler's inner ear. The right ear continued to bleed for several days. Giesing wanted to carry out a simple cauterization, but Morell proposed instead a miracle-working hemostatic called Nateina which had aroused controversy in the 1930s when sampled, allegedly successfully, by the hemophilic Spanish royal family.

Meanwhile Hitler proved the perfect patient. Dr. Giesing found that he could carry out the most painful cauterizations without even a local anesthetization of the damaged eardrum. "I will get over it," said Hitler, waving the anesthesia aside. "I've suffered worse in my life, and let's hope it's not all that painful anyway." The bleeding continued.

"Well, my dear professor," Hitler sighed to the elderly von Eicken when he reappeared. "It appears there is more wrong with my ear than we thought. Morell gave me another of his blood staunching injections last night, and I've been taking all the styptic tablets too, just like the doctor ordered. The bleeding's got to stop sometime! Perhaps I'm just a natural bleeder . . ."

On the next day the ear was still bleeding internally. Hitler asked Giesing to cauterize it again. "I stopped feeling pain long ago," he said pathetically. "Besides, pain exists to make a man of you."

July 28, 1944

Wolf's Lair. Patient A, injections as always. Glucose, Tono-phosphan-forte, Glyconorm.—Apparently the ear dressing is still in place; it's not bleeding any more.

July 29, 1944

Wolf's Lair. Patient A. Note that since the moment the bomb blast occurred the tremor has vanished from his leg and the trembling of his hands is down to a minimum.

July 30, 1944

Nothing to report.

INDIRECTLY, the injuries affected the strategic direction of the war. In the middle of June 1944 Hitler had still been able to jump into a plane and rush to France for a special conference with his western commanders, Rundstedt and Rommel. Now that kind of hustle was impossible. On July 31 the shorthand reporters took down Hitler's words about his new and accursed debilities. "I would so much have liked to get over to the west," he lamented. "But now with the best will in the world I cannot. Certainly I will not be able to go up in a plane for the next week or so on account of my ears. Obviously, if all the dams burst, I would do anything and wouldn't care—I'd go as gunner in a single-engined plane to get there as fast as possible."

Early in August the dams did burst in the west: at Avranches the Americans finally fought their way out of their bridgehead in Normandy and poured into open countryside. In the next three weeks the whole of France was lost to Hitler. He could not fly, and remained at his headquarters.

In a special note dated August 1, the following data were recorded showing that Hitler's condition was still dominated by the injuries sustained on July 20: "Adhesive bandages show blood seeping through the skin on the arm and buttocks. Over the coccyx there is a hand-size rainbow-colored area which has now shrunk somewhat. On the right forearm on the little-finger side the wrist is thicker (caused by blood emanating from the large internal hemorrhage in the vicinity of the elbow). General condition good. In the evening two Optalidons and two spoonfuls of Brom-Nervacit."

August 1, 1944

Wolf's Lair. Patient A. Blood pressure. Injected twenty percent glucose intravenously, plus liver, Glyconorm, Tonophosphan-forte intramuscularly. [*Data card*: double glucose. * * *]

August 2, 1944

Wolf's Lair. Patient A. Gave two Optalidons last night to help him sleep, and two tablespoons of Brom-Nervacit. Has a throbbing over his right eye.—At three-thirty P.M. to see Patient A: blood pressure 160+ (compared with 135–140 of late); not possible to inject him with iodine because of the ear bleeding recently; the left eardrum is almost healed; there is a serous secretion on the right one. *** Bloodletting 200 cc! Ten drops of Sympathol.—The relief is very great.

August 3, 1944

Patient A. Injected glucose intravenously, and Vitamultin-Calcium, liver and Tonophosphan intramuscularly.—The colored area [a hematoma or blood effusion] over the sacrum has extended to both sides and is colored bluish-yellowish-green. Blood pressure 133–135 mm.

August 4, 1944

Wolf's Lair. *** Around evening went for tea with Führer and [secretaries] Wolf[7], Schroeder and Daranowski.

August 5, 1944

Intravenous injection of glucose, and intramuscular of Vita-multin-Calcium, liver, Tonophosphan-forte. Says his ear has not bled for five days. But ENT specialist [Giesing] did not bother to inform me of that. The patch on the small of his back is being reabsorbed.—Romanian state visit (Antonescu).[8]

ACCORDING TO Giesing, Hitler persuaded Morell to resume his use of Ultraseptyl, although in Morell's diary we find no explicit reference to his giving it to Hitler between May 7 (when he noted, "Ultraseptyl doesn't help him any more") and October 15, 1944 ("at his request"). Hitler had confided to Giesing, "Professor Morell has such a good drug, called Ultraseptyl, it's helped

---

[7] Johanna Wolf, born June 1, 1900, in Munich, Hitler's senior private secretary since January 1930. Lives now outside Munich.

[8] Marshal Ion Antonescu of Romania was paying his last visit to Hitler. A few days later he was arrested by the king; he was executed by the Russians after the war.

me a lot in the past with head colds or at the onset of flu." Giesing was worried, as he knew that the sulphonamide level in blood could not be kept high for long without it losing its antibiotic properties. But Hitler told him, "When he comes in after you I'm going to ask Morell to give me a couple of shots."

To Dr. Giesing it seemed no coincidence that as the Ultraseptyl course began, so Hitler became irritable and sleepless, and began suffering terrible nightmares as scenes from the battle fronts haunted his sleep. A few days later Hitler told him he was puzzled that despite the Ultraseptyl the inner ear infection had worsened. "Morell wants to give me another iodine shot today," he told Giesing, "as well as a heart-, a liver- and a Vitamultin-Calcium injection. That's what he learned in the tropics," Hitler added, "that these things have to be shot straight into your veins."

Giesing began treating Hitler in that second half of August with cocaine too—a ten percent solution to dispel the growing sinus pains. Giesing afterward wrote, "Hitler told me that after the treatment with the cocaine he felt quite light-headed and he could think much clearer." He asked the doctor whether he might not have this agreeable daubing with cocaine done once or even twice a day in future. The army doctor agreed, but warned of the danger of a cocaine overdose as cocaine is virtually entirely absorbed by the mucous membrane of the nose and enters the blood stream very rapidly. A few days later Hitler complained, "Good that you came, doctor. I've a scorcher of a headache today—probably from that head cold." He complained again of stomach pains and lack of appetite and said he had not slept well. "The worries about the future and Germany's existence are just eating me up inside," he said.

Giesing indicated that the Ultraseptyl might be the cause of the stomach problems. In fact he had begun dosing himself with the drug to test its side effects, and after five days he experienced the same stomach pains. Hitler still refused to take note, and began to look forward instead to Giesing's cocaine treatments every other day. Giesing humored him. "It's as though I am not ill at all," was how he described the effects of the cocaine. "I just wish my head could always be so clear." He added, "I hope you're not making me into a coke addict." Morell knew none of this.

August 6, 1944

Traveling. Midday reached Berlin-Schwanenwerder. Air raid!

August 7, 1944

Back at Berlin-Schwanenwerder. [Morell's sister] Emilie and Kurt. My twenty-fifth wedding anniversary!

August 8, 1944

Berlin. *** Twelve-thirty P.M. saw General Zeitzler at the practice.

August 9, 1944

Traveling back to Wolf's Lair. Patient A's blood pressure 133 mm, almost everything fine, injected glucose intravenously and Vitamultin-Calcium, liver, Tonophosphan-forte intramuscularly. Injected myself with glucose.

August 10, 1944

*** Afternoon tea with the Führer, and Wolf, Schroeder and Daranowski.

August 11, 1944

Patient A. Intravenous glucose, plus intramuscular Testoviron, Vitamultin-forte and Tonophosphan.

August 13, 1944

Patient A. Injected intravenous glucose, plus Vitamultin-forte, Tonophosphan-forte. *** [With Hitler to visit] General Schmundt [in the hospital] on his birthday.

HITLER was missing Schmundt badly. The general had been his chief Wehrmacht adjutant since February 1938. His concern is evident from the diary kept by Frau Anneliese Schmundt. July 23, 1944: "Three professors—Brandt, Hasselbach and Wustmann—are working around the clock to keep Rudolf alive." July 24: "Rudolf slept a lot thanks to the morphine. Big hopes that Rudi will pull through. The Führer visited him." Hitler also visited on August 1 and 13. On September 4, however, she noted: "Big doctors' conference on Rudolf's inexplicable high fever. Hasselbach, Morell, Lonicer, Brandt and Gohrbandt are unanimous that the fever can only be caused by the major injuries and his generally weakened constitution." On September 19: "Afternoon, the Führer comes again. It works like a tonic."

August 15, 1944

Wolf's Lair. Gave Patient A glucose, Glyconorm, Vitamultin-forte, Tonophosphan-forte.—Called on Ribbentrop at Gross-Steinort and injected intravenous Ultraseptyl and iodine.

August 17, 1944

Wolf's Lair, Patient A. Intravenous glucose, plus Vitamultin-forte, Tonophosphan-forte, and Testoviron intramuscularly.

August 18, 1944

Professor von Eicken is here!

ICKEN recorded in his own notes: "Consultation. Both tympanic membranes healed. Whispered figures: more than four meters on both sides. No nystagmus, not even after shaking his head, but does still feel unsteady when walking in the dark. In general he feels considerably better than on July 23."

August 19, 1944

Wolf's Lair. Patient A—Injections as always. [*Data card*: Double glucose.]

August 21, 1944

Wolf's Lair. Patient A, glucose plus Vitamultin-forte, Tonophosphan-forte, Testoviron. *** Telephoned the Karlshof field hospital during the evening (Schmundt and von Hasselbach).

Fury and Frustration

TO HITLER'S FURY over the "July 20 traitors" was now added his frustration over the failure of Göring's air force in the west. He called for increasingly drastic measures. He ordered fighter training squadrons thrown prematurely into action in France, where by mid-August 1944 the encirclement of the Seventh Army at Falaise was complete. The air force generals protested vehemently. In the east the Russians had already reached the frontiers of East Prussia; on the threatened shores of Lake Goldap the tombstone marking the grave of Hans Jeschonnek, the chief of air staff who had committed suicide twelve months before, was uprooted and buried. Hermann Göring played sick, and put in no appearance in Hitler's headquarters for several weeks. The Gestapo arrests continued. There were rumors that the circle of traitors had been much bigger than officially admitted. Day by day SS General Ernst Kaltenbrunner's interrogation reports were laid by Martin Bormann on Hitler's desk.

Hitler's health declined. On August 11 Lieutenant-General Werner Kreipe saluted before him in the rebuilt war conference room at the Wolf's Lair. Kreipe was to succeed Korten, killed in the bomb blast, as chief of air staff. After returning to Luftwaffe headquarters nearby, he wrote in his private diary: "The Führer's back has become very bent. Cotton wool in his ears. He often trembles violently. You can only give him your hand gently." And on August 14, he added this description of a conference with Hitler: "Charged atmosphere. Fegelein drops broad hints that further generals and field marshals were involved in the 20th of July."

On that evening the news was that the Americans had landed in southern France as well. The Luftwaffe's failure was evident. On the twentieth, Hitler asked sarcastically of Kreipe, "How long is Göring planning to remain sick?"

August 1944 was not Hitler's month at all. Antonescu was arrested, and a few days later an uprising broke out in Slovakia. When Kreipe now approached Hitler with the request that he abandon his order for the Messerschmitt 262 jet to be built only as a bomber, Hitler interrupted him. "In mounting anger he sharply dismissed my objections," noted Kreipe. "Now I was stabbing him in the back too." Over the following days Hitler foamed with allegations against the air force.

In east and west, collapse seemed inevitable. While Finland also abandoned the sinking ship (Kreipe: "At today's war conference: incantations against Mannerheim, and immediate decisions"), military police units manned the Rhine bridges to round up fleeing troops and deserters. Hitler formulated a short-lived plan to dissolve his evidently useless air force altogether. He waved aside Kreipe's horrified objections. "You're just another expert," scoffed Hitler, "and like all the rest of the General Staff you're not receptive enough to new ideas."

Morell caught whiffs of these difficulties in his diaries:

August 22, 1944

[SS-Obersturmführer Hans] Junge killed in action [in Normandy]. That's why the Führer has been in great anguish these last two or three days, which I couldn't fathom at the time.

A FEW MONTHS EARLIER Junge—then one of Hitler's SS valets—had married Hitler's most recently recruited secretary, Traudl Humbs. He had left to join an SS panzer division. Hitler broke the news to her himself. The death of people that he knew personally affected him far more deeply than the thousands who were dying anonymously every day. The routine injections continued.

August 23, 1944

Patient A. Injected glucose plus Tonophosphan-forte, and Glyconorm, Vitamultin and liver.

August 27, 1944

Patient A, intravenous of glucose, plus Testoviron, Tonophosphan-forte, Vitamultin-forte. Treated French Minister de Brinon
(at Belfort) for a cyst.

August 29, 1944

Patient A. Intravenous of glucose and Glyconorm, Vitamultin-
forte and Tonophosphan-forte. Telephoned Conti. Still treating
Brinon. Evening with the Führer.

August 31, 1944

Birthday of Dr. [Otto] Dietrich, press chief. Birthday too of
Gretl (Braun) Fegelein, and of lord mayors Liebl of Nuremberg
and Fiehler of Munich.—Injected Patient A with glucose intravenously plus Vitamultin-forte and Tonophosphan-forte, Glyconorm intramuscularly. Blood pressure 143 mm.

IT SEEMS that early in September 1944 Hitler did attempt to
reduce all this medication. "Now Morell is giving me his injections only every other day," Hitler told Dr. Giesing. "I hope that
later on, when I'm well again, I will only need them twice a
week." But when Giesing warned him emphatically against
Ultraseptyl, Hitler remained adamant. "I'm going to keep taking it," he said. "Anyway, it's well known that the faith a sick
man has in his doctor and in his medication is necessary for a
cure—I'm sticking with my dear old house doctor, Morell."

However, Morell's notes make few references in these
months to administering Ultraseptyl. The data cards show him
methodically continuing with the "double glucose" shots every
other day.

September 4, 1944

Patient A. Double glucose intravenous, plus intramuscular
injection of Testoviron, Glyconorm, Vitamultin-forte. Visited
Schmundt. * * *

September 6, 1944

Patient A, double glucose injection and Tonophosphan-forte, Vitamultin-forte, Glyconorm. Visited Schmundt in the evening, high fever (40.9 degrees) treated with *penicillin*.

September 7, 1944

Schmundt's shivering fit has subsided, fever down to 39.6 and then 38, injected four shots of penicillin intramuscular.

September 8, 1944

Double glucose and 10 cc of Septoid plus Testoviron, Vitamultin-forte, Glyconorm. Blood pressure 155, throbbing around right eye. In the afternoon it was 143 mm.

O N SEPTEMBER 1, 2, 7, 10 AND 16 Morell jotted down in his agenda that it was again time for blood tests and an electrocardiogram, but again Hitler would not agree.

In the west, the Allies had by now run into intractable logistics problems—because the most important ports in liberated France were still held by fanatical German troops. And on September 11, at the Führer's war conference, he touched for the first time upon the possibility of striking back at the Allies in the Vosges Mountains.

September 14, 1944

Intravenous injection, double glucose and intramuscular injection of Tonophosphan-forte, Vitamultin-forte and Testoviron.— Blood pressure highly variable, 146–150, after great agitation.

H ITLER had now taken the decision to shelve the Vosges idea and launch a major strategic winter counteroffensive in the west. He revealed this decision to a selected few. In a secret conference, General Jodl estimated the balance of strength in the west—about ninety-six German divisions were faced by fifty-five Allied. Hitler announced his decision: "A counterattack from the Ardennes, with Antwerp as its objective."

Field Marshal von Rundstedt would command the attack. It was relatively easy to hold the present front line, explained

Hitler. Meanwhile they would create a strike force of Volks-grenadier and panzer divisions over the next few weeks and rip open the front line at the precise spot where the British and American army groups met. His strategic target was clear: "A new Dunkirk!" He wanted this bold thrust to take place early in November. By then there must be a reserve of 1,500 fighter planes; he stipulated that the attack would be begun under cover of bad weather, so that the enemy's strategic air power was at a disadvantage.

September 15, 1944 (special note)

Patient A, at six P.M. Blood pressure 150 mm, heart tones pure and regular, 84 beats per minute. Pulse good and full. Complains of dizziness, throbbing head, and return of the tremor to his legs, particularly the left, and hands.—A lot of worries!

Right Ankle	*Left Ankle*	—Left ankle is swollen, particularly on left shinbone above the ankle. Some time ago there was an eczema on the shinbone which vanished because of the Mutaflor cure. Up to the bomb attempt on his life, the left leg particularly showed a transitory tremor when sitting down.
23 cm	21 cm	
26 ( )	28.5 ( )	

I recommend: adequate oxygen intake either by an eight or ten day stay at the Berghof or by going for drives in an open car every other day, with or without interrupting the drive for half an hour's walk. Also massage to improve the blood supply and treat the swollen left foot and ankle. In injections for the time being concentrate on the cortex of the suprarenal gland, testes and combinations of vitamins (Vitamultin-forte).

Brom-Nervacit causing it. Is this possible?

As it contains saccharine and yeast, yes. Fermentation of the sugar.

I ought to have it chemically analyzed.

Should try and put his left leg up as often as possible. Only perform the really vital functions [*Bearbeitungen*] himself. Shed as much load as possible. (Signed) Professor Morell.

ON SEPTEMBER 16, 1944, Morell telephoned SS-Brigadeführer Dr. Blumenreuther of the SS Medical Stores for his view on Brom-Nervacit, the tried and trusted sedative which Morell administered to Hitler in periods of tension. This consisted of four percent potassium bromide, 0.1 percent sodium phosphate, and one percent naphrodyl, the rest being diethylbarbiturate acid, phenyldimethylpyrazolon, alcohol, saccharine and flavoring. Morell learned the result in a telephone conversation with Dr. Mulli in Hamburg on October 13: the sedative was bacteriologically above reproach; when yeast was added fermentation took place; when pepsin and trypsin were added no gases were formed. "We still have to try it with diastase," said Mulli, "which is particularly important if we are to draw conclusions about the formation of gases in the intestine. We are out of diastase until tomorrow."

Morell had also sent to Mulli a sample of drinking water from the Wolf's Lair. Mulli reported, "The water that arrived here was bad. Although neutral, it was exceptionally hard (carbonates), and the sample sent had an exceptional number of germs, in other words bacteriological impurities. . . . An additional, larger sample in a sterile vessel is requested." On October 23 Mulli added, "In bacteriological terms that water is impure. The bacteria were neither coli nor typhus . . . but the possibility cannot be ruled out that in consequence of this content of non-disease bearing bacteria, this water, if drunk by people whose stomachs do not produce enough hydrochloric acid, might result in digestion problems."

September 16, 1944

Patient A, blood pressure 153 mm, highly variable. Injected intravenous glucose, and Prostrophanta, plus Glyconorm, Tonophosphan, and Vitamultin-forte.

September 17, 1944 (agenda)

Ask Chief about Ultraseptyl.

September 18, 1944

Patient A. Blood pressure 145 mm, variable. Intravenous glucose, plus Tonophosphan-forte, Vitamultin-forte, Testoviron intra-muscular. Visit by Croatians.

Wolf's Lair. Patient A, blood pressure 153, constant. Glucose intravenously, and Tonophosphan-forte and Vitamultin-forte and Glyconorm. Head X ray! Left maxillary sinus.

THREE X-RAY PLATES dated September 19, 1944, were found among Morell's files. "The plates were made to assist in diagnosing pain complained of in the sinus regions. Four views were taken, including a left lateral of the sinus cavities. This, however, could not be found. The three plates available include one each of the frontal sinus (nose-forehead position), the sphenoidal sinuses (mouth-chin position), and the maxillar, ethmoidal and frontal sinuses (chin-nose position)." (OI/CIR/4.)

Dr. Giesing summarized on October 18, "A sinus infection on both sides which was caused by a cold contracted from the barber has completely disappeared. X-ray examination of sinuses on 19 September 1944 revealed a slight shadowing of maxillary sinuses. All other sinuses, including sphenoid, clear on both sides."

September 23–24, 1944

During the night at 4:30 A.M. he sent for me on account of intestinal spasms he was suffering after some overexcitement. I gave him 0.02 of Eukodal and 0.03 of Eupaverin intravenously. Heart findings inconclusive except that as usual the second heart beat accentuated, with pure sounds, regular heart action. Right eye: conjunctivitis and a little vessel burst in the right corner. Gave him cocaine-adrenaline solution as an eyedrop twice daily.

September 24, 1944

Wolf's Lair. Made electrocardiograms of Patient A (negative T_I, T_{II} isoelectric). Dr. Mulli is here.

MORELL sent these electrocardiograms to the cardiologist Professor Weber at Bad Nauheim. Again the diagnosis was a rapid progressive coronary sclerosis. That night, Hitler again suffered violent stomach cramps:

At four A.M. I injected Eukodal and Eupverin intravenously again because of renewed spasms. This afternoon I injected intravenous glucose and intramuscular Testoviron, liver, Vitamultin-Calcium. Blood pressure variable between 143 and 153.

Jaundice

THE CATASTROPHE happened one morning late in September 1944: he simply refused to get up. "The Führer sends his regrets," his staff were told, "but he'll be eating alone."

His bulldog of an adjutant, Otto Günsche, told the other staff members: "The Führer is completely apathetic about events around him. We don't know what to do. He's not even interested in the eastern front although we've a real crisis on our hands."

The buoyant mood inspired by initial planning for the great winter counteroffensive in the west had been destroyed by reports of renewed air force shortcomings in the east. The Luftwaffe had proven incapable of destroying even one railroad bridge at Constanza to obstruct the Russian sweep into Romania. Göring's generals had plundered and looted and enriched themselves. Now the General Staff and Guderian were maintaining that the western offensive would not work.

Hitler's own belief was that these colossal rows during September were making him ill. For a while the Allied airborne landings in Holland on September 17 and 18 had threatened to drive a wedge deep into the German western front. Göring's generals claimed the weather was not good enough for flying. "The Führer loses his temper," recorded the new chief of air staff on the eighteenth, "and rages over the Luftwaffe's failure." He demanded to speak to Göring—"I imagine you are still capable of arranging that?" he said sarcastically to Kreipe on the phone. At the next morning's war conference, the mood was frosty; Kreipe was ignored.

He could see that the witchhunt was really aimed at Göring. But for some reason Hitler was reluctant to speak his mind to the fat Reichsmarschall, and was taking it out on Kreipe instead. Around one A.M. on September 20, SS-Gruppenführer Fegelein transmitted to Kreipe the order that he was banned from the Führer's headquarters. On the twenty-first Hitler sent for General Ritter von Greim, instructing him not to breath a word to Göring first, lectured him on the sins of the air force, and offered him the (brand new) position of deputy commander in chief, Luftwaffe. Greim was no fool—he asked for time to make up his mind.

These were not the actions of a rational man, perhaps, but Hitler was now becoming significantly ill. On September 20, Professor von Eicken, the ENT specialist, telephoned his colleague Dr. Giesing. Giesing told him, "The Führer has been hoarse these last three weeks." That was not a good sign. There was slight secretion, but only in the morning. Eicken entered in his records, "An X ray has revealed a shadow on the left maxillary sinus, the other sinuses are clear. After discussion with Professor Morell and dentist Blaschke, decision taken to wait a week. Patient will get microwave treatment, and a microwave diathermy set has been ordered. If the secretion does not cease, Captain (med.) Giesing will irrigate."

Two days later Eicken wrote, "Two small flecks of pus in the left maxillary sinus. Sweating procedures." And Dr. Giesing summarized on October 18, "Irrigation of left maxillary sinus performed by Professor von Eicken . . . as check yielded two flecks of pus. Nose clear on both sides at final examination. No complaint. A slight laryngitis has also subsided. The slight tiring of the voice is due to a slight weakness of the vocal cord muscles (paresis of internus muscle)."

But that was by no means all, as Morell shortly found. Now jaundice came into the medical picture.

September 27, 1944

Midday, intravenous injection of glucose with iodine, plus Vitamultin-forte, Tonophosphan-forte and Glyconorm. Pulse 72, blood pressure 143.

At nine this evening (after afternoon tea) I commented to the Führer that he was looking a bit yellow. I said I would come over in the morning and make out a prescription (Calomel, et cetera).

September 28, 1944

Patient A got Arndt[1] to telephone and tell me not to come.

But at six-thirty P.M. Führer sent for me, said he was suffering violent spasms. Said that immediately after lunch he had violent colic pains and nausea. His stomach was very taut and he had a lot of wind, his cardia very tender, his pylorus somewhat less. The duodenum and gall bladder region also tender. His pulse was 78, he was nauseous and his face was yellow, he had no fever but said his urine is as brown as beer. [*Data card*: Feeling dizzy.]

Injected 0.005 of Eukodal and an ampoule of Eupaverin intravenously, and liver and Glyconorm intramuscularly, and ordered heating pads and hot unsweetened tea. Later his pulse had slowed to 66. Not to take milk or alcohol, and is to fast tomorrow.

September 28–29, 1944

[Written at] one-thirty A.M. I was called in at fifteen minutes after midnight. Still suffering spasms but considerably less, still nauseous, appendix free. The pit of the stomach! Injected intravenously 0.02 Eukodal plus one and a half ampoules of Eupaverin. The pains and cramps subside slowly. Pulse 72, regular and full, sweating freely, temperature normal. Says his urine is brown as beer. Left at one-thirty A.M. as Führer wanted to sleep, was tired. Führer had eaten mashed potatoes and other light things but had had some milk in his soup and apparently got the nausea and cramps immediately after the meal.—Ordered a day's fasting, with only unsweetened tea and no milk or alcohol.

MORELL was frantic to find his patient becoming genuinely ill, and began three or four parallel diaries of the case. In a separate note on this day's events he recorded: "Back at one-thirty A.M. Says he has had a lot to anger him over the last few days.[2]

[1] Arndt was one of Hitler's orderly officers, killed in April 1945 when one of the last planes to leave Berlin crashed in what is now East Germany.

[2] On September 26 Heinrich Himmler had visited Hitler with a special dossier, headed "Treason since 1939": it revealed that Vice-Admiral Wilhelm

Violent flatulence and periodic cramps. Gave double glucose, Progynon B Oleosum forte and Cantan-forte—and 0.3 Calomel and cod-liver oil."

September 29, 1944 (Friday)

Wolf's Lair. Visited at eleven-fifty A.M. Patient says he had only slept until three A.M. Agonizing winds (he has had some terrible rows on recent days, particularly on Tuesday and Wednesday. His body is still pretty taut. He has kept getting cramps (calls them "contractions in his intestines") and is in considerable pain. To fortify him generally I injected intravenously glucose plus Cantan and intramuscularly Progynon B Oleosum and Vitamultin-Calcium. He got down some oatmeal gruel (but not much) and 0.3 Calomels and three tablespoons of cod-liver oil.

Four P.M. He tried to take two Calomel powders but vomited them up instantly. At seven P.M. he took two Calomel powders (0.3) and hot tea, with heating pads. Between nine and ten-thirty P.M. the tension relaxed, he has had no more spasms since noon. But despite the Calomel and cod-liver oil there has been no bowel movement. The winds are agonizing. Gave him two more table-spoons of cod-liver oil, and sliced lemon for attacks of nausea (but none came).—Twenty drops of Sympathol. Pulse 96, heart sounds were a bit weaker before he took the Sympathol.

From 11:45 P.M. to one-thirty A.M. A chamomile enema (one liter) resulted in his passing a number of small hard crumbs.

He stayed confined to bed all day and did not eat anything.

HIS STAFF agonized over him. On September 30 Martin Bormann wrote to his wife in a private letter that Hitler was suffering "incredibly painful stomach cramps," but that Morell was treating him with cod-liver oil and the Führer had lost six pounds in the last three days. "I am still convinced that Morell's treatment is right," Hitler had assured Bormann. Bormann privately had doubts: "I would prefer another treatment, more based on biology."

Canaris and other Abwehr traitors had continually betrayed Hitler's most vital military secrets—like the times and dates of his 1940 offensives—to the enemy.

The upshot was that for the second time in three years Hitler found himself trying to fight the war from a sickbed. His restless brain was not idle: it began working over his grand plan for a winter counteroffensive. Under interrogation a few months later, on July 26, 1945, General Jodl would recall: "When Hitler conceived the first idea he was ill in bed with jaundice." Hitler had spread out the map of the Ardennes across his bedcover, and discussed the best direction and depth of attack. Jodl's recollection is confirmed by the shorthand writer Reynitz: "He threw himself into preparing the Ardennes offensive down to the last detail, calling Jodl and General Walter Buhle into his bedroom, where he lay sick. . . . The planning of this offensive was . . . entirely Hitler's brainchild from everything I saw and heard."

Every evening his naval adjutant von Puttkamer—also a victim of the 20th of July—would hobble into the bunker on crutches and read out the situation reports typed on Hitler's special large-face typewriter. "On the first day," the rear-admiral would recall to this author, "Hitler just lay there, without making even the slightest comment or reaction. On the second day he gestured wearily with one hand. . . . Thank goodness that nothing much was happening at this time."

September 30, 1944

From one-thirty to five A.M. A further chamomile enema. One bowel movement, and the stool has come down a bit farther. Pulse 96, and greater epigastric suppleness, the pit of the stomach and the gall bladder region can also be palpated with little tenderness, but there are still winds present. Appendix free.

From noon to two-thirty P.M. There has been no bowel movement for five hours, so he's in a lot of discomfort from gas. The patient claims it is not getting better but much worse than before. I countered that his objective condition is far better—no more spasms, a considerable relaxation and tenderness only in the pit of the stomach and he is very tender near the liver and gall bladder. He flatly refused to allow me to administer an enema of oil or chamomile in bed, but on the contrary took an irrigator and tried to administer one to himself in the W.C.: the patient sitting upon the toilet bowl for the purpose. I had to wait outside (in fact he even locked me out). But the enema liquid did not stay in, he said, and he had to eject it immediately (unfortunately!). After the enema the stool came down farther from above. Electric warming pads and moist compress on stomach and liver. Twenty drops of Sympathol, pulse 90, blood pressure 143 mm, temperature 36.8 and 36.9. Took six Boxberger pills. We must wait. Führer should try to get some sleep (without sedatives!).

At seven-thirty P.M. I was sent for. There had been four bowel movements between four and six, two of them weak and two very violent. In the second one, after releasing a blockage there was an explosive watery evacuation. The third and fourth were extremely foul smelling and especially the fourth. (Probably fingerlike stools present before, but disintegrating balls of it remained behind and were the cause of the gases and poisonous substances.) Pulse 96, temperature 37.2 thanks to the heating pads. Body still quite taut, but not completely. Pit of the stomach still resistant in depth, and there is still some stool before the left flexure of the colon.

Otherwise relatively strong improvement, and there is a change in facial expression. He said he had only sent for me to tell me the good news about the effect. He must take 5 grams of Karlsbad mineral salts dissolved in 20 cc of warm water each morning and evening, sipped over a period of about four hours. Continued heating pads. Only gruel, nothing else. No drugs, but await further bowel movements. From time to time the Führer should perform enemas of chamomile tea using the rectal syringe (as he will not allow me to perform these). Also necessary are a change of air, as there is too much carbon dioxide in the bunker and not enough oxygen, and exercise (walks). I propose after two days' stay in the bunker having an X ray made by [Professor] Chaoul of the gastrointestinal region and gall bladder for changes in the mucous membrane, defects in the pylorus, and of the duodenum and gall bladder region for possible gallstones (though not likely as there is no tension there) and then recommend a stay of about fourteen days at the Berghof.

Midnight: two more stools since the last one, brown and not as evil smelling. Pulse 88, temperature 37.3, he was using heating pads until one hour previously. Performed chamomile enema which resulted in a lot of watery and crumbly feces afterwards. Gall bladder, liver and left flexure somewhat resistant. Twenty drops of Sympathol. No sedatives tonight. One glass of Karlsbad mineral water.

GENERAL RUDOLF SCHMUNDT, Hitler's faithful chief adjutant, who had been badly injured on July 20, was still at the field hospital near Rastenburg. But he was now suffering from septic erysipelas. In September Hitler had proposed to his escort doctor von Hasselbach that Morell should take over the treatment of Schmundt. "Perhaps Schmundt could still be saved with penicillin," said Hitler, and had Morell's product fetched by plane from Olmütz. Morell cursed when he saw the two packages, each containing three penicillin ampoules—his factory had not labeled them and he had no idea how much to inject. When Hitler visited Schmundt on September 19, there were tears in his eyes because it was obvious that his adjutant's life was inexorably ebbing away. "I was called in too late," Morell regretted. "Otherwise I could have saved him with penicillin." Schmundt died on October 1, at eleven-ten P.M. Four days later his widow called on Hitler for one last time at the Wolf's Lair. Hitler received her in his sick quarters. "Führer in bed," she noted. "Says he's lost his best man."

October 1, 1944

One P.M. There have been two bowel movements since last night, containing disintegrating fragments. He looks better but limp. Pulse 96, temperature 36.8, blood pressure 140 mm, heart examination shows second heartbeat accentuated as usual. No epigastric tension, some tenderness still, deep down near the left flexure and deep in the pit of the stomach, but that in the gall bladder region is virtually gone. The yellow color has also largely vanished.

For lunch he had oatmeal gruel made with water, steamed fruit and an Acidol-Pepsin tablet as an experiment. Still confined to bed. Massage with Franzbranntwein lotion would seem called for but is not desired. The positive effect of the chamomile enemas is recognized, but the patient wants to continue to perform them by himself. Apart from the irrigator I have held out prospect of a Klystier syringe so that measured quantities can be independently administered by the patient in bed. Injected twenty percent glucose solution intravenously plus Vitamultin-Calcium, Glyconorm and Progynon B Oleosum intramuscularly.

At seven-thirty P.M. temperature 37.15, pulse 84, heart good and abdomen supple, just a little tenderness in the pit of the stomach again and some gases there. Complains about lack of appetite. For lunch he had gruel and apples and an Acidol-Pepsin tablet. Two tablets to be taken each evening. The yellowish coloration has almost completely vanished.

I again proposed most urgently a change of air (to Berlin) either for two or three days and then the mountain for twelve or fourteen days or just Berlin for eight to ten days. He rejects the Berghof out of hand and says Berlin is unsuitable as he (the patient) would have to keep going down into the bunker, and he cannot walk much at present, he is too weak. I referred to the unsuitability of the new bunker for him, the living and sleeping quarters are tiny and despite the ventilation system there is far too little oxygen. He is much too undemanding as the top man and leader of the Reich. He gave me a promise that he would go on more walks. "You say that but then you don't," I argued, and said: "I consider it vital that you build up a physical reserve by taking in as much oxygen as possible, thereby creating better food-combustion conditions for the likely exertions of the coming months." As I went, the Führer suddenly sat bolt upright, and said he had painful wind and stabbing pressure on his heart.

At ten P.M. his temperature was 37.2, his abdomen supple, irrigation with chamomile tea. Unfortunately he had taken no more Acidol-Pepsins. In two hours' time a Tempidorm suppository is to be inserted. With his steamed apples he can have some sugar. The Führer calls for saccharin as a sweetener. It will be taken care of.

([Postscript] The Hungary decision is allowed in, but the news about Schmundt is delayed until tomorrow morning.)

Strychnine

IN KEEPING with the Nietzsche image of the superman, Hitler tried to keep his suffering to himself. On October 3, 1944, Professor Morell wrote this account of a conversation in which Hitler confided to him how much he had in fact suffered.

"He says that the weeks since July 20 have been the worst of his life. He has fought and won a heroic struggle the likes of which nobody, no German, can ever imagine. Despite the most agonizing pains, and despite hours of faintness and nausea of which he's never breathed a word to anybody even when they inquire, he has kept a stiff upper lip and fought back with iron determination and energy. Often, he says, he has been in danger of crumpling, but by sheer willpower he has always managed to overcome his condition.

"These disclosures," recorded Morell further, "were made after my remark that I regarded his present condition, outward appearances apart, as a minor breakdown stemming from the 20th of July, albeit a belated one.

"The nervous disturbance in his left leg as well as in his hands are not as Brandt claims a consequence of his eating strychnine but of the trauma to the convolutions on the right side of the brain, since such symptoms increase in frequency with worry."

During the summer of 1944 Hitler's stomach spasms had increased in severity and frequency. The opinions of Hitler's doctors as to their origin differed widely. But in September the ENT doctor Erwin Giesing chanced on what he believed to be the reason. He noticed Hitler's breakfast tray being carried in—

a plate of porridge, two thin slices of bread, a glass of orange juice—and a small hospital dish containing several white Vitamultin pastilles and six black pills. It was not until about September 15 that he began to speculate on those black pills. Their composition was printed on the flat aluminum tin they came in: they were Dr. Koester's anti-gas pills, and 120 of them contained half a gram of extractum nucis vomic (better known as strychnine) and half a gram of extractum belladonnae (deadly nightshade or atropine), as well as one gram of extractum gentianae (gentian). Giesing's rough calculation showed that, judging by the numbers of pills on that plate, Hitler was taking a near overdose of strychnine and atropine, both deadly poisons, each day.

At first Giesing kept this extraordinary deduction to himself. Almost certainly he recognized a chance of getting rid of Morell. But he wanted to be sure. He purloined a few and sent them for analysis. And from Königsberg he obtained E. Poulsson's *Handbook of Pharmacology*. In its pages he read this: "Atropine acts on the central nervous system first as a stimulant, then as a paralyzer. In humans it primarily affects the forebrain, coupled with vivid flights of ideas, talkativeness, and restlessness, visual and aural hallucinations, and fits of delirium which may be peaceful and serene but may equally degenerate into acts of violence and frenzy."

The maximum daily dose of extractum belladonnae was listed as 0.4 grams. By Giesing's calculations just ten of the pills contained this dose.

As for strychnine, Giesing read in the handbook that it was capable of causing tetanus (lockjaw) as it would increase the reflex sensitivity of the spinal cord to its maximum. "One or two milligrams of strychnine have no really perceptible effect on people," the handbook stated, "but closer examination shows that there has been a clear effect on the acuteness of the senses. . . . After heavy doses the accentuated sensitivity to light may turn into downright aversion to light; and the other senses undergo similar changes. The senses of hearing and touch are accentuated, and for a time the sense of smell and taste may become more acute." If many small doses were taken over a long period, a sudden cumulative poisoning might result. "For nonspecific conditions of tiredness and weakness as well as for

sexual debilities strychnine is used as a stimulant and 'fortifier.'" According to Giesing's arithmetic, ten pills per day would
contain more than the maximum permitted dose of strychnine.

This was all Giesing needed to know. The anti-gas pills were
to blame for everything, it seemed. "After all, Hitler was permanently in a euphoric condition," he would write in November
1945, "and there was no other way of explaining this, and his
exaltation when taking decisions after major political or military reverses can probably be explained largely by this too."

Even so he was careful how he went about connecting
Hitler's recent jaundice and these unprepossessing little black
pills. Morell maintained that Hitler's hepatitis had been brought
about by nothing more sinister than a retention of bile caused by
a nervous cramp at the gall bladder exit. Giesing would write
a year later, "I think that highly unlikely: a nervous constriction
of the gall bladder exit would not have resulted in the lengthy
period of icterus, nor in a confinement to bed lasting almost
four weeks, and Morell would not have had to refuse so fiercely
any kinds of blood and urine analyses."

These remarks show how subjective the hostiilty of the other
doctors to Morell was. The files show that Morell was almost
superstitiously conscious of the need to carry out frequent blood
and urine tests on Hitler.

Giesing then let the cat out of the bag, and soon the whole
headquarters was whispering that Morell had treated Hitler
negligently. Some people said that he had not even known that
the anti-gas pills contained strychnine. The jockeying for position began. Brandt, Hasselbach and Giesing seized the chance
to intrigue against Morell. But Bormann saw it as a chance to
get rid of Brandt. Professor Brandt was a powerful protegé of
Bormann's enemy Albert Speer, whose star was rising now that
Göring's was on the wane. As Reich Commissioner for Health
and Safety, Brandt came under Speer's ministry.

The closing act of this intrigue came early in October 1944.
Giesing began to dose himself with the suspect black pills. He
began to experience the same symptoms as Hitler—extreme
sensitivity, photophobia, acuteness of taste and increased thirst.
When Brandt arrived from Berlin, Giesing told him. Brandt took
the matter to Hitler.

Brandt also denounced the fat doctor to the SS chief, Himmler. Himmler thought it not impossible that Morell had made a deliberate attempt to murder Hitler, and made no bones of his distrust of the doctor. Himmler intimated to Morell that he had hanged so many men that one more would make no difference to him. Morell's patient SS-Gruppenführer Hans Hinkel, head of the German film industry, informed Gestapo chief Kaltenbrunner that Morell had an assistant, Richard Weber, in Berlin. Weber was fetched from the Kurfürstendamm practice and grilled at Gestapo headquarters—did he think it possible that Morell was systematically poisoning the Führer? Weber's answer had the ring of authenticity. "Out of the question," he said. "Morell's too big a coward for that."

What was the truth? Analysis of the actual composition of the anti-gas pills suggests that Brandt, Giesing and Hasselbach had willingly exaggerated their toxicity in their attempt to dislodge Morell.

Professor Schenck, by no means an admirer of Morell, has told the author that the pills ("Indications: excessive acidity of the digestive juices, flatulence, constipation, tonic") were the product of an otherwise unknown Berlin firm, Dr. Koester & Co., with premises in 1937 in Wilmersdorf and somewhat later out in Mecklenburg. He performs the following arithmetic on these pills: in 120 pills there would have been 0.075 grams of hyoscamin, the effective and toxic alkaloid of atropine, and 0.035 grams of strychnine. So if Hitler had taken a dozen pills he would still only have consumed one tenth of these amounts. But the maximum permissible dose of strychnine was far more, 0.01 grams a day. Moreover, strychnine cannot cause hepatitis. Most probably Hitler had contracted *infectious* hepatitis, which is not infrequent among troops living under crowded conditions.

All this was little solace for Morell, as he now faced the biggest challenge of his career.

On the way to the Battle of Tannenberg monument to attend Schmundt's funeral, Hasselbach foolishly mentioned the strychnine affair to officers with him. It was a violation of his medical oath of secrecy, and it would cost him his job.

On the following day, Hitler told Dr. Giesing that his stomach cramps had subsided somewhat. Giesing pointed out that the Führer was no longer taking the anti-gas pills, and he told of how he had been taking them himself as a test. "I have told

Hasselbach about this," he concluded. His pride was misplaced. Hitler flared up. "You ought not to have done that! I want this anti-gas pills affair dropped. Say what you want against Morell, he is and is going to stay my physician. I have complete faith in him."

Weighing every word, Hitler added: "I'm going to get to the bottom of this entire business. I have asked Brandt to see me this afternoon."

His attitude shocked the doctors. Hasselbach tried Bormann, but the Reichsleiter would not interfere. So he went to Himmler instead, and took Giesing with him.

The SS-Reichsführer became thoughtful. "Well, gentlemen," he said, "you are clearly no diplomats. You're going to have to tackle Morell far more cleverly. Why not meet Morell for tea, or invite him to a schnapps and talk it all over with him—you know, as one comrade to another? You've got to realize that the Führer trusts him implicitly, and we must do nothing to disrupt that."

Hasselbach was furious, and said, "This business is so grave that a medical or even a civil court would have punished Morell for causing bodily harm by negligence, at the very least."

Himmler pitched his voice higher as he answered. "Herr Professor, you seem to forget that as minister of the interior I am also the supreme public health authority. And I do not want any action taken against Morell."

On their way out they ran into a young SS doctor. It was Dr. Ludwig Stumpfegger, Himmler's personal physician. Hasselbach related to him how Giesing had used himself as guinea pig to test the little black pills. Stumpfegger grasped Giesing's arm and said mockingly, "Colleague, I shall put your name forward for the Knight's Cross for this."

He drove off with Himmler, heading for Hitler's bunker.

Morell continued his treatments.

October 2, 1944

One P.M. Pulse 82, blood pressure 148/53, temperature 37.3. General malaise in abdomen with localized pains, general weakness and complaints of frequent belching. Cramps have ceased. Yesterday evening he had a bowel movement an hour after the Tempidorm suppository was inserted, and says that's why he has not slept.

For breakfast (at two P.M.) oatmeal gruel mixed with water and a little salt, pears, grapes.—Vitamultin-forte tablets. One Acidol-Pepsin tablet with the meal. Refused to drink the Karlsbad mineral water set before him because of its evil taste. I rubbed his arms and legs with Franzbranntwein lotion.

Intravenous injections of glucose and Cantan plus Vitamultin-Calcium, Glyconorm, and liver intramuscularly.

He was handed an important despatch this morning at five A.M. Before I went in, Dr. Brandt had called on the Führer and told him that Schmundt had died, and stayed a long time going over exact interpretation. (Cause of death was an embolism.)

The yellow coloration of his skin has gone. Two stools between ten P.M. last night and one P.M. today.

Five P.M. Führer has had a war conference in his room! Made a very limp impression on the gentlemen. Objective condition: considerable improvement, is capable of getting out of bed and dressing himself. Irrigation with chamomile, nine P.M. Pulse 78, temperature 37.05 and 37.1 degrees, abdomen supple but still some gases present.

Injected Vitamultin-Calcium, Glyconorm and Testoviron intra-muscularly. After supper he must take two Euflat pills, and with the meal an Acidol-Pepsin tablet, and a few Vitamultin-forte pas-tilles from time to time.

Discussed [different] supper with Miss Manziarly,[1] but Führer talks her out of it and takes only oatmeal gruel and puréed fruit again, and some grapes.—He wants to have five oranges, as that's what he has a craving for at this moment. Asks me to see if I can find any at the Berghof or in Berlin.

Reichsmarschall Göring and Field Marshal Keitel inquired after him.

O N OCTOBER 2, 1944, Morell sent fecal samples for analysis in-dependently to Freiburg and the chemical analysis division of the Berlin Military District at Zehlendorf. The latter reported

[1] Constanze Manziarly, successor to Frau Exner as Hitler's dietician. Miss-ing in Berlin, May 1945.

three days later: "Bacteriological examination of the fecal sample yielded no pathogenic growths. Every possible test was made, only coli could be identified."

To Nissle, Morell had written, "Please examine *immediately* the enclosed fecal sample for food remains . . . and for fermenting and putrefactive agents and pathogenic bacteria. Please telephone your findings to me in advance of the written report." But the transport conditions in Germany were chaotic and the sample did not reach Freiburg until October 19. Another week passed before Nissle completed his analysis. "Numbers of coli bacteria . . . and a few relatively sparse aerogenic bacilli," he reported. "This rather meager number of the aerogenic bacilli that are capable of causing increased fermentation and gas formation is probably of little significance. But I point out that the colonies of Mutaflor bacilli have significantly lessened, so to be on the safe side I would recommend a further Mutaflor course."

Professor Schenck doubts the value of these findings, as modern analysts would consider a fecal sample which had been traveling for three weeks useless for purposes of examination.

Hitler sent for Dr. Giesing. The ENT specialist noticed incidentally that there was a revolver lying on the table next to Hitler's camp bed. As he prepared to examine the inner ear as usual, Hitler said, "Doctor, how did you first hit on this anti-gas pill business?" He was trying to find out who was behind the intrigue. He added, "Why did you not come and tell me all this in person?" Giesing stuck to his guns and accused Morell of negligence, because it was now quite plain that it was Morell or his assistant, Corporal Makkus, who had supplied the pills to Hitler's bunker.

"Well," said Hitler, "you've given Morell a terrific shock. He's looking quite pale and distracted, and he's blaming himself over and over again. But I've calmed him down! I myself always thought they were just charcoal tablets for soaking up my intestinal gases, and I always felt rather pleasant after taking them."

October 3, 1944

At two A.M. his pulse was 78, temperature 37.5 degrees. Still has some stomach gases, and these are putting pressure on his heart. His abdomen is supple. Gave him 0.6 of an S.E.E. injection to help him sleep.

As I injected him he became very tired and his pains went. (The patient stated that if the pain would only go away he could definitely get to sleep. But I could not persuade him to take a sleeping tablet—it had to be an injection.) I sent a fecal sample yesterday to Berlin *** for chemical analysis by Military District III. Took a urine sample today for analysis ***. The result on this at eleven A.M. was:

> Reaction acid, specific gravity 1.019, albumen traces, sugar negative, sediment: masses of bacteria, a very few leukocytes, moderate numbers of erythrocytes, urates, oxalates, small round epithelia.—An Indikan test could not be performed because of a shortage of reagent, but it will be carried out at Karlshof and if not possible there either then in the war department's field laboratory.

It's one-thirty P.M. *** He slept until seven P.M. Still complains of winds in his stomach and the pressure on his heart. His abdomen is supple, stomach still resistant in depth, gall bladder hardly at all resistant now. *** Injected two 10 cc shots of twenty percent glucose intravenously, and Vitamultin-forte, Glyconorm and Tonophosphan-forte intramuscularly. His left tonsil is very inflamed and is slightly furred, the left sublingual gland is swollen.

For breakfast this morning he had oatmeal gruel, stewed apples with glucose and a heap of grapes.—For lunch, rice gruel, semolina and stewed apples.

Eight P.M. *** Two bowel movements since midday without an enema, one very copious including one thick lump. Facial expression good, voice firmer. Intramuscular shots of Vitamultin-Calcium and Glyconorm. Führer in good mood, says that Miss Schroeder[2] and Miss Christian should come over after the war conference.

Before I went over to see the Führer I had a conversation with Dr. Brandt which I then discussed with the Führer. Brandt said the

---

[2] Christa Schroeder, born March 19, 1908; Bormann's private secretary until 1933, then Hitler's until April 1945. Typed among other historic documents Hitler's August 1936 memorandum on the Four Year Plan, and his August 1938 paper on the West Wall. All four secretaries basically were used as conversation partners, however. See Albert Zoller, *Hitler Privat, Erlebnisbericht einer Geheimsekretärin* (Düsseldorf, 1949), largely based on interrogations of Miss Schroeder by Zoller. She now lives in Munich.

Führer had been swallowing sixteen anti-gas pills every day, which contained so much strychnine that it came perilously close to the maximum dose; he claimed that the present illness and all the previous ones were a chronic case of strychnine poisoning. I declared that I never prescribed this intense consumption of the anti-gas pills and that I had heard of it these last few days with horror. In his (Brandt's) opinion the Führer was getting better now because over the last five days in which he had been confined to bed the Führer had stopped consuming the anti-gas pills, for the reason that there aren't any more there. He said the tremor could also be attributed to this cause. (I am of different opinion, as the tremor in the leg and the hands vanished at the instant of the bomb explosion even though—as we now know—he continued to take the anti-gas pills; I would further comment that the Führer—as he himself maintained this evening—has suffered from these stomach spasms and accumulations of gas ever since 1929 and the major upsets he encountered at that time. Later he suffered them again very badly after taking some [Neo-Balestol] capsules that Brückner[3] had recommended, in which Dr. Grawitz[4] was able to identify traces of methyl alcohol. And later still he suffered them after any large upset, and he has been having a lot of those lately.) He said he has been taking the anti-gas pills for about two years, and for the last few months at the rate of about sixteen pills a day. He had also told Brandt that I had not prescribed them, that he had been taking them on his own initiative and that he had thought that these pills were similar to charcoal tablets.

Dr. Brandt talked gloatingly of my responsibility in this, even though I never issued any such directions. "Do you seriously think anybody will believe you when you claim you did not prescribe them?" he said. "Do you think that Himmler[5] will treat you any different from anybody else? So many people are being strung up now that they'll pass stone-cold judgment on this whole thing. If

[3] SA-Gruppenführer Wilhelm Friedrich Brückner, born December 11, 1884, was a World War veteran comrade of Hitler's and his chief adjutant until October 1940. Died August 1954.

[4] SS-Obergruppenführer Dr. (med.) Ernst-Robert Grawitz, born June 8, 1899, in Berlin, was chief doctor of the SS. A specialist in internal medicine since 1929, he was the last acting president of the German Red Cross under Hitler. In April 1945 he took his family down into the cellar of his house and blew them all up with a bazooka.

[5] Heinrich Himmler, born October 7, 1900, in Munich. Reichsführer of the SS and national chief of police. Suicide in June 1945.

anything had become of the Führer, you can picture for yourself what would have happened then. They wouldn't have made Hasselbach,[6] say, responsible but you and probably myself too. That's why it would be better if I am always briefed on everything that's afoot. I've got all I need to prove this was a clear case of strychnine poisoning. You must be able to see the strychnine level in the urine! I might as well tell you frankly that I've only stayed here these last five days because the Führer is so ill."

Brandt's remarks during this conversation about the pylorus and duodenal canal and about a blockage reaching back to the gall bladder, with resulting icterus, were identical with the data I had given Dr. von Ondarza[7] when he telephoned, in the Reichsmarschall's name, and it was because of this that I declined to give Ondarza any further medical data a few days later, as the information had sprouted legs and got back to me (via Reichsmarschall Göring) at which time Greim and Loerzer[8] were also present. Göring claimed to have learned details of the Führer's illness from Schaub[9] on the evening before. Evidently Brandt and Ondarza had quite a talk about the whole thing. H. H[immler] dropped some interesting comments.—

Then I went to see the Führer. I told him I'm getting flak from the doctors for allegedly never making X rays of him and never ordering an analysis of the contents of his stomach. The Führer flared up. "Just let these gentlemen come and try telling *me* that! How often have you made these very suggestions, and how often have I refused! What is this stupid bunch after?"

"Even so," I countered, "I urge you Mein Führer to let me do both things in the near future!"

[6] Professor Dr. (med.) Hanskarl von Hasselbach, born November 2, 1903, in Berlin-Wilmersdorf. Was Hitler's deputy escort surgeon from 1936 until this anti-gas pills episode in October 1944. Some of his papers are in the Bundesarchiv, Koblenz, under file Kl.Erw.441–3, including studies on Hitler's intellectual ability, his ignorance of character, and his attitude toward Christianity. Died at Christmas 1981.

[7] Dr. Ramón von Ondarza, personal physician of Reichsmarschall Hermann Göring.

[8] Bruno Loerzer, Luftwaffe general in the Mediterranean theater, a particular crony of Göring.

[9] SS-Obergruppenführer Julius Schaub, born August 20, 1898, in München. Party veteran, chief adjutant of the Führer. Trained as a druggist, entered the party in 1928 with membership number 81.

He said, "That can't be done at all just now!"

So if we can't undertake it in a major radiological institute in Berlin, then we will have to have a set installed in a bunker room in the Reich Chancery, and he said I should talk with Chaoul about that. I recalled that I had earlier wanted Brückner to get me the files of X rays made before my time in Munich, but I had never got them.

October 4, 1944

One-thirty A.M. His pulse is 80, blood pressure 120, temperature 37.2. Had one more bowel movement since last evening, but that was virtually all wind. Still a lot of gas higher up. Says he's been working a lot and had therefore a degree of restlessness which prevented him getting to sleep before the morning.

I said, "You ought to be able to take a month off. But that time is bound to come sooner or later."

"My dear doctor," he replied, "then you would have to come with me, so you get some respite too. Miss Schroeder and Dara [Miss Daranowski] have been here and they have made another assault on me—the Schroeder girl operates in a very cunning way, discounting all my arguments in advance so that I have no option but to agree. But I already promised you that I would work in the *big* rooms with the *big* windows, and just use these inner sancta for sleeping."

He is not to take any sedatives tonight, I would even draw the line at giving him an injection. Earlier, I mentioned that my colleagues are blaming me for giving so many injections; but I think it better to bypass the stomach and shoot the drugs straight into the body than to irritate or overload the stomach. As I was going, he called out, "Little doctor [*Doktorchen*], I'm always so happy when you come in the mornings!"

He has taken one Chineurin dragée and twenty drops of Sympathol. Because of the work this afternoon and evening he was a bit dizzy—which has happened quite frequently since the bomb blast; for several weeks since then he has been able to keep upright only by summoning up every ounce of energy. He says he has noticed that he is suffering more or less the same symptoms as almost all the others. As I left I took Arndt aside and emphatically forbade that Führer should receive any kind of drugs without my permission. I asked about the anti-gas pills, and was told there weren't any left. The Führer, he said, had taken sixteen of them a day, whereupon, Arndt said, he had telephoned me about two weeks ago and I had given permission for only two.

Fifteen minutes past noon: *** abdomen supple, submaxillary gland only half the size of yesterday. Injected two ampoules of 10 cc glucose (Glycovarin) and 5 cc of Cantan-forte intravenously, and Vitamultin-Calcium, Glyconorm and Tonophosphan-forte intramuscularly. The feces were brown, partly watery (because of the Karlsbad mineral water) and partly firm.

Called Major (med) Dr. Giesing because of the enlarged submaxillary gland and the angry inflammation noticed by me yesterday of both tonsils, but particularly the left one, which also manifests purulent excrescences. His examination confirms my suspicion, and by squeezing them out he established the presence of four such excrescences.

Called in Professor Blaschke to check the dental cavity forming in the upper jaw. No connection with the swollen gland. Gave the Führer another Chineurin, as it has had a beneficial effect. In addition one Acidol-Pepsin with the meal and two Euflat pills after it.

Seven P.M.: *** Abdomen somewhat distended. General health said to be even better than yesterday. Gave him two Chineurins, and Karlsbad mineral water for supper.

October 5, 1944

Saw him at twelve-thirty A.M. *** Administered an arm and leg massage with Franzbranntwein lotion. Two Chineurin dragées, with two Euflat tablets before that, followed by Karlsbad mineral water. Dinner had tasted good to him. On the inside left of his mouth there is some pain caused by a slight injury by Dr. Giesing's sharp fingernails. Führer is going to try to get to sleep without an injection and without tablets.

Noon: *** blood pressure 118 mm (after a bath). *** Stomach supple, pit of the stomach a bit resistant deep down, and the left flexure of the colon resistant when deep pressure applied. Gave him two Hamma Dry Coli capsules,[10] two Chineurins after my examination and thirty drops of Sympathol. He breakfasted on thin porridge, slices of pear, and glucose; injected 10 cc of twenty percent glucose

[10] Hamma Dry Coli was a Morell product, successor to Mutaflor.

solution and Cantan-forte intravenously and Vitamultin-Calcium, liver and Tonophosphan intramuscularly.

This was his second night without sleeping tablets. The Führer thinks the gentle massaging of his limbs with Franzbranntwein did not do him any good as he could not get to sleep, and during the night he felt first freezing and then feverish. But he feels stronger than he did yesterday.

When I visited the Führer last night I asked him—if I might ask for this one tiny favor—to give me a brief note confirming that I never issued any instructions that he should take quantities of anti-gas pills every day and furthermore that I have repeatedly called for a gastrointestinal X ray and an examination of the contents of his stomach, but that he had never given permission for this. The Führer agreed to this and said he would do this in the form of a letter to me.[11]

With regard to the things Brandt said, it now occurs to me that he claimed he could *prove* that strychnine was present. As he then spoke of the eight pills the Führer had allegedly consumed at every meal, I did not at first pay attention to this claim. But later he also mentioned that it would be possible to prove the strychnine level in the urine (clearly, if there was any strychnine in any of the drugs there would be a positive result). Evidently Brandt has had the urine sample which I sent to the clinic for analysis, and which had to be sent on to the Karlshof field hospital for the Indikan reaction,[12] analyzed for strychnine.

During my discussion of Brandt's remarks, the Führer flared up angrily and asked whether Brandt had been maintaining, then, that it was I who had ordained the taking of the anti-gas pills. Because, he said, *he* had already told him that he had been taking them on his own initiative.

"No," I replied, "but I would be grateful if I could have that in writing as a safeguard for myself." Besides, I said, Brandt had gone from me to him. The Führer declared that that was not true, because Brandt had gone *first* to him and only after that to me.

I replied I thought there must be some mistake, because Brandt had already told me that he would naturally have to inform the Führer and was about to go and see him.

The Führer repeated, "No, he went to you after leaving me."

[11] No such letter is however in Morell's papers.
[12] See the entry for October 3.

SMALL WONDER that with what he took to be the shadow of the gallows looming over him for having nearly poisoned Hitler, Morell fell ill. On October 7 he noted in his diary, "At midnight on October 5–6 I was with the Führer. After I got back home I had a brain edema and a slight hemorrhage behind the left eye, with resulting double vision, change of optical axis and restricted vision from extreme left to bottom of field, also slight nausea without vomiting, tenesmus (but only one stool during the night); there was no headache, but dizziness when walking—I took three Koagovit tablets, Brom-Nervacit, and opened a vein to let some blood; unfortunately intravenous injections of glucose and iodine were not at first possible because of my thin veins, but I managed them three quarters of a day later; I at once took one ampoule of Thrombovit and Vitamultin-Calcium, went to bed, applied an ice bag and fasted." He added, "Toward evening I called briefly on the Chief." On December 2 he would recall it to Professor Weber like this: "A few months ago I had a hemorrhage behind my left eye caused by a sudden aggravation, but this was rapidly reabsorbed."

October 5–7, 1944

I was ill.

October 6, 1944

Half an hour after midnight [visited Hitler:] *** Epigastric suppleness, little wind. During the day he took: two Chineurins three times, two capsules of Koli Hamma, two Acidol-Pepsins twice, two Euflats twice, twenty drops of Sympathol three times, and a bottle of Karlsbad mineral water.

At six P.M. his pulse was 80, blood pressure 120 mm, temperature 36.6 degrees. Abdomen supple. Large bowel movement. Good appetite. Continues to feel much better, says "best day so far."

Gave him a Profundol tablet during the night to get to sleep, but it had no effect, so one tablet of Tempidorm, after which he slept for three and a half or four hours.

October 7, 1944

One-fifteen P.M. The Führer telephoned and when I inquired whether I might come over, replied he was feeling fine, he had no temperature at all and he wanted me to stay in bed, so I would recuperate quickly.

MORELL was touched by the many visits he received during his two days in bed. On October 7 he wrote in his pocket diary, "Wolf's Lair. Von John [one of Hitler's adjutants] was here and [Flight Captain] Baur at my bedside. Stayed in bed all day! Christa Schroeder and Dara (Frau Christian) also called on me."

On the following day his Berlin assistant, Dr. Weber, had arrived but was none too well himself so Morell struggled over to see Hitler alone. Hitler consoled his ailing doctor with a startling decision: all three rival doctors would be dismissed from the Führer's Headquarters—Morell alone would stay.

October 8, 1944

Dr. Weber[13] arrived, but with angina.

Visited Führer, but made only normal diagnoses. *** Abdomen soft, particularly the gall bladder. Injected 10 cc of glucose intravenously and Vitamultin-Calcium, Glyconorm, Tonophosphan-forte and Progynon B Oleosum intramuscularly. In his right eye, outer corner, the conjunc. bulbi, a tiny vessel has burst (the second time recently). Applied a few eyedrops of cocaine adrenaline solution.

Führer told me that Dr. von Hasselbach was being sent back, and that Dr. Brandt would in future concern himself only with his Berlin duties.[14] As surgical escort, said Hitler, a young doctor would be taking over who had until now been staff doctor to the Reichsführer SS, called Stumpfegger.

DR. LUDWIG JOSEPH STUMPFEGGER had been born on July 11, 1910, in Munich. A tall, nonsmoking, muscular and well-built SS-Obersturmbannführer, with blue eyes and thinning blond hair, his appointment as Hitler's escort doctor would officially take effect from October 24. He had been a personal assistant to Professor Gebhardt until 1939, working in his famous Hohenlychen Clinic as a surgeon.[15] He would stay at Hitler's side until the end, and survive him by only one day. He is considered

---

[13] Dr. Richard Weber, Morell's Berlin assistant; now lives in Hoya in northern Germany.

[14] Brandt had been the Führer's commissioner general for health and public safety for some years.

[15] See Himmler's files, National Archives microfilm T-175, roll 40, pp. 1073 et seq.

to have been killed attempting to escape with Martin Bormann from the Reich Chancery on May 1, 1945. The two corpses were exhumed from a Berlin street recently.

From his pocket diary of October 9, it is plain that Morell still believed himself in no shape to treat Hitler. "Wolf's Lair. Weber is here. Chief is okay (I telephoned). Dr. Weber gave *me* an intravenous shot of 10 cc of glucose and Prostrophanta and intramuscular of Glyconorm and Testoviron."

October 9, 1944

When I telephoned, the Führer came to the telephone himself and said he's getting along magnificently and I should stay in bed so I can get well again soon.

A T FIVE-THIRTY P.M. Brandt was called to Hitler's bunker and formally dismissed by him. Hasselbach was also sent into the wilderness. An hour later, as Giesing described, he was summoned to Reichsleiter Bormann and also released from Hitler's service. "We have nothing against *you*," Bormann said, "on the contrary the Führer has only the highest praise for you." Hitler confirmed this a few minutes later. "You see, Herr Doktor," he said, "this anti-gas pills business had to be cleared up somehow." Hitler added, "It was very bold of you to go to Himmler about it, but you have always been straightforward with me, and I am going to be the same to you."

Himmler was content, and Bormann was smugly pleased as well. He wrote in a private letter on October 10, "Yesterday Hasselbach was dropped as escort doctor to the Führer and is to be replaced by Dr. Stumpfegger, who was Uncle H.'s physician until now. The new man seems very pleasant. Brandt too is no longer to act as escort doctor. There have been fresh rows between Morell on the one hand and Hasselbach and Brandt on the other; but now this state of affairs, so unpleasant for the Führer, no longer exists."

On October 23, Morell wrote to General Walter Warlimont, who was recovering from the bomb blast effects. "A number of weeks have gone by in anything but a pleasant way for me, and there was a lot of aggravation in them for me. But the Führer was so charming to me that this has more than made up for everything else. I think I will now be able to pursue my duties and responsibilities in greater peace. I just wish we could exchange the swampland around here soon for a healthier German climate. It's real autumn here, with dense fogbanks everywhere."

October 10, 1944

One P.M. The patient is making an excellent impression and claims that he has never had such a clear head since July 20 as now. He feels liberated. His pulse is 72, temperature 36.2, blood pressure 108, after taking a Tempidorm tablet last night. Injected twenty percent glucose intravenously, plus liver and Glyconorm intramuscularly. ***

ON OCTOBER 10 a urinalysis was performed by the headquarters clinic and doublechecked by Morell's assistant, Weber. "Completely normal," was the result. In particular there were no signs of permanent liver damage after the jaundice attack. On the same day Morell had a throat smear sent to the Chemical Research Laboratory of Military District III, "the smear from a tonsil that yielded four pustules when squeezed out eight or ten days ago." He asked the laboratory to identify the responsible bacteria. Two days later they sent him an interim reply. "No harmful bacteria were identified." All in all, records like these go a long way toward dispelling the myth of Morell as an incautious, haphazard physician.

October 11, 1944

The patient is feeling excellent and for this reason asks me not to come, saying I should take a rest myself, so that I get well again soon. For the first time the Führer went outside, to inspect the big new bunker. But from time to time he had to sit down for a rest as he did so.

October 12, 1944

One P.M. His pulse is 72 and regular, no heart problems (second heart beat still accentuated), temperature normal, blood pressure 116 mm. Abdomen soft and hollow—he has lost around thirteen pounds over the last two weeks. His neck glands are no longer swollen, and his throat has stopped hurting.

From today I'm going to give him only three more Chineurins a day for two days and then stop. During meals he'll get two Acidol-Pepsin tablets and two Euflats afterwards. He'll keep getting Hamma Dry Coli. Injected glucose and Cantan intravenously, and Vitamultin-Calcium, Glyconorm and Tonophosphan intramuscularly.

ON HIS MEMO PAD Morell reminded himself: "Patient A—I must write up his case history." It deserves comment that as soon as Morell ceased visiting, Hitler's health improved.

Throat, Heart and
Other Problems

THE HITLER of the autumn of 1944 was no longer the man he had been in 1940. From Field Marshal Gerd von Rundstedt we have a word picture of Hitler in the war conferences constantly fumbling with Vitamultin tablets or whatever other "junk" Morell had given him. "His posture is stooped," described Rundstedt, "and he trembles with both arms—the right more than the left. Since September 1944 Hitler loses himself in details, questions why this pillbox or that has not been fortified."

Dr. Brandt had also noticed that Hitler's legendary memory was seriously impaired. He sometimes had difficulty in following the thread of a conversation. "He was noticeably flighty," he told interrogators, "and rambled on and on about inconsequential matters, only to slump into silence."

Hitler himself recognized this—his self-insight at least was intact. One day he had confessed to Brandt, "There was a time when I could recall the names of thousands of people in all walks of life, but since this summer I just don't seem able to place people any more."

October 13, 1944

By telephone I am told that the patient is feeling very well. Last night at eleven-forty-five P.M. he himself telephoned to ask whether he might drink some watery chocolate, which I approved as he would also be taking the Karlsbad mineral water as an aid to digestion. He says he has now lost altogether sixteen pounds. Then the Führer said he would like to tell me some agreeable news, something that had come from Reichsleiter Bormann: Bormann has had the anti-gas pills analyzed by Gruppenführer Dr. Blumenreuther's office and has received the result: the pills are quite harmless, containing only the tiniest doses of belladonna and strychnine. If as stated two to four of them were taken at mealtimes they were completely innocuous; and even if twice as many were taken, or if there had been excessive consumption of a dozen or more, they still could not have caused any damage.

"The pills," he said, "were only meant to harm you!"

I reminded him that when it had first became known that he had been taking so many anti-gas pills I had expressed the selfsame view.

MORELL did not want to go through the same nightmare twice. On October 13 he telephoned Blumenreuther—chief of the SS medical stores—about Mitilax, before prescribing it for Hitler. Blumenreuther reassured him: "It consists virtually entirely of paraffin, with no noxious additives. The samples you sent were completely free of bacteria."

October 14, 1944

Twelve-fifty P.M. As he was feeling okay, the Führer did not have me sent for.

Eleven P.M. He had me sent for immediately, as the gland on the left of his neck had swollen up again, and he was complaining of an obstruction in his larynx. His left tonsil had reddened after a slight daubing with iodine [potassium-iodide] glycerine. Pulse 72, blood pressure 110 mm. Started the inhaler going, but unfortunately it could only be used for a few minutes. He refused neck pads, and also rejected hot milk and honey for fear of flatulence. Must get lemon juice to work on the tonsil for a while. Gave him two Chineurin dragées. I won't try any injections until tomorrow.

October 15, 1944

One-thirty P.M. Führer had already breakfasted, had slept only three hours as there had been major conferences during the night. Apparently there have been some big rows, and he was in a grim mood.[1] *** Left neck gland had gone down a lot, the reddening was

---

[1] Operation Bazooka—a lightning Nazi swoop on the Hungarian government and the arrest of its leading members—had begun early on October 15. On the evening before, October 14, his favorite field marshal, Erwin Rommel, had been forced to commit suicide, which was reported to Hitler during the evening war conference.

almost gone. To be absolutely certain I gave him at his request Ultraseptyl and 10 cc of Septoiod intravenously and intramuscular shots of Omnadin and Vitamultin-Calcium. From now on he must take one bar of Vitamultin three times a day and not forget lemon juice and a heart drug (Sympathol three times a day). The Führer asks if he can have Brom-Nervacit without the sugar. I will have some manufactured quickly.

A NOTE in Morell's papers says that this latest infection was caught from the headquarters' barber, Wollenhaupt, who shaved Hitler each morning. Dr. Giesing—who had however left Hitler's service by this time—quotes Hitler as telling him: "That fellow had a cold for five days and told me nothing about it. I spoke with Morell about it yesterday evening, and he's giving me Ultraseptyl again."

Morell was still occasionally reminding himself in his agenda, "Write up Patient A's case history."

October 16, 1944

Daubed left tonsil with Lugol's iodine. Outer gland has almost subsided. Injected 20 cc of glucose intravenously and Vitamultin-Calcium, Glyconorm and Tonophosphan-forte intramuscularly. Instructed that he must use inhaler and allow lemon juice to take effect. His vocal chords are still inflamed. Said he had been working and telephoning until seven A.M.

October 17, 1944

One-thirty P.M. Says he has slept well, but is in a hurry. The left neck gland is coming up again. Daubed the left tonsil. Injected 10 cc of Septoiod and Ultraseptyl intravenously. If the tonsil does not get better soon, I will have it taken out sometime after it heals. At ten in the evening I injected one cc of Bismogenol intramuscularly. The gland has gone down perceptibly.

October 18, 1944

One-thirty P.M. Slept well, but spirits not very high. The gland on left of the neck is scarcely palpable. My yesterday's opinion was

caused by the turning of his neck and the tension of the sterno-
kleidomastoid muscle [which turns the neck]; there is only a very
slight swelling left in the larynx. The left tonsil is much less
swollen, the inflammation is almost gone, and when I daub it with
Lugol it is possible to penetrate deep into the lacuna. I have ordered
further radiation (twice a day). Injected glucose, Septoiod and
Ultraseptyl intravenously plus Vitamultin-Calcium, Omnadin and
liver intramuscularly. Pulse 78, blood pressure 118 mm. Giving
Cardiazol now instead of Sympathol, 15 to 20 drops three times
daily.

October 19, 1944

One-thirty P.M. His sleep was good. * * * The neck gland is still
swollen near the left tonsil, a slight swelling extending down to near
the larynx. His heart tones are pure and weak, with a strong
accentuation of the second heart beat. Left tonsil inflamed near the
top. Injected glucose, Ultraseptyl intravenously, and Cantan-forte,
Tonophosphan-forte, Vitamultin-Calcium and liver intramuscularly.
The Führer regrets that when the tonsil was squeezed out recently
no sample was taken or culture examination made. Von Eicken will
have to come tomorrow. The Führer had Chineurin sent for. If I
am not careful when I make the intravenous injections I now pierce
right through the veins (there is much less blood in them as the
pressure is 118 mm now compared with 143 mm earlier).

At three P.M. I ordered through Arndt (but just for today) that
the Führer should take three Ultraseptyl tablets three times as a
shock treatment. Unfortunately we've no Iodex here for rubbing
into the neck. The Führer does not want neck pads. Sent over to
Arndt today 300 Luizym dragées, two to be taken with each meal.

Seven P.M. the Führer telephoned that he cannot take any more
Ultraseptyl, as after three tablets he gets a taut stomach just like
recently and he attributes his recent condition [when he had
hepatitis] to the large Ultraseptyl intake. I declared this was absurd,
but we'll stop giving further Ultraseptyl. Of course, his cold's going
to linger on, I said. I only wanted him to take as much as he did
because I thought he wanted to get well again *immediately* whatever the cost. I added that tomorrow I would be getting in some
Neo-Pyocyanase and Tonsiosan, which had not arrived today as
they had missed the train.

October 20, 1944

At two P.M. The Führer again has badly swollen tonsil and glands on the left. Tells me that in consequence of having taken the three Ultraseptyl tablets he again had bad stomach pains and could not sleep at all last night—just a few hours this morning. Daubed the left tonsil with Neo-Pyocyanase and gave him Tonsiosan (a Schwabe product)—one tablet to be taken three times a day. While I was swabbing the tonsil two blockages were released from the lacunae. I refrained from making any injections today, to give the punctures made these last few days a chance to heal. Inside the right elbow there are red dots still visible (but no pustules) marking where the last injections were made; but none inside the left elbow. The Führer thinks there weren't any such marks visible on previous occasions. *** Heart sounds clearer than yesterday.

October 21, 1944

Professor von Eicken arrived,[2] and we went over to see the Führer together at twelve-forty P.M. The left nasal cavity still manifests some secretion. It is possible that this is draining off into the larynx and that this is causing the rather hoarse voice. The left tonsil looks relatively good today. The right tonsil is slightly inflamed. Throat gland barely palpable. Swabbed (by von Eicken) with Neo-Pyocyanase. There must now be an X-ray check on the left maxillary sinus, following which we will decide whether there should be another sinus irrigation.

The Führer looked to me very limp and pale. He told us he had worked eight and a half hours yesterday. So I injected him with 20 cc of twenty percent glucose solution intravenously and with Vitamultin-Calcium, Tonophosphan-forte and Testoviron intramuscularly.

Drove to Karlshof field hospital at six P.M. for the X rays. Dr. Stumpfegger went with us; the chief surgeon and Dr. Brinkmann were present. Linge[3] *** was with us. Two X rays made; these showed the frontal sinuses clear, the right maxillary sinus free and a small degree of lateral shadow on the left one. Double-checked by

---

[2] Eicken noted only, "October 21: consultation."

[3] Heinz Linge, Führer's valet; born March 22, 1913, in Bremen; former bricklayer, served Hitler with rank of SS-Hauptsturmführer until the end. Died in 1981 in Hamburg.

Eicken, who declared the X-ray results too meager to make any specific diagnosis as to whether the secretion is what is inflaming the larynx. A further X ray must be made later.

October 22, 1944

One-fifteen P.M. The Führer had lengthy conferences yesterday so he was talking for a long time. *** Left tonsil quite good; swabbed it and applied Neo-Pyocyanase to the lacuna.

At nine-forty-five P.M. again treated left and right tonsils with Neo-Pyocyanase and applied ten drops to the right and ten drops to the left nasal cavity. His voice had been hoarse when I spoke on the telephone to him several hours earlier; after this treatment he was better.

October 23, 1944

One-thirty P.M. Injected glucose intravenously and Vitamultin-Calcium, Glyconorm and Tonophosphan-forte intramuscularly. Pulse 78 after breakfast. Swabbed tonsils with Neo-Pyocyanase. Applied about fifteen drops of this to each nostril, and repeated the treatment at midnight. No complaints, though voice is still causing a bit of concern. He slept about six hours last night, in two stretches.

October 24, 1944

Two P.M. *** Abdomen very good but sunken; tonsils almost normal, lacunae visible in depth. Swabbed with Neo-Pyocyanase and applied ten drops to each nostril. Führer complains that despite a treatment that has now lasted nearly five weeks his voice is still not free. Of course I myself have been handling this treatment only recently. I referred to the sulphonamide-proof nature of the bacteria, resulting from the fact that Wollenhaupt, who passed the infection on while shaving the Führer, has been taking Ultraseptyl for a long time. The Führer would like me to make an attempt at killing off the bacteria by means of a different sulphonamide (but only one that can be injected). In his opinion there must be another focus of these bacteria somewhere else, one that is *not* in the tonsils. I suggested Tibatin and Antiphlogistine applications. The latter should be applied—if absolutely necessary—for a few hours in the evenings. The Führer has been fully advised as to the difficulty in procuring them. He says he slept only two hours last night so his spirits are rather low.

October 25, 1944

At one-forty-five P.M. *** Feeling well, his hoarseness has almost cleared. Swabbed both tonsils and applied Neo-Pyocyanase drops to them and both nostrils. Injected intravenous glucose plus intramuscular Testoviron, Tonophosphan-forte and Glycovarin.

O N THE TWENTY-FOURTH, Morell had ordered from Dr. Blumenreuther by telephone camphor, menthol, and hydrargyron oxide flavon, which with liquid paraffin would provide the ingredients for a medicine to be prescribed to Hitler with the directions: "Apply one pipetteful to each nostril morning and evening. Shake well." He also at last ordered two boxes of Tibatin, the sulphonamide ampoules which competed with his own patent Ultraseptyl product, and two boxes of Antiphlogistine poultices, which were regularly used for inflammations of the glands and lungs, pleurisy, arthritis, effusions, and bruises.

October 26, 1944

At noon *** the gland on the left of his neck was still slightly palpable. Swabbed both tonsils. For the larynx, Neo-Pyocyanase is to be pipetted into both nostrils twice a day, and twice a day also a paraffin mixture (0.05 camphor, 0.1 menthol, 0.2 hydrag. oxid. flav., with paraffin liquid to 20 cc). Yesterday I left the patient with Cardiazol-Aphidr. (fifteen to twenty drops to be taken three times daily) in addition to the regular Cardiazol: if his heart weakens he is to use the Cardiazol-Aph., otherwise the liquid Cardiazol for the time being.

T HE MILITARY SITUATION had not improved during these weeks. Hitler however had abandoned his idea of replacing Göring with Greim. On October 7 the Russian attack on East Prussia began. On the eighth, Hitler had to approve the evacuation of his forces from eastern Hungary. His SS troops had smashed the uprising in Warsaw, but now the political situation in Hungary became acute as the government made a vain attempt to get out of the war; the Regent, Horthy, was arrested on the fifteenth and taken to Germany.

Hitler intended to stay in East Prussia. But he was not blind to the coming crisis. The first refused columns streamed past his headquarters at Rastenburg. On October 21 the Russians broke through German defenses onto the Rominten Heath and Soviet artillery fire began to rain down on Goldap. "The influx of visitors from Berlin has slackened," General Kreipe observed laconically in his diary the next day, "now that we are coming under fire." In the war conference that day Field Marshal Keitel urged an immediate move to the safety of Berlin. Hitler refused to budge. His forces counterattacked. The Hermann Göring panzer corps recaptured Gumbinnen and found the first grim evidence of Russian atrocities against the native population—murdered women and children nailed to the doors of farm buildings. Though it seemed to Hitler like a miracle, the situation in East Prussia somehow stabilized.

October 27, 1944

One-thirty P.M. F. is in a very sour mood today, says his voice is bad again—how can he be expected to stand before the microphone and speak to the German people like this? Could I not hear for myself how rough his voice is?

It is true that his voice is a bit hoarse, but not all that much. I referred to the fact that the new nose drops that we have now begun to apply, in line with [Dr. Rudolf] Franck's standard work, *Modern Therapy*, in cases of chronic catarrh of the larynx, may indeed cause some slight inflammation; as there is camphor and menthol in these, I said, temporary irritations are possible; but I added that these would have a beneficial effect, causing hyperaemia [the presence of excessive blood] in the mucous membranes, which would result in the production of more antibodies.

"But what use is the increased blood supply," he asked, "if the bacteria are not killed off? *They* are what matters!"

"It doesn't have to be bacteria that are causing the hoarseness," I rejoined, "it might be the mechanical irritation that your vocal chords are permanently subjected to."

An examination of the pharynx showed that the left wall of the pharynx was of normal color, and the right tonsil looked absolutely normal too (both of which were slightly inflamed yesterday, by comparison). The left tonsil, which has a few brighter spots in its fork, is still a bit reddened at its upper extremity. I daubed both tonsils with Neo-Pyocyanase penetrating deep into the left lacuna as I did so (without any resulting expression of pain).

Before this treatment I had injected 10 cc of twenty percent glucose solution intravenously and Tonophosphan-forte, Vitamultin-Calcium and Glyconorm intramuscularly.

The patient then again started off on the topic of killing off the bacteria, and about how he had been undergoing medical treatment now since July 20 and yet his voice was worse than ever. I pointed out that I have only been dealing with his upper respiratory tracts since recently (about one and a half weeks), and that I am proceeding precisely according to the best textbooks and that everything has now been cured except for the throat irritation.

"Yes," he said, "but that's the most vital of all. When you were using the Ultraseptyl you ought to have given me a powerful series of doses and not just frittered it away in isolated applications."

"Mein Führer," I said, "I injected you two days running with intravenous shots of Ultraseptyl!"

"Evidently that was not enough. You should have gone on with it!"

"From this afternoon or tomorrow morning," I explained, "you're going to get another sulphonamide course, using Tibatin this time because this is the swiftest to be excreted, in fact in twenty-four hours. At the same time I'd like to stuff some pure paraffin up your nostrils, which will sooth your voice box a bit."

"That's no use, is it! The bacteria have got to be killed off. That's just the same as you've been squirting up my nose all this time, and that's not cured anything either."

"Mein Führer," I said, "both camphor and menthol are painful on raw mucous membrane, and they inflame it; but they also disinfect. The inflammation is soothed by paraffin however; the mucous membrane relaxes and gets a chance to heal. Can I begin this treatment this afternoon?"

"No," he said, "tomorrow!"

Entirely objectively judged, at the moment his health is quite good apart from a really very minor hoarseness. As the patient has conferences all day and talks all night until around three A.M., and as he stays all the time inside his bunker quarters without any natural light and only gets ten or fifteen minutes' daylight and fresh air at most each day, while there is a constant cold draft in the bunker caused by the extractor fans, and as he will neither agree to wear a neck comforter nor undertake to use an inhalation apparatus, it is small wonder that it is taking so long for him to get better.

I drew attention to the need for greater vitamin consumption to increase his resistance, and instructed him to take two Vitamultin-Calcium tablets three times a day. He said he is afraid of getting constipated because of their cocoa content, and he has only been taking two of them a day; so I agreed that we might try two—taken twice daily—for a while.

I sent over to the Führer bunker this midday the following: 100 cc of ersatz Brom-Nervacit; Acidol-Pepsin tablets, and a factory package of Euflat dragées.

October 28, 1944

Saw him at two P.M. Daubed both tonsils with Neo-Pyocyanase. Tonsils and pharynx clear. Voice is better (according to the patient himself, it is "better but not much so"). [*Data card*: Has a cold.] Injected two grams of Tibatin and Cantan-forte intravenously.

At ten-thirty P.M. Intravenous injections of Tibatin and of glucose solution. Voice almost better. We talked about the water supply here—it is hard and crawling with bacteria that are not pathogenic but can upset the metabolism. I said his urine was certainly full of bacteria again. We conversed then about hypos-padias,[4] about spina bifida, and about cysto-pyelitis with pathogenic coli bacilli with their main focus in the prostate. I said it would soon be time for me to give the latter a thorough examination too. As for the administering of the nasal drops, the patient says he wants to do this himself.

October 29, 1944

At one-thirty P.M. His pharynx and tonsils were clear; I swabbed them nonetheless with Neo-Pyocyanase. Injected Tibatin and glucose intravenously. When I proposed that he should go for some days almost without speaking at all, he said this was quite im-possible and rejected the suggestion. When I again proposed that we might soothe the inflamed mucous membranes of the larynx by

---

[4] The reason for Hitler's interest in hypospadias is not evident. It is a developmental abnormality in the male, in which the urethra opens on the undersurface of the penis or in the perineum.

flooding them with egg white or paraffin, he very angrily rebuffed me explaining that the bacteria, and not the inflamed mucous membranes, were at the bottom of it.

After that he exclaimed that this illness has been going on now for months and he wasn't getting any better despite all the doctors and specialists called in. I reminded him that I had not been in charge of this treatment, but that it had been initiated by the specialists. It was only in the very recent past that I had begun treating his upper respiratory passages, and after all I had managed to cure his tonsils. As I myself could not see very well, I said, I had had to leave the investigation of the larynx to Professor von Eicken; and the diagnosis and decision whether to irrigate the sinuses or not had been left to him too. Ought I to call him in tomorrow morning?

The Führer said I ought to wait one or two more days to see what effect the Tibatin injections might have. He said that he's not a little boy any longer, and that he's had enough catarrhs in the past to know that it's bacteria and nothing else that cause them. Over the past few years they had always been nipped in the bud by a few Ultraseptyl tablets, or they hadn't even got started at all. But now this, he said—meaning the illness—had been dragging on for months and he wasn't getting any better. So far he's turned down: neck comforters and poultices, a facial vapor bath, wearing a woolen shawl at night, drinking milk with bee's honey, nasal inserts of paraffin and moving into a warm room without a draft, and much else.

October 30, 1944

At six A.M. I was sent for. I must come immediately and bring some Eupaverin with me. I was with him twenty minutes later. The Führer said he had worked right through the night and had had to face up to a *very* tough decision, as a result of which he had got highly worked up. The worry had built up more and more inside him until suddenly, as always happens when he's really worried sick, his stomach knotted up into this painful cramp. He said I was not to give him any examination as this would just add to his pain. I rapidly made up some Eupaverin and Eukodal and gave him an intravenous injection. This was by no means easy because of the many recent needle scars. So I again said he ought to give the veins a rest for a while. As I had to pause once during the injection, I noticed that he was already becoming less tense, and the pain then went. The Führer was very pleased about this and gratefully pressed my hand, saying, "What good fortune it is that we have this Eupaverin."

"Mein Führer," I said, "but this time there hasn't been any preceding consumption of anti-gas pills! And Br[andt] tried to tell me that all your pains these last years were just a result of the anti-gas pills."

The Führer: "These dimwits and idiots—they would have done better to work out ways of getting rid of my throat problems, and that goes for the specialist Giesing. My dear doctor, you wouldn't believe how much grief I have had over all that!"

I then lectured the Führer on tackling such grave affairs far into the night—it was robbing him of any chance of getting any sleep. But he retorted that he had no choice, and he had to dispose of such a burden, grave though it was, first.

As I made to leave he again thanked me profusely and apologized for having deprived me of my sleep. I reassured him that I sleep only from two to six A.M. and that I am always wide awake on the dot of six. Sometimes I am able to snatch another two hours' sleep later in the day, and I often do.

At two P.M., the Führer said he is now quite free of pain but that he did not go to sleep and worked right on. The pharynx and both tonsils look good. A slight swelling on the left, near his larynx. Swabbed the tonsils with Neo-Pyocyanase and made an intramuscular injection of Vitamultin-Calcium and liver extract. *** Abdomen supple, no tenderness.

I advised him to drink large quantities of liquids, particularly warm Karlsbad mineral water, and take some Boxberger pills to prevent constipation.

The Führer confided to me that after this renewed attack of pain the trembling in his leg and hands was much more violent than before. Yesterday, he added, he had had a major upset and during the night a very worrying job.[5] So there was no wonder that

---

[5] Almost certainly Hitler's annoyance had been kindled by renewed Luftwaffe failures.

he had ended up doubled up in pain. He moaned about the dis-
loyalty of a certain general, and about the meager performance of
so many General Staff officers. Their motto of "Be More than You
Appear!" was the sheerest self-delusion. If you've got it, you
shouldn't be shy of showing it—that was his view. When I suggested that these bad qualities had only turned up in the General
Staff officers after World War I, he replied that even during that
war this clique had begun to isolate itself from the rest.

O N OCTOBER 30 Morell's Olmütz laboratory sent him their report
on the latest fecal sample. "*Diagnosis:* slight presence of coli
and aerogenic bacteria, otherwise normal. As for anaerobe
bacteria the main traces are of apathogenic butyric acid bacilli."

October 31, 1944

At two P.M., checked his pharynx and tonsils. Swabbed tonsils
with Neo-Pyocyanase, findings good. Voice is also scarcely impaired. The slight swelling to the left of the larynx has almost
entirely subsided. As I was leaving, the Führer had me called back
from the adjutants' room and told me that thanks to my rapid
intervention yesterday morning he completely recovered and that
there had been no further spasms and he had had a substantial
bowel movement. I said that if he was ever in such a condition
again he should not hesitate to send for me even if it was in the
middle of the night. He said his only worry was that he might be
depriving me of my sleep like that, but I reassured him once again
that I never get to sleep before two and I'm wide awake again by
five-thirty or six A.M., and anyway I'm only here for his sake and
I can always be at his side within twenty minutes of getting the
call. I said that the greatest satisfaction he could give me was the
chance of being of help to him.

November 1, 1944

Two-thirty P.M. The Führer had been in a huddle with Schaub.
He had a long face and was in a bad mood.[6] Said he had slept well

[6] From the diary of shorthand reporter Karl Thöt we get this glimpse of
Hitler's new life-style: "October 31, 1944: from 10:50 to 11:21 P.M. took
shorthand note of a conference between General Buhle and Gruppenführer
Fegelein in Führer's sleeping quarters. As only *one* stenographer was called

thanks to a sedative until one-thirty P.M. I injected him with glucose intravenously and with Vitamultin-Calcium, Glyconorm and Tonophosphan-forte intramuscularly. As I made the intravenous injection the Führer thought I was not massaging the place long enough with alcohol first—said I always did it too little—and suggested this was why he kept getting little red pimples lately where I had made the injections. (In fact because of his squatting for months at a time in his bunker without natural light or fresh air his blood lacks oxygen and is venous, as is evident when his arm is gripped to stop the blood flow, and the blood in consequence is less coagulant and the punctures remain red.) But despite all this the Führer attributes it to bacteria and thinks that it is perhaps the injections themselves that are responsible for the bacteria getting into his body.

When I was about to swab the pharynx and tonsil and check them, he asked me to desist, saying that there was no point, because that was not going to get rid of his sore throat (incidentally there was virtually no hoarseness perceptible!). So I refrained.

The Führer then pointed out, "But you've got a hoarse voice too now!"

"Yes," I said, "since yesterday, since I often open the window in my bedroom at night for a few minutes when it gets too hot."

"No," he insisted, "you've been hoarse now for several days." (In fact my voice is a bit rough today because I went to the farewell party for Lieutenant-Colonel von Amsberg[7] yesterday evening, and what with sitting in a smoke-filled room and eating and drinking a lot I vomited it all up during the night and brought up some bile in my larynx.) "It comes from the cold draft, when I've been perspiring," I added.

"No, it's the bacteria that do it."

I then suggested getting an X ray made today and booking a visit by von Eicken tomorrow. He postponed agreement to this. Nor

---

for and Krieger did not think he could accept responsibility for a solo shorthand note because he has a bad hand, I went; it went better than expected. The Führer lay in bed, but was no less lively than usual, and I sat behind his two visitors at a round table with a lamp."

[7] Lieutenant-Colonel Erik von Amsberg, born on October 21, 1908, had been attached to Hitler's staff as Wehrmacht adjutant (Army) on January 21, 1944. On October 24 he was posted to the Nineteenth Army as adjutant. He now lives near Munich.

would he allow me to fix an appointment for Professor Blaschke.[8]
I then left him.

November 2, 1944

Führer did not send for me, is said to be in good spirits and
good health.

November 3, 1944

One P.M. His pulse is 72. Injected glucose intravenously and
Tonophosphan-forte, Vitamultin-forte and Testoviron intramuscularly. He had slept well (six or seven hours) admittedly after taking
a sedative, a Phanodorm tablet. The Führer complains a lot about
the tremor in his left leg and in his hands. However the latter,
when extended with fingers spread, showed no visible tremor.
"When the 20th of July happened," he said, "all this shaking
suddenly stopped. But now it's crept back again, and it's worse than
ever."

I said that I attributed it to his constant burdens and worries
and irritations.

"What is to be done against it?"

"Peace and quiet," I said, "and keep out of arguments." But
those are all things that are impossible. One might try electric
currents or water treatments (four-cell baths, pure high-frequency
methods and Bro-Valoton baths, et cetera).

"Isn't there some kind of drug or shot you can give me against
it?"

"Vitamin B_1 and nicotinamide along with tranquilizing medicines. But if you take them to excess they'll put a damper on everything."

He said he already takes Brom-Nervacit when the going gets
rough. I said, "What would be very much to the point here would
be massages!"

Professor von Eicken is only to come after we have X-rayed the

8 Professor Johannes Blaschke, born November 14, 1881, was the dentist
attached to Hitler's headquarters. He had studied in Pennsylvania and London, and opened his first Berlin clinic in 1930; there he had treated Göring,
and Hitler too, since 1934. He was promoted to professor in June 1943, and
became chief dentist to the SS with the honorary rank of Brigadeführer. He
would leave Berlin on the night of April 20–21, 1945, and be taken prisoner
by the American forces.

jaw. And Professor Blaschke must estimate how long he will need for the teeth (three sessions, altogether about a week).

November 4, 1944

Führer is okay, so no need for me to come.

November 5, 1944

Two o'clock. Injected glucose intravenously plus Tonophosphan-forte, Vitamultin-forte and liver intramuscularly. Left him some Neo-Pyocyanase to gargle with (a teaspoonful every few hours). His voice is a bit hoarse again. * * *

November 6, 1944

Führer did not send for me.

November 7, 1944

Slept well with one Phanodorm from five-thirty A.M. to six-thirty P.M. At two P.M. pulse 78, blood pressure 118, gave him Eukodal and Eupaverin on account of stomach spasms, and injected intravenous glucose and intramuscular Homoseran (Homoseran administered to him for the first time). Checked his pharynx and throat: left in order, pharynx of normal coloration, right tonsil slightly inflamed (gargled too violently?). The Führer thinks he has had an infection in his right Eustachian tubes all along; incidentally, he says, his right nostril is bunged up. His voice is only barely perceptibly hoarse. The gargling with Neo-Pyocyanase has had excellent effect, he says, and I should keep him supplied with it at all times. Says that during the night before last he only got to sleep yesterday morning, but there was a dull throbbing right across his head and an uneasy feeling and a distinct lack of appetite for work. He mentions that Himmler also felt the same symptoms yesterday.

"I can say the same goes for myself," I said, "just as you described it. It comes from a kind of Föhn mood—it's an effect of the climate."

The Führer then stood up and showed me how thin he's become in the midriff. Under his ribs there was a deep pit, and as the Führer is very concerned to keep slim he was very pleased at having lost so much weight! I jogged his memory again about the need for getting away for eight or ten days.

He still had a few major decisions to take before then, he said; he had to make up his mind.

"Professor Blaschke has been waiting to give you dental treatment," I said. "He's been here since the day before yesterday.[9] Incidentally I recently gave him Homoseran too, and I also prescribed it for his wife, and it's had a very favorable effect on both."

When I reminded him about the X ray of the sinuses, he said he would not make up his mind until after five P.M.

[*Data card*: Still up at two A.M.!]

November 8, 1944

At half an hour past midnight I was suddenly sent for—the Führer has had a sudden spasm near the sternum with a violent accumulation of gas in his abdomen. From what he told me, the patient is facing the biggest decisions of his life at the moment and is suffering more and more nervous tension in consequence.[10] Intravenous shots of Eukodal and Eupaverin relieve the pains and the spasms only partially at first. When he asked me to give him another half syringeful, even if only intramuscularly, I sent for my bag and saw that I had only given him 0.01 of the Eukodal instead of 0.02. After injecting another 0.01 of the Eukodal intravenously and some more Eupaverin too (since I had previously used the 5 cc syringe as well, and had not injected the last two tenths on account of blood and air bubbles), an immediate cessation of the pains and cramps began.

The Führer thanked me profusely for this rapid aid. After retching several times, which brought up a lot of wind, he relaxed completely; the Führer was absolutely delighted and told me I would never know how much he had been upset by the recent intrigue against me.

"The idiots had never paused for a moment to think of the harm they would have been doing to *me*!" he said. "I would have found myself all of a sudden without a doctor—and these people ought to realize that you have saved my life several times in the eight years you have been with me. Look how I was before! Every single one of the doctors who was dragged in failed. Well, you will find, my dear doctor, that I know how to show my gratitude. If we both

[9] Hitler was treated by Blaschke at 6:45 P.M. according to Linge's log.
[10] Hitler had now provisionally fixed the date of his vital counteroffensive in the West.

get through this war intact, you will see how I am going to reward you in peacetime!"

I referred once again to the blamelessness of the anti-gas pills, at which the Führer said: "The stupid people were just looking for a pretext."

"My Führer," I said, "if a normal doctor had had you for treatment you would have been off the job for so long that the Reich would have gone to the dogs because of it. I have always *had* to resort to crash treatments with maximum dosages; I have *had* to go right to the limits of the permissible, even though I might be condemned by many of my colleagues for so doing. But I am the man with this responsibility, and I am prepared to take it, because if you ever had to take things easy for any length of time, then Germany would end up on the rocks."

"My dear doctor," he said, "I am pleased and happy that I have you." He took my hand in his as he said these words, squeezed it warmly, and fastened a long, grateful look on me.

"My Führer," I replied, "I do ask one favor of you: as far as medical instructions are concerned you must toe the line, because I have to take the responsibility and I really cannot be expected to if you will not do as you are told. For instance you ought to have got out of this bunker long ago and gone away for a few weeks, and you must still do so. It is so vital for you to get fresh air and sunlight, and a change of climate too."

"I'll move over to the big bunker tomorrow," he promised, "and I'll work in the big outside room."

"That's all well and good for the present, but it still can't take the place of a change of climate. I beg you to get away from here at least for eight or ten days, if you cannot make it longer than that."

"I'll try and manage it in the coming week. But at present I still have a number of the most momentous decisions to take."

"And while you are about it, my Führer, I must ask you to permit Professor Chaoul to make a complete X-ray and radiological examination of the gastrointestinal tract and the gall bladder in Berlin. X rays of the *heart* and lung could be made at the same time so as to complete the set. For years now I've been asking you for an X ray of the gastrointestinal tract, and my colleagues might try to make an issue of it that I have not done so.[11] I won't telephone

---

[11] They did. Both Hasselbach and Brandt commented on this in their postwar interrogations.

Chaoul about this, so that the news does not get around; but as soon as we get there [Berlin], I'll get a big X-ray machine and have it set up in the [Reich Chancery] bunker so that we can make the pictures there without attracting attention. I'd like to ask your permission for this."

"Yes," he said, "that would be the best way. Don't telephone, but wait until Berlin to discuss it."

Very cordially and still thanking me profusely for everything, and apologizing for having deprived me of some of my sleep, he took leave of me.

At two P.M. I saw him again: pulse 78, blood pressure 118 mm, heart quiet and keeping perfect time, but a slight degree of resistance palpable deep down in his upper abdomen and a minimal degree of glandular swelling is still evident deep down on the left of his neck, near the tonsils. Despite this, however, the Führer has asked that Eicken should not be sent for tomorrow and will not permit X rays of the area today, because, as he says, that's not going to make anything better; he finds most relief from the Neo-Pyocyanase I have prescribed for him, and asks me always to have a lot of it on hand for him.

There's a constant draft in the bunker room [at the Wolf's Lair], and I already asked the Führer yesterday to wear a woolly scarf, particularly in view of the ease with which he perspires; but he declared he could not stand them.

After that I showed him the letter H[einrich] Hoffmann had sent[12] and photocopies of the fecal analysis. As the latter did not clearly show the names of the hospital or the analyzing laboratory or doctors and there was no accompanying medical report, the Führer sent for Detective Superintendant Högl[13] and instructed him to investigate when Hoffmann was hospitalized, and which

[12] Heinrich Hoffmann, born 1885, had been Hitler's personal photographer since the twenties and had the lucrative monopoly in publishing official Party photographs; a Nazi Party member since 1924 (No. 59), Hoffmann had fallen foul of Martin Bormann, who had circulated rumors that Hoffmann had contracted an infectious disease, knowing that this would effectively bar access to Hitler's headquarters. He was rapidly given a clean bill of health, and Bormann, as usual, escaped unpunished. Hoffmann died in December 1957.

[13] Kriminalkommissar (Detective Superintendent) Högl was head of Hitler's personal security squad.

was the hospital, the doctors treating him, the diagnoses and the treatments, et cetera. The Führer is disposed to believe that Hoffmann is not in a hospital at all and that the doctor, probably a *** Brother, is not giving him any treatment, because of the lack of any accompanying letter.

November 9, 1944

At five-thirty A.M. The Führer's abdomen is distended, and he has some pain (more to the right of the sternum). The origin: a decision on certain steps that will later have the most powerful consequences and which is at present (see the first such attack several days ago[14]) causing him an enormous burden of worry which will be with him for several weeks yet. I injected him with intravenous shots of Eukodal and Eupaverin, which as always brought immediate relief from the pain and cramps.

The Führer is now in his new bunker (he made the move on the afternoon of November 8). The Führer's sleeping quarters and working quarters are 23 cubic meters larger than in the old bunker, and there are no drafts. In the mornings he works in a really big outside room that has large windows and a view of forests and meadows. The Führer told me how he had a premonition when he was leaving the Berghof before the 20th of July[15] that he would very shortly find himself in mortal danger. He said he also told E[va Braun] this when he said good-bye to her, and told somebody else as well and made his dispositions accordingly.[16]

After the injections he took four Boxberger pills and, a while later, some Karlsbad mineral water.

Saw him again at two P.M. *** Abdomen a bit resistant in depth near the liver. Injected intravenous glucose and intramuscular Homoseran. He asked me to send him over some Sympathol as this was the heart drug that agreed with him best. As for the Neo-Pyocyanase he said that foam built up when he shook the second bottle of it and it did not seem as effective as the first (perhaps because of [not?] having been stored in a cold area). Schaub was

[14] On November 8.
[15] He had left the Berghof on July 14, 1944.
[16] Hitler had also told his forebodings to the wives of Colonel Nicolaus von Below and Dr. Karl Brandt on the evening of July 13, as Frau Maria von Below told this author.

at once instructed to get me a refrigerator so I could keep sufficient supplies on hand. The Führer at last gave half-hearted approval for X rays to be taken of his gastroenteric region and gall bladder and of his heart and lungs if we make a stop in Berlin. But he was less enthusiastic about having the contents of his stomach investigated at the same time, and inquired whether Frau [Ruth] Krause could not come again to take some blood samples to check his blood sentimentation, blood serology, et cetera.

O N NOVEMBER 10, 1944, Morell had obtained a urinalysis which showed positive readings for urobilin and bilirubin, which he attributed to a transitory blockage of the flow from the liver and gall bladder.

November 10, 1944

The Führer did not send for me, and is said to have a bit of a hoarse voice.

November 11, 1944

His tea session last night is said to have gone on until four-thirty this morning.

Saw him from three-thirty to five P.M. He said he had slept very well and for a long time, until three-fifteen P.M., thanks to a Phanodorm tablet. He's looking very good and healthy, says the tremor has gone (probably as a result of the Homoseran treatment, while he says the present batch of Vitamultin-forte is not as effective as the previous one). I injected glucose intravenously (did not get in with the first jab as my hand was a bit unsteady as a result of the news I just received of my brother's death), and then gave him an intramuscular shot of Homoseran, Vitamultin-Calcium and Progynon-forte.

After I told him of my brother's death the Führer was very alarmed at the idea of my going to the west as there is a lot of danger there. I suggested that I might go by plane (he said that that was out of the question as there are always hordes of enemy fighter planes about); or by car (he said that I could not stand such a long road journey whatever I might say to the contrary); or by train (you could not rely on them much as their timetables are in chaos because of the air raids). He said he would have a word about all this with some gentlemen.

He asked me to arrange for Dr. Weber to come at once to make the injections. When I suggested Dr. Stumpfegger, he objected that he might not be so good at making injections, which I found hard to believe since the man is after all a surgeon.

After these attacks of his, I notice that his abdomen is always supple and palpable in depth, and that it can be probed into without any resistance; this leads one to assume that these are purely spastic conditions. However, as stated, X rays are absolutely necessary by way of confirmation.

MORELL'S BROTHER Adolf had died aged 61 of a brain embolism. Morell had got the news at noon, and left for Berlin that evening. Dr. Weber would arrive the next day at the Wolf's Lair, but Hitler evidently did not call for him until the thirteenth. From Weber's notes we obtain the following data.[17]

November 13, 1944 (Weber's notes)
On account of spasms *** intravenous injections of Eukodal and Eupaverin at five-thirty A.M. At nine-thirty A.M. intravenous injection of 0.01 Eukodal and 0.03 Eupaverin. At two-forty-five P.M. intravenous injection of twenty percent Glycovarin, and intra muscular of 10 cc Homoseran. At ten-thirty P.M. one Dolantin suppository. Palpation findings on November 13: slight meteorism, some tenderness in region of gall bladder and one finger's breadth below the xiphoid cartilage. Heart clinically in order. No palpable tumors.

November 14, 1944 (Weber's notes)
At one P.M. intramuscular injection of Vitamultin and Glyconorm. Gall bladder region slightly tender. Urinalysis: urobilin positive, otherwise no remarks, sedimentation also in order. Abdomen supple.

[17] Heinz Linge's register shows Dr. Weber calling on Hitler as follows: November 13, at 3:45 P.M. and 6:00 P.M.; November 14, at 1:45 A.M. and 1:00 P.M.; November 15, at 12:25 A.M., 2:10 A.M., 1:15 P.M. and 11:45 P.M.

November 15, 1944 (Weber's notes)

Abdomen no remarks. Intravenous shot of twenty percent Gly-covarin, intramuscular of 10 cc Homoseran.

Morell had arrived at his native Trais-Münzenberg at midday on the thirteenth, viewed his brother's remains, met his young nephew Karl-Heinz and spent the night at Schloss Camberg in the Taunus Mountains. The funeral followed on the next day. Morell recorded, "Noon, learned from Detective Schmidt of the death of Professor Becher. Sad, not so much because of the works we published together as that I was counting on him as my replacement here! B was a vegetarian, shunned nicotine and alcohol, a fine scientist, particularly on the gastrointestinal tract and bacterial flora (wrote books about them)." Evidently quoting Weber, Morell also noted on November 14: "Führer states that when he had his attack for the first time he was violently sick, but without any blood." He returned to Berlin from Hesse at midday on November 15, attended a simple family reunion at Schwanenwerder, where his wife sang a hymn, then left at six P.M. for the Wolf's Lair, by train.

November 16, 1944

I returned here at noon. I hear that there was widespread annoyance over the fact that I had gone, particularly among the military gentlemen. But the Führer had given me his consent, and as I assumed that there would be no attack in my absence, I set out on the journey, particularly since neither my sister nor my wife would be able to go to the funeral and the fourteen-year-old boy would then have stood at the graveside alone without even his mother.

At three-thirty P.M. I was with the Führer. The patient was unfriendly ***. When I again suggested he should go to Berlin for an X ray, the Führer became *very* irascible (more so, in fact, than he has ever been in the last eight years toward me).

According to Morell's other notes on this day, Hitler had said, "I'm not a silly schoolchild, I know precisely what I have to do." Hitler had looked very sickly, his face hollow, his attitude limp; but his pulse and blood pressure were both normal.

His voice was hoarse. When I again suggested von Eicken should visit him, he was in agreement. I injected intravenous glucose and intramuscular Vitamultin-forte, Glyconorm and Tonophosphan, but no more Homoseran as the course of five injections is over. * * *

November 17, 1944

Three-thirty P.M. Went with von Eicken to see the Führer and examine tonsils, throat, sinuses and pharynx.[18] Injected intravenous glucose and Cantan. The Führer had a long talk with von Eicken about the intrigue by Brandt[19] and Hasselbach against me and other things.

The Führer stayed up until four-fifteen A.M. with tea.

MORELL'S OTHER PAPERS describe Hitler as "lively" that day, while Morell was himself invited to dinner by Field Marshal Keitel until he was called for at one-thirty A.M. by Hitler. On this evening Morell began administering Gallestol once or twice daily to Hitler.

November 18, 1944

At five P.M. I went to the Karlshof field hospital with the Führer, von Eicken—who had stayed the night—and Stumpfegger. An X-ray picture showed his left maxillary sinus to be shadowed. Back at the Führer's bunker Eicken examined him, found divided tonsils, a small focus of bacteria on the right. Irrigated the left maxillary sinus, examined the larynx and discovered a small polyp (about 2 mm long) on his right vocal chord. The Führer refused any fortifying injections for today, saying I really must go home and rest (I had gone pale once or twice—what with my great fatigue, renal disorder and *heart!*).

[18] Eicken would note in his papers, *"November 16–18:* Wolf's Lair. Anterior part of vocal chords cannot be seen. Ordered Reichert spatula to be sent by courier from Berlin. *November 18:* Hoarseness has increased. X ray shows distinct shadowing of left maxillary sinus. A small polyp on left vocal chord." Morell, of course, had not detected this polyp, not having the right spatula.

[19] Linge noted a visit by Brandt to Hitler at 7:25 P.M. on the next evening.

November 19, 1944

Tea until four A.M. this morning, and a lively conversation.

Saw the Führer again at three P.M. looking far better than yesterday and apparently completely well though the voice is rough. *** Doesn't want an injection at present. We talked about anti-gas pills and strychnine.

November 20, 1944

[Hitler] had tea until four this morning, talked well and ate well too. Was wakened at eleven A.M.

IN A DATA CARD Morell noted this day that he gave Hitler the usual injections of 20 cc of glucose, Testoviron, Vitamultin-forte, liver extract, and Glyconorm, then "Departure for Berlin."

Reluctantly, Hitler had decided to leave East Prussia and the Wolf's Lair for Berlin, persuading himself it would only be for a minor operation to remove this polyp from his throat. But his fears could not be easily concealed—he might lose his voice for weeks or even months; and the growth might turn out to be cancerous.

The loss of voice worried him more almost than the fear of cancer now. It was his only asset. Stenographer Dr. Ewald Reynitz would afterward recall, "The most striking feature . . . was how Hitler actually dominated everybody around him not by bullying but simply talking, talking and talking. There was never such a thing as might be called discussions, only monologue after monologue. . . . Göring sometimes would *start* contradicting but his arguments were mostly so poor that Hitler simply waved them aside. Jodl was the only one who in fact spoke up."

And Reynitz's colleague Thöt noted in his secret diary, "On the afternoon of this day the Führer left the Wolf's Lair and arrived at Berlin's Grunewald Station at five-thirty A.M. on November 21. Sworn to secrecy!" The secretaries who sat with him in the train had never seen Hitler so grim. "His voice scarcely rose above a whisper," wrote Frau Junge. "His eyes remained rooted to his plate or gazed distantly at a spot on the white tablecloth." The Red Army was pouring into East Prussia. Refugees were streaming westward and now he was heading westward too. But that millet-seed-size polyp would have to be cut out. Hitler had confidence in von Eicken, but he had his worries too. "He has a heavy responsibility," he told the secretaries. "But he is the only man who can do it. I may end up losing my voice."

November 21, 1944

Berlin. At six P.M. von Eicken, with Sister Maria in attendance, irrigated left maxillary sinus: a thick blockage caused by secretion; treated the nose and tonsils too.[20] It would appear in general that any major worries or burdens coupled with great upsets immediately result in meteorism and a violent buildup of gas in his stomach; and of late there has been tenderness in the area of the gall bladder, liver and deep down beneath the left costal arch extending as far as the flexura lienalis. After the spasms everything becomes supple again.—Owing to the colossal upsets since the 20th of July and the continual aggravations, frequent attacks have been brought on (see my Eukodal and Eupaverin injections).

November 22, 1944

At eleven-thirty A.M. the Führer is feeling fine; his stomach is no longer distended, has no discomfort. Injected 0.01 morphine, and 0.0001 atropine subcutaneously. At twelve-thirty P.M. von Eicken operated on the polyp, with Dr. Stumpfegger holding the [surgical instrument] tray. Sister Maria assisted. The polyp was as big as a linseed. Was taken to his bed in the bunker.[21] I went there, ran into Miss E, his pulse was 66 and full. At nine P.M. I was fetched from my dinner table to see the Führer immediately, who asked if he was permitted to have some oatmeal gruel. I said yes. At ten P.M. I was to come at once; he had spat up some blood; von

[20] See too von Eicken's notes for November 21, 1944: "Left maxillary sinus, balls of secretion." And he wrote to Morell that day, "We might carry out the operation this same day. A prerequisite would be that he has his last nutrition intake four hours before. Then half an hour before we operate, a dose of 0.01 morphine (or 1 cg subcutaneously).—Von Eicken."

[21] Linge recorded that Hitler was "in private" from 1:00 P.M. to 8:35 P.M. when Morell was sent for. And Eicken's own succinct record of the feared operation was this: "November 22: after one milligram of morphine the polyp was excised, with the use of a Reichert spatula (in Reich Chancery)."

Eicken prescribed 10 cc Sangostop and twenty drops of codeine, and Sister Maria had seen to these herself. The bleeding is of no significance as it is only slight. I called on the Führer altogether four times during the evening, and gave him two Optalidons to help him get to sleep. Ran into E. again as I was leaving. At noon while standing and in the evening his blood pressure was 120. Checked patient's abdomen while lying in bed: supple all around with no resistance and no tenderness.

November 23, 1944

Führer had me asked about permission to eat. I checked with von Eicken, who said he can eat anything he wants and as much as he likes. When I visited him [at noon] he said he was feeling very well. *** Discussed Professor Chaoul and those X rays and again emphasized the need. Professor Blaschke worked on one dental cavity. Meanwhile [one-thirty-five P.M.] von Eicken had come and pronounced himself very pleased. Dr. Stumpfegger was also present. The Führer is free of any kind of discomfort. Toward evening the Führer went upstairs [from the bunker] and paid a visit to the secretaries. He ate well. Later that evening I had him asked, but the Führer did not send for me.

November 24, 1944

One-thirty P.M. *** He had only slept two hours. I considered that the injections would not be necessary, but the Führer said he would like some so as to get strong and well quicker; so I injected 20 cc of twenty percent glucose solution intravenously and Glyconorm and liver extract intramuscularly.

At six P.M. von Eicken saw him.[22] Second irrigation of maxillary sinus, blow-clean of tonsils and cauterization with five percent silver nitrate. During the afternoon the Führer went for a short stroll in the Chancery garden. Ate well.

November 25, 1944

The Führer has an excellent appetite, is feeling fine and went for an hour's stroll by himself in the garden. Said it was not necessary for me to come over today.

---

[22] Eicken wrote simply, "Left maxillary sinus: negative."

THERE WAS one anomaly in his blood checkup at this time. While the blood sugar analysis (Seiffert's Test) carried out by Morell's medical assistant Frau Ruth Krause on November 24 yielded a value of 80 mg percent (as compared with a normal value of 90 to 120 mg percent), the blood sedimentation rate determined by the Westergreen method turned out to be greatly increased—33 millimeters per hour against a normal rate of ten. Morell speculated guiltily on the possible cause, and noted his own comment on the analysis: "N.B.: On November 9 I ended a course of five Homoseran injections." As a comparison he added, "On May 11, 1943, the blood sedimentation average rate was 2.5 millimeters." It remained a mystery.

On November 26, Morell had a fecal sample analyzed for blood traces and for the digestion of fat and starch; and he ordered a full analysis of a urine sample for diastase and bilirubin, but all these tests produced normal results.

November 26, 1944

At twelve-thirty P.M. sent for Frau Krause, my former medical technical assistant at the practice, to perform certain tasks on the Führer. [*Data card*: Frau Krause and I took blood samples.]

[One-fifteen P.M.] we started by taking samples for a blood count and tests on blood sugar, blood sedimentation and hemoglobin content. I then drew off further samples (of thirty and fifteen cc) using a 5 cc syringe, to check the levels of calcium, diastase, bilirubin, bile acids, cholesterol, and we also obtained urine and fecal samples for the Schmidt-Burbach Institute to analyze for fat and blood content. *** The Führer had held his war conference until five A.M. this morning.

At six P.M. von Eicken telephoned that Professor Rössle's histological examination of the excised polyp had been very satisfactory.[23] At seven P.M. Professor von Eicken was here and removed

---

[23] Professor Rössle of the Pathological Institute of Berlin University had written to Eicken on November 25: "The operation specimen which you personally brought to me on November 22, 1944, after removal from the larynx, was a nodule the size of a millet seed and of virtually smooth surface. *** It was prepared in the usual manner and a series of sections mounted on slides. *** Diagnosis: taken as a whole, it presents the typical picture of a so-called singer's nodule in an early stage. Verdict: this was certainly not a genuine tumor, but a displacement and thickening of the surface of the mucous membrane resulting from the inflammation and aggravation of the vocal chord."

two blockages of secretion from both the right and the left tonsils.[24] He attributes the dramatic rise in blood sedimentation rate to the tonsillitis. [*Data card*: blood sedimentation rate 33—maxillary sinuses, tonsils and trachea in inflamed condition.] The nasal cavities were cauterized with 5 percent silver nitrate solution. Diagnosis: an early stage in the formation of a so-called singer's nodule [on the vocal cord]. Verdict: certainly not a tumor. *** Frau Krause and Dr. Weber informed the Führer of these diagnoses. Dr. Stumpfegger was present while Eicken was treating the Führer.

November 27, 1944

Twelve-thirty P.M. Word is that the Führer ate *very* heartily yesterday. But he slept only two hours because of interruptions (doors banging, a clamor in the kitchen, air raid, et cetera). From today there are to be sentries down in the bunker to ensure he gets his peace and quiet. Having been awake and working so long there is some redness of the eyes. Because he has a lot of strenuous work ahead of him the Führer wants his injections: I gave him 20 cc of twenty percent glucose solution, and Vitamultin-forte and liver extract. Palpated his abdomen while in standing position: supple, and he said he was not suffering the slightest problems. He credits the Gallestol with this. His voice is loud and clear and carries well.

Three-thirty P.M. Diagnostic results of the Schmidt-Burbach Institute.[25]

November 28, 1944

Two P.M. The Führer had gone for an hour's stiff walk with General Bodenschatz. Voice is good and precise; appetite healthy. *** Told him the findings of the Schmidt-Burbach Institute (everything normal). I did not treat him. Had a talk with Reichsleiter Bormann and in the evening with Rattenhuber.

[24] Eicken noted, "*November 26*: injury to right vocal chord almost healed; blow-cleaned tonsils, applied silver nitrate to pharynx and nose. Voice good. Handed over Rössle's diagnosis."

[25] According to Morell's data card on Hitler, Schmidt-Burbach assessed the diastase in the blood at 16 units, urine the same, residual nitrogen at 22 mg percent, cholesterol at 182 mg percent (slightly above the normal range of 160–180), calcium at 9.7 mg percent, bilirubin negative (direct) and less than 0.3 mg percent (indirect), "—that is, everything normal."

November 29, 1944

He went to sleep around six A.M. Took a stroll for three quarters of an hour this afternoon. Appetite very good. At seven P.M. Eicken came to see him (irrigated the maxillary sinuses, blow-cleaned the tonsils and cauterization with silver nitrate). Some secretion. I did not undertake any treatment of him today.

November 30, 1944

One-thirty P.M. I called to ask if I should come and see him or not. "No, you don't need to come." No treatment undertaken.

December 1, 1944

Führer took leave of his staff at 4:30 this morning, was wakened at eleven-thirty A.M. Had had a *huge* appetite yesterday and gone for an hour's walk. Everybody said he was bursting with energy.

One P.M. I went over to the Führer, injected 20 cc glucose solution intravenously plus Vitamultin-forte and liver extract intramuscularly. Says he would like a Homoseran injection, as that causes his trembling to go away. I always do a course of five injections (5 cc) separated by intervals. He has had really major spasms after violent emotional upsets—the 1924 trial (matter of life and death); the 1929 due date on the loan (to *Völkischer Beobachter* and Eher Verlag), the 1935/36 crisis of military unreliability.[26] Added to this was the dysbacteria that the spasms probably generated. Then again in 1943 before his meeting with the Duce at Feltre [on July 18, 1943] at which time he already had a foreboding, or even foreknowledge, of the forthcoming betrayal by the Italian army; and in 1944 after the Bomb Plot.

December 2, 1944

The Führer was in conference until five-thirty this morning. Was awakened at 12 noon, is in good health and full of energy, they say. He now goes for an hour's stroll every day. No treatment today!

[26] During 1935 a dangerous dispute had smoldered between the Party, the SS and the Wehrmacht; and during the spring of 1936 the military leadership had, in Hitler's view, lost its nerve over his plan to remilitarize the German Rhineland.

MORELL knew that in the coming weeks the strain on his chief would reach its peak. For Hitler to succumb to a heart attack in the middle of his coming desperate counteroffensive in the west might make the difference between final defeat and victory. On December 2, 1944, Morell composed a concerned letter to the cardiologist Professor Weber and sent it to Bad Nauheim by courier. It is quoted at length below because it throws light on Morell's treatments and intentions:

"I have several times already submitted to you the electro-cardiograms of a foreign ministry gentleman," wrote Morell, alluding to the secret cover he had concocted for his patient Adolf Hitler, "asking for your opinion. These produced the diagnosis of coronary sclerosis. Unfortunately the patient was never able to lay his work aside but has been subject to constant burdens, particularly in recent times, and to major upsets and irritations. These last years he never went to bed before four or five A.M. as his final conferences and labors were never finished before then. He had become a stranger to the idea of going for walks, as he became accustomed to taking only fifteen minutes' fresh air for a day for months on end, spending the rest of his time without natural light in bunkers! Nevertheless I managed by injecting a lot of 20 percent glucose—in intra-venous shots of 10 cc at a time—often for months on end, and by adding iodine from time to time (in the form of Septoiod), to ward off an even more rapid progression of the coronary sclerosis. To fortify him further I frequently administered Vitamultin-Calcium (which contains vitamins C and B$_1$, nico-tinamide and calcium, et cetera), Glyconorm (the extract of cardiac muscles, suprarenal gland cortex, liver and pancreas) and from time to time liver extract too. The patient lives a vege-tarian existence without nicotine and alcohol, with restricted liquid intake. Iodine-Calcium-Diuretin was not administered, as his stomach is hypersensitive and reacts violently with spasms."

Morell continued, "So far there have been no anginal com-plaints. I would be very grateful to you for any opinion and suggestions for further treatment, if you consider a change is called for. I did recommend massage, but this was not per-mitted."

Finally he also included some of his own electrocardio-grams. His own heart was causing him concern, and the symptoms of a coronary insufficiency had become more marked since 1941. As he told Weber, he had had his first attack of angina pectoris two years earlier, after a miserable airplane flight. He had taken electrocardiograms of himself on July 28 and again on October 9, 1944, and these appeared to show some improvement. He had been taking Cardiazol and Iodine-Calcium-Diuretin for several weeks. "The QRS opening is gradually enlarging," Morell explained, "and due to the constant responsibility and several hateful intrigues against me I have begun feeling constantly a little depressed. I perspire at night and get breathless easily. Also the edemas on my lower legs have become more pronounced, so I have been getting massages every few days now. Altitudes of 800 to 1,200 meters do not agree with me at all, and that goes for air that is low in oxygen too. I have had to have a series of Glucadenose injections more than once already, and things go better after that; but as my burdens increase so it becomes evident that I am not getting permanently better. There are unfortunately certain reasons why I cannot take time off."

Weber sent his reply on December 4, 1944, by the same courier. "I am replying to your courteous letter from my cellar," he wrote, "while hordes of enemy bombers thunder overhead." There was little he could recommend for Morell's own heart condition. "I can well understand," he wrote, "that your present way of life is not actually good for your coronary arteries. But all of us are wishing that in the foreseeable future there may be a change for the better which will also have a favorable effect on your health. May I suggest adopting a philosophical attitude toward all the petty intrigues that are bound to occur, given the position that you occupy." He suggested that Morell should try to take one day off a week and should meanwhile continue to take Iodine-Calcium-Diuretin while avoiding any kind of sudden muscular exertion such as lifting a heavy object.

As for the electrocardiograms of "Patient A" dated August 1941, May 1943 and September 1944, Weber repeated his earlier diagnosis. "There is a slowly progressive symptom of left coronary insufficiency," he reported, "and probably also a left retardation." He repeated his earlier recommendation too —Hitler should try to take complete days off, and eat a low salt diet. Above all, the vegetarian nutrition must avoid resulting in a shortage of albumen. "If Iodine-Calcium-Diuretin is not compatible with this patient then please try administering Deriphyllin, one or two tablets to be taken daily. Of course there is no drug that can make up for the harm done by an unhealthy way of life, but that is just another cost of this war."

December 3, 1944

Sent for at two P.M., injected [10 cc of twenty percent] glucose intravenously and 10 cc of Homoseran intramuscularly. In good health. Had a pea soup hotpot yesterday (with two Luizyms and two Glyconorms), and it went down well.

December 4, 1944

Führer got up at eleven A.M., is in good health. The Hungarians are here.[27] Gave no treatment.

December 5, 1944

He worked until seven this morning. At eleven A.M. there was an air raid alarm. Went over at one P.M., injected Homoseran intramuscularly. Courier brought the opinion of Professor Weber, of Bad Nauheim, on the electrocardiograms. [He recommends] one tablet of Deriphyllin twice daily, and low-salt diet; interpolation of complete rest days; a nutrition not too low in albumen, and occasional checks on his daytime weight to assess his water balance.

December 6, 1944

Führer sent for me at twelve-thirty. His blood sedimentation rate is now 38 millimeters per hour.[28] Injected 20 cc of twenty percent glucose intravenously. He asked me to send for Professor Löhlein to see to his left eye. Says that there's no real need for [radiologist] Chaoul at present—on which score I contradict him; but the Führer says that since he is now completely free of complaints and his appetite is good, such an X-ray examination would by wholly superfluous.

[27] The Hungarian prime minister Ferenc Szálasi visited Hitler, who persuaded him of the need to defend Budapest against the Soviet onslaught.
[28] There is a small note on Morell's headed notepaper in his files: "December 6, 1944. Blood sedimentation after one hour 38, after two hours 71, after 24 hours 116. The day before, I injected Homoseran (a placenta drug); possibly test its effect on sedimentation rate by test on animals."

A telephone inquiry establishes that Professor Löhlein is at present away and will be back at the end of the week. The Führer declares that his illness was the result of eleven years of anger at "the generals of the 20th of July."

In the evening I telephoned Dr. Mulli and commissioned him to test on rabbits whether injections of Homoseran might cause an acceleration of blood sedimentation, as Homoseran is manufactured from placenta and pregnancy accelerates sedimentation too. At the end of May 1943 the blood sedimentation rate was right down to 2.5 millimeters. Before the visit to the Duce at Feltre around July 20, 1943, there was a massive attack that began in the Wolf's Lair and continued the next day down at the Berghof. The next attack was a big one, the worst of the lot, after a showdown with the Luftwaffe on or about September 28, 1944, preceded by a number of trembling fits beginning with July 20, 1944.

December 8, 1944

Summoned by Arndt at six-fifteen this morning. He said the Führer had had a lettuce salad for lunch yesterday without any immediate subsequent problems. That was noon. For supper he had had a green salad. He had immediately realized that it disagreed with him. Three hours later he got pains at the same spot as before (the right upper abdomen), and three hours later still these were so bad that (at six A.M.) he had me sent for. Yesterday afternoon he had had a major row (caused by the situation in the air war and on the ground—a generaloberst who had disobeyed an order).

Findings: gall bladder region resistant and some tenderness, but less than on other occasions. The spasm is more to the left (toward the right lobe of the liver), becoming weaker; the pyloric region is supple and without complaints. Injected intravenous Eukodal and Eupaverin. Spasm at once began to go gradually away. Right now he claims he's facing the worst burdens of his entire life. His nerves are taking a beating from coming events and the constant terror air raids on German cities. Result is it only takes the tiniest thing to trigger off these spasms. He says he's quite clear in his own mind there's nothing objectively wrong with his gastrointestinal tract because he's never had blood in his stools or vomit. He has a bowel movement once a day, but it is of normal coloration and neither weak nor very hard.

I left at seven-fifteen A.M. after I had satisfied myself that the injections were working. The Führer said I ought to go downstairs very slowly so I did not suffer heart troubles. Before that we had spoken about the little sleep he is getting as he usually works right through to seven A.M. I thought it vital for him to change this. But he said there is no other way at the moment.

Visited him again at seven this evening. He said everything was okay again, and the attack of cramps had passed by. *** His left leg has stopped trembling now, but his left arm and left hand have started to shake. Blood pressure 136, abdomen supple, gall bladder region a bit resistant in depth and slight tenderness.

I told him that Dr. Stumpfegger was waiting outside to inquire about his condition; could he come in and might he also palpate the Führer, so that *he* could see for himself how supple the abdomen was and how good everything looked. But the Führer said it was enough for me to confirm all that, and he did not want other people poking around. I replied that I would have preferred to get a second opinion on his condition from another doctor.

When I asked the Führer what medicines he is taking now, so that I can enter them up, he listed: one tablespoon of Gallestol two or three times daily (today he only had two), some Chineurin a couple of days ago when he was frightened of catching a cold, and yesterday ten drops of Cardiazol solution twice running. As for meals he is taking oatmeal gruel (I added that he can have that twice a day), and he is having the heat treatment advised every hour (with heating pads).

I asked if I might call in once more this evening to see him.

"If I'm feeling bad I'll send for you soon enough," declared the Führer. "But there's no need otherwise."

"Can Dr. Stumpfegger come in now?"

"Yes."

"Should I stay for that?"

"No, I'd like to speak to him alone for once."

I then took leave of him. I might note that during the night of December 7–8 there was a sudden drop in the barometer, and the result was that for an hour and a half I had such heart pains that I had to walk around the room for hour after hour. These atmospheric conditions must have affected the Führer too. ***

December 9, 1944

Eleven A.M. The Führer has slept altogether *eleven* hours (five plus six) and feels very well and looks good too. He informs me that his abdomen is completely supple, which I find confirmed by my own examination. As I reach the gall bladder region he says I should press deep as there's not even any swelling there now and there is only a small degree of irritation deep down; and it is true!

I said, "This condition ought to be seen by certain gentlemen who claim that you are being badly treated and that the diagnoses are all wrong, and who keep prophesying doom as a result."

I had planned to lay off the injections for a while, but at his request—on account of the forthcoming great exertions[29]—I gave him 10 cc of intravenous glucose and 10 cc of intramuscular Homoseran.

Professor von Eicken has been reminding me every day, and he was due to come finally this evening, but this has been postponed again. Professor Löhlein has been noted down for Sunday [December 10]. The Führer only went for forty-five minutes' walk. Unfortunately quite a big war conference was held.

December 10, 1944

I was summoned at four-thirty this morning by Arndt saying the Führer has his spasms again. Injected intravenous Eukodal and Eupaverin.—Checkup showed gall bladder region resistant, but during my examination it softened up. Said these are the most dramatic days of his entire life—"We have *got* to win a great victory!"

At eleven-thirty A.M. The Führer still has spasms and has not slept a wink, on top of which he is permanently in conferences which he cannot avoid. Our departure [for the West] is dependent on a few vital pieces of information we are expecting—it may be postponed until tomorrow. Impossible to administer major injections in his train as he must be wide awake when he detrains, but in his view it is vital that I should make one more big intravenous injection. I gave him an intramuscular shot of Eupaverin.

At one-thirty von Eicken saw him. Irrigation of right tonsil yields three blockages of secretion, otherwise everything is well.[30]

[29] The Ardennes counteroffensive.
[30] Eicken noted only, "*December 9*: final checkup."

"Dr. Giesing ought to have detected that polyp," said the Führer. Von Eicken was rather embarrassed and told an anecdote about a professor who ministered to Kaiser Wilhelm II[31] and only partially excised a polyp. It was not until Professor Spiess of Frankfurt am Main saw him—he had to provide phonetic aftercare—that the remaining portion was found and excised.

Five P.M. Our train left Berlin's Sonnenwald railroad station. He still had some spasms in the train, but they were only slight. Gave him (one) Spasmopurin suppository to use, and this brought him relief despite the lengthy rail journey.

December 11, 1944

At 2:42 this morning we arrived at a railroad station on the Werra and transferred to cars for the journey onward to the Eagle's Nest.[32]

[31] He evidently meant Kaiser Friedrich III.
[32] The Führer's headquarters adopted for this final great counteroffensive in the West. It was near Frankfurt.

The Battle of the Bulge

THE HOURLY RECORDS show that during these, the final months in Hitler's career, the doctors were increasingly frequent visitors. Morell of course attended him almost every day, sometimes two or three times a day. Stumpfegger, clad in the elegant gray uniform of the SS, Professor von Eicken and Morell's own deputy Richard Weber also often called. Increasingly, Morell was sent for around six A.M.—proof of Hitler's growing insomnia.

His convoy of cars reached the Eagle's Nest at six-thirty A.M. on December 11, 1944. He seemed well, but in his diary Morell noted that Hitler's urine had seemed ominously dark the day before ("beer brown"), so he asked him to provide a sample the next day. Hitler had not exaggerated in calling these the most dramatic days of his life. It was his last chance of victory.

At five-thirty-five A.M. on December 16, his carefully husbanded reserves tore off their cover and fell upon the unsuspecting American lines. Hitler's aim was to breach the enemy front and head straight for Antwerp; he would Dunkirk the British for a second time, and the Americans would get the blame. In his diary that day, shorthand writer Karl Thöt depicts the euphoria at the Eagle's Nest. "When Reynitz and I went over to the war conference at three P.M., an impressive number of German fighter planes passed overhead and Major Büchs, evidently recovering at this instant from the perpetual inferiority of our air force, turned to everybody present and declaimed with a glance skyward, 'Now let me hear one of you say any-

thing against the German air force!' . . . As we approached the
conference room we saw that the Führer was already present,
contrary to his custom. We could read only too clearly in his
expression how engrossed he was in the first favorable news
about our offensive."

It seems significant that as soon as the offensive had begun,
and was apparently running well, Hitler scarcely sent for his
doctor, Morell.

December 11, 1944

We arrived at the Eagle's Nest in the Taunus Mountains at
six-thirty A.M. When I inquired I received the information that the
Führer is fine.

At eleven-thirty A.M. Führer free of complaints but says his
urine was brown as beer yesterday and today. Whites of his eyes
inconclusive but facial skin manifests a scarcely perceptible yellowish hue. He must take a tablespoon of Gallestol three times
daily, apply warmth, and follow his diet strictly. Invited to evening
tea with him from eight to eleven. Before that the Führer had a
conference with about forty or fifty generals, lasting many hours.
He is said to have been very alert and lively, inspiring and com-
pelling.[1]

After the three-hour conference he became, according to Fegelein, rather tired. When tea began at eight P.M., however, he
became an excellent conversationalist for the rest of the evening,
alert and in a particularly good humor. As I left him I inquired
once more how he felt. "No complaints at all."

December 12, 1944

The Führer turned in at four this morning and was wakened
at eleven. No problems, said there was no need for me to come
over.—I asked for a urine sample to be brought to me. Findings:
albumen, opalescent, sugar Ø, bilirubin 1+, urobilinogen normal,
urobilin Ø; sedimentation: 4–6 erythrocytes, 3–5 leukocytes, a lot
of mucus and urates in the whole sample. No treatment.

---

[1] A shorthand text of Hitler's famous speech to his commanding generals
on the western front, inspiring them to this one final exertion, was published
by Helmut Heiber in *Hitler's Lagebesprechungen* (page 713). The speech
began at 5:40 P.M.

December 13, 1944

Saw him at 12:45 P.M., injected 20 cc glucose intravenously. He had slept six hours, was feeling well.

THE ENTRY in Hitler's data card this day adds, "The elevation here is 240 meters above sea level, like Linz on the Danube"— which had been Hitler's home town. From the valet's log we see that Morell was a frequent guest at Hitler's nocturnal tea parties, a sign that he was again high in the Führer's favor. For example, on December 13, 1944, we find Heinz Linge recording: "One P.M.: Professor Morell. . . . Eight P.M. dinner with Frau Christian, Miss Schroeder, Miss Manziarly, Professor Morell."

December 14, 1944

One P.M. The Führer has slept well and is in really good health. I went for over an hour's walk with the Führer in the tempting woods and valleys along with his adjutant [Albert] Bormann and Dr. Stumpfegger. The Führer got his Alsatian Blondi to carry a wooden exercise block. No treatment!

December 15, 1944

Führer in good health, is always of excellent appetite. No treatment.

December 16, 1944

At five-thirty this morning the great offensive began! Visited the Führer at twelve-thirty P.M.; he is very alert and lively, but he got no sleep because of the coming offensive. Blood pressure 147–153 mm, varying by the hour, and there is a permanent tremor in his left hand. [*Data card* adds: Great emotional crisis because of the offensive.] *** Says his abdomen is completely free of pain so there is no need whatever for me to examine it. On account of the coming mental strain I injected 20 cc of intravenous glucose and an intramuscular shot of Vitamultin-forte and Hamma liver. Immediately afterward [at one P.M.] the Führer had a dental treatment from Professor Dr. Blaschke with Frau Hensing[2] as assistant.

[2] Probably Frau Käthe Häusermann, Blaschke's assistant, who now lives in Düsseldorf.

December 17, 1944

Tea lasted until four this morning; the Führer was wakened at eleven. The offensive is making slow but sure headway. No treatment!

December 18, 1944

Führer very well. No treatment!

December 19, 1944

Twelve-fifteen P.M. Führer in good health. Injected 20 cc intravenous glucose solution, plus Vitamultin-forte, liver and ***[3] at his request because of the overload of work at present. He goes for over an hour's walk every day now. [*Data card*: Appetite remains very good.]

December 20, 1944

No treatment!

December 21, 1944

No treatment!

December 22, 1944

One P.M. The Führer is feeling well. Injected 20 cc intravenous glucose plus intramuscular Vitamultin-forte and liver extract. Pulse 72, blood pressure 145 mm. Without the slightest complaints still, and is sleeping adequately without sedatives. His appetite is good.

December 23, 1944

No treatment!

December 24, 1944

No treatment!

December 25, 1944

Christmas Day. *Blood pressure now 151*. Injected 20 cc intravenous glucose plus intramuscular Vitamultin-forte and liver. Is feeling well but says there is a growing tremor in his right hand ([deteriorating] situation in Hungary!).

---

[3] One word illegible, "Per——," but not the narcotic Pervitin.

THE MILITARY PROBLEMS now came thick and fast. As the weather cleared, the Allied air forces were able to throw in their full weight against Hitler's offensive. Shorthand writer Thöt observed how the war conferences now dragged on through the night until the early hours on December 24, 25 and 26, and complained in his diary about the hours of shorthand record that had resulted: "There is a huge amount of work—nine and three-quarter hours of shorthand! On Christmas Eve I did not get to bed until two-thirty A.M., on Christmas Day it lasted until three A.M. and on the next day it was four-thirty A.M. before I turned in." Given this work burden, it was unlikely that Hitler's fine health would hold.

December 30, 1944

Three P.M. For two days he has had a queasy stomach with gaseous buildup allegedly resulting from a green pea soup he had, but in my view it comes from nervousness over what lies ahead: composing a speech and delivering it, and secondly, evidently some major military event. At his request I had summoned von Eicken from Berlin to give his larynx a going-over; during the afternoon von Eicken checked larynx, tonsils, left maxillary sinus and nasal cavities and found them in order.[4] To me the right tonsil and the mucous membranes in the nose on the right seemed to be inflamed. Swabbing and irrigating the left maxillary sinus yielded a clear secretion. The larynx has healed well, but the patient feels there are minor irritations there.

Following this I gave him intravenously 20 cc of glucose and intramuscular shots of liver, Vitamultin-forte and Progynon B Oleosum forte. Tremor in his left hand very pronounced. He asked me to return at midnight to check his blood pressure before the speech and possibly to measure out a dose of liquid Cardiazol.

---

[4] Linge logged on December 30, 1944: "Woke him at 12:00 noon. . . . 3:00 P.M. Professor von Eicken, Professor Morell, Obersturmbannführer Stumpfegger." And during the night that followed, "12:10 A.M. speech. 1:15 A.M. war conference; 2:00 A.M. tea; 4:45 A.M. Professor Morell; 5:00 A.M. bed." Hitler's speech was the nationwide New Year's Day speech being pre-recorded for broadcast twenty-four hours later. Professor von Eicken noted only: "Further examination in Führer's headquarters." He never saw Hitler again.

December 31, 1944

At midnight I checked his blood pressure—*154* mm, in other words heightened (on account of the slight spasms), so I advised him against taking any Cardiazol. After that he delivered his New Year's Day speech, then checked the transmission quality, after which we sat up for tea until five A.M. [*Data card*: voice good.] At five A.M. I injected him with intravenous Eukodal and Eupaverin. He went to bed in the bunker because his morning sleep is now disturbed by enemy planes.

At eleven-fifteen P.M.: the Führer has calmed down almost completely. The trembling of his left arm and the tremor in the hand are only very slight now. At eleven P.M. this evening a second major offensive began on the western front.

THIS NEW OFFENSIVE, code-named North Wind, was opened by a mighty strike of the entire available Luftwaffe force against the Allied air power: 1,035 fighter aircraft and fighter bombers struck at the forward Allied airfields as the new year, 1945, dawned. But the Allies had foreknowledge from codebreaking. This attack misfired, and the offensive was not the strategic success that Hitler had hoped.

1945:

The Final Months

A T THE END Hitler was a physical wreck. "The rot had set in on the 20th of July," wrote Captain Heinz Assmann, "and it was made only worse by his illness of September 1944 and by the questionable treatments and methods of Dr. Morell." Stalingrad, the retreat in Russia, the loss of North Africa and the Mediterranean, the military collapse in Normandy, the events of the 20th of July, Hitler's growing mistrust and now finally the realization that his offensive in the Ardennes was failing —the chain of circumstances was one unbroken litany of catastrophe, and this was bound to have an annihilating effect both on Hitler's body and on his soul. As Assmann would write, "Upon a man who believed with unparalleled fanaticism in his own mission and in Final Victory, the gradually dawning realization of the inevitable defeat lying before us must have had devastating effect."

January 2, 1945

One-fifteen P.M. The Führer is feeling well if one discounts the tension about the offensive that is under way. He asks me if we can eliminate the tremor from his left hand; I said that he would have to take sedatives and tranquilizers, but that these could not be used as he has to keep his wits constantly about him and these drugs would be inhibitory. Electric therapy might have some effect, but not much. Gave him 20 cc of glucose intravenously.

January 5, 1945

One P.M. The Führer would like to have glucose injections because of the strain of these days—lots of conferences, with Dr.

Goebbels yesterday, then Speer, Saur, Ganzenmüller,[1] et cetera. On account of the palpitation of the left arm I gave him 10 cc of twenty percent Calcium Sandoz intravenously, followed by 10 cc of glucose intravenously, and intramuscular injections of liver and Vitamultin-forte.

January 7, 1945

One-thirty P.M. Injected twenty percent Calcium Sandoz intravenously and intravenous glucose.

January 10, 1945

One-thirty P.M. Twenty percent Calcium Sandoz and intravenous glucose and intramuscular Vitamultin-forte and liver. He's feeling good, but his hands tremble. Recently when we had late night tea he mentioned to Frau Christian and Miss Schroeder that he had had his violent spasms for the first time in 1929.

BY JANUARY 10, 1945, deep snow lay around Hitler's headquarters, and the thermometer had dropped to minus six Centigrade. It was a beautiful scene, but not the kind that agreed with Hitler. Two days later, on January 12, the Soviet winter offensive began from the Red Army's bridgehead at Baranov on the Vistula. Hitler had to take the fateful decision to abandon his thrust in the West and to return to the Reich Chancery in Berlin, for the last battle to be fought there. In the following weeks Poland was finally overrun by the Russians, and much German territory too: East Prussia was lost, and Upper Silesia; the river Oder became the new front line, just east of Berlin. Thöt, the shorthand writer, commented grimly in his diary, "We've got to summon up every scrap of nerve we now have, if we are not to succumb to despair."

January 12, 1945

After our nighttime tea party ended at five A.M. I asked him how he was feeling. The Führer knocked on wood three times and said: "Very good!"

---

[1] State Secretary Alfred Ganzenmüller, transport chief.

January 13, 1945

One-thirty P.M. Injected twenty percent Calcium Sandoz and glucose intravenously. In good health. At present he is, he says, under *very* heavy strain and he will be for the next few days.

January 16, 1945

Arrived Berlin during the forenoon.[2] Injected 20 cc glucose and two ampoules of Omnadin intravenously on account of a sore throat. I further ordained that he should speak as little as possible, and gargle with a solution of salt water and glycerine. On the railroad journey from the Eagle's Nest to Grunewald it was *very* cold. The Führer has had a lot of upsets on account of the Russian breakthrough at Baranov (toward Cracow and the Upper Silesian industrial basin).

January 18, 1945

Yesterday's evening war conference lasted right through from four to eleven P.M.! (Security of Budapest, Cracow.) Then tea until four A.M. When I saw the Führer at two P.M. he was fresh. I injected 10 cc of twenty percent Calcium Sandoz intravenously and Omnadin, plus 5 cc glucose, and an intramuscular shot of Vitamultin-forte and liver extract. The Omnadin is because he has a cold and a sore throat.

January 19, 1945

His cold has gone, and his voice is normal.

January 20, 1945

One P.M. Führer seen, is well. Injected Calcium Sandoz and glucose intravenously. Reminded him of the need for an X ray, and explained why.

January 22, 1945

At noon his appetite is said to be good, and slept well without sedatives. Injected 10 cc of twenty percent Calcium Sandoz and glucose, and Vitamultin-forte and liver extract.

---

[2] Linge noted in the log on January 16, 1945: "9:00 A.M. wakened; 9:40 A.M. arrival Grunewald; 10:00 A.M. arrival at Reich Chancery; 10:45 A.M. Professor Morell; 11:00 A.M. war conference, Colonel-General Guderian."

January 24, 1945

Tea last night lasted from three to five A.M. this morning, as his war conference went on until three A.M. Saw him at one-forty-five P.M. and injected 10 cc glucose and 10 cc Calcium Sandoz intravenously and Vitamultin-forte liver extract and 25 milligrams of Testoviron intramuscularly. Slept badly last night.

January 25, 1945

Gave him 0.1 of Luminal this evening before he went to bed.

January 27, 1945

One-twenty-five P.M. He didn't take the Luminal to get to sleep. As a consequence of the critical military situation a stronger tremor in the left arm and leg has appeared. Otherwise no complaint whatsover. Injected intravenous glucose and Calcium Sandoz.

January 30, 1945

One P.M. Injected intravenous glucose and Calcium Sandoz and intramuscular Vitamultin-forte and liver. Completely complaint free. A major speech this evening!

February 1, 1945

One-twenty-five P.M. Injected intravenous glucose and Calcium Sandoz; blood pressure up to 153 mm. Says his health is perfectly okay.

February 3, 1945

Midday, injected intravenous glucose and Calcium Sandoz and intramuscular Vitamultin-forte and liver.

February 5, 1945

One P.M. Intravenous glucose and Calcium Sandoz and intramuscular Vitamultin-forte and liver.

February 7, 1945

One-fifty-five P.M. Intravenous glucose and intramuscular Vitamultin-forte and liver.

February 10, 1945

One-ten P.M. Tried unsuccessfully to let some blood from an

artery using a very broad needle. (The blood pressure was only 154 mm, but despite this he still requested the bloodletting.) Injected glucose plus Betabion-forte. When I asked the Führer's valet Krüger what the Führer is now taking, he states: one Gallestol three times a day, one Pepsin wine twice daily, Brom-Nervacit or Brom mixture every third day—two or three tablespoons in the evening—Acidol-Pepsin tablets, about one tablet every other day at mealtimes.

February 11, 1945

Twelve noon. Injected intravenous glucose and Betabion-forte. The tremor has diminished, particularly in the left leg. The Führer's valet Arndt states that he *is* still taking Euflat, one tablet with every meal. He says only very little liquid is consumed, he calculated with the Führer that it amounts to only one liter or 1,200 cc per day.

February 12, 1945

One-five P.M. Drew off 230 cc of blood from an artery! There was no real need for this, but it was requested. After the bloodletting the blood pressure was 143; before it, it was 156 mm. His right hand was shaking strongly on account of a violent emotional upset he had yesterday.

February 13, 1945

One-thirty-five P.M. Injected intravenous glucose and Betabion-forte. The Führer is rather strange toward me, curt and generally irritable in manner.

O N THE FOLLOWING NIGHT the undefended Saxon city of Dresden was set aflame by two RAF bomber command attacks. More than one hundred thousand civilians, mostly refugees, were killed in the flames of this beautiful city. As the air war climaxed, the Soviet onslaught continued in the East and Southeast. General Fritz Hossbach surrendered the fortress of Lötzen in East Prussia and was dismissed his command. Hitler sensed treason all around him.

February 15, 1945

One-forty P.M. Injected intravenous glucose and Benerva-fortissime. *** Has no complaints! His morale is low, he seems mistrustful, evidently on account of the eastern front situation and the air raids on Dresden.

February 17, 1945

Two-five P.M. Injected Strophantin and 25 milligrams of Benerva-fortissime intravenously. He said that he had no health problems of any kind apart from the tremor that had now become powerfully evident in his left hand too, as I had noticed for myself during tea last night. During the conversation he expressed the wish that I might make a few (say three) injections of Strophantin as these had earlier lasted a whole year. I reminded him of the electro-cardiogram that I had wanted to take a week ago.

These last four or five days the patient has become extremely pensive and appears tired and short of sleep. His eyes—particularly the right one—are reddened but he refuses treatment for them. The Führer says he wants to try to get by without tranquilizers and won't even touch the Luminal tablets I give him.

February 18, 1945

Two P.M. Injected intravenous Strophantin II and Benerva-fortissime.

February 20, 1945

Two-five P.M. Injected intravenous Strophantin II and 25 milligrams of Benerva-fortissime.

February 22, 1945

Twelve-forty-five P.M. Injected intravenous Strophantin II and Benerva-fortissime.

HITLER'S LEFT ARM and hand now trembled uncontrollably. All the witnesses saw it, and it embarrassed them. His right hand was almost incapable of signing documents for the same reason. His spine had lost its symmetry. His face was haggard, masklike; his voice quavered. He faced these growing infirmities with puzzlement and hoarse defiance: "And if my whole left side were paralyzed," he declared to the gauleiters assembled in the Reich Chancery on February 24, 1945, "I would still call on the German people again and again not to capitulate but to hold out to the very end."

When Dr. Giesing happened to see Hitler again in mid-February 1945, he suspected that the tremor was not an organic ailment so much as a nervous, even hysterical, affection. Giesing wondered whether Hitler's evident exhaustion and irritation at this time might be a withdrawal symptom from the strychnine and atropine in the anti-gas pills. "But," Giesing would write in November 1945, "perhaps only a pharmacologist can really answer this question." Morell appears to have been in two minds—on the one hand associating the attacks of trembling with external events and emotional upsets, and on the other prescribing the kind of drugs that would be called for by an organic ailment.

February 24, 1945

One-twenty-five P.M. Injected intravenous Strophantin II and Benerva-fortissime.

February 26, 1945

Two P.M. Injected intravenous Strophantin II and 25 milligrams of Benerva. No physical complaints. He took two Luminal tablets to get to sleep, but then the air raid sirens went shortly afterward.

February 28, 1945

Two-twenty P.M. Injected intravenous Strophantin II and Benerva.

March 2, 1945

Midday. Injected intravenous Strophantin II and Benerva. Added intravenous Omnadin because of a developing head cold.

March 3, 1945

Midday. Injected intravenous Strophantin and Betabion-forte on account of his trip to the front line. Head cold has gone.

THAT DAY, Hitler and a small entourage visited the troops on the eastern front, at Wriezen, where five weeks later the troops were to make one of their most notable stands against the

Soviet advance. The Russians now had their armies on the Oder and the Pomeranian coast, while Eisenhower's armies had advanced to the Rhine and were threatening Cologne and Düsseldorf.

March 4, 1945

I am confined to bed by thrombophlebitis of the lower left leg, caused by an attempted intravenous injection of Strophantin II by Dr. Stumpfegger a week ago, and a small metastasis on the inside above the left ankle. The Führer pays a visit on me and remarks how fortunate it was that he would not allow me to accompany him on the drive out to the front line at Wriezen yesterday. * * *

March 5, 1945

The Führer called on me with Schaub. He said that I should not accompany him on major journeys, let alone visits to the front line, because the only things likely to happen would be serious injuries as a result of an accident or fighter-bomber attack. And if anything were to happen to *me*, he said, he would have no doctor left, or at very best I would be out of action for some time. When he was on the road, he said, it meant much more for him to know that he would always find me standing by at home for him.

March 6, 1945

Midday. Injected intravenous Strophantin and Betabion-forte. He rejects a massage of his left arm. Electric therapy also out. As long as he's not upset, the trembling does not appear. But he gets so infuriated by the blunders that are made, and afterward it always turns out that he was in the right, he says. I injected two ampoules of Omnadin into Reichsmarschall Göring because of a very bad cold, and gave him an intramuscular shot of Vitamultin-Calcium. * * *

March 8, 1945 [*and on four days thereafter*]

Injected intravenous Strophantin II and Betabion-forte.

March 19, 1945

Midday. Injected two ampoules of Omnadin, Strophantin and 25 milligrams of Benerva intravenously. Rather more noticeable tremor in the left forearm and hand. Has slept badly despite sedatives—incredible crises! I proposed electrotherapy. He replied that if he finds any time during the afternoon he would let me know. Remained without directions.

March 21, 1945

Midday. Injected Strophantin, one Omnadin and 25 milligrams of Benerva intravenously.

DURING MARCH 1945 the final major German counteroffensive of the war, near Lake Balaton in Hungary, failed. To postpone the inevitable defeat as long as possible, Hitler ordered his gauleiters to scorch the earth ahead of the advancing enemy armies. These orders met with resistance from Albert Speer and the army's chief of staff, Guderian; the latter intended to put out peace feelers to the western powers through Himmler or Ribbentrop (on March 21–22), but Hitler learned of this and told him bluntly, "I've gained the impression your heart is causing you problems—you're beginning to get irritable and fatigued. You are to go on leave." Guderian was dismissed on about March 29. Keitel recommended Bad Liebenstein for a cure, but the army general replied drily that the Americans had already overrun the spa.

March 23, 1945

I saw him at midnight (22–23). Slight conjunctivitis in eyes probably caused by the dust blowing around, as there is a lot of debris from buildings in the courtyard. The Führer declared that he had only very limited vision with the right eye anyway. His left hand is somewhat swollen, perhaps because of the trembling motions; there also are swellings on left ankle and part of the lower left leg (the circumference of the lower left leg was about an inch more than the right, above the ankle, a year or two back). For about seven years he had constant eczema on his lower left leg, which only disappeared when I began my Mutaflor treatment about eight or nine years ago. But the swelling remained.

I applied eye drops of cocaine-suprarinin solution, and forbade him to read. He was also to protect the eyes from wind and dust. I recommended chamomile poultices, but he did not follow this up. The Führer does not want to wear an eye shade. But the night war conference is to be arranged as briefly as possible and if possible without any maps to be read. (Told of illness of Minister Lammers —is edgy and has high blood pressure, 180 mm/85.)

Midday injected Strophantin and Benerva-forte intravenously, plus Omnadin, and electrotherapy of the left forearm.

March 25, 1945

Midday. Injected Strophantin, Omnadin and Benerva-forte intravenously, plus electrotherapy. No complaints.

March 27, 1945

Midday. Injected intravenous Strophantin, two Omnadin ampoules and Benerva-forte, and electrotherapy. The tremor in the left leg is barely perceptible now; he claims that the tremor in the left forearm has increased with the crisis, but objectively it is in fact considerably weaker than before.

March 29, 1945

Midday. Injected Strophantin and Benerva intravenously; electrotherapy.

March 31, 1945

Midday. Injected Strophantin and Benerva intravenously. Electrotherapy. I again suggested he should have his right eye reexamined (by Löhlein). I also reminded him of the X ray. Asked him if he has any complaints. He said he had not. When I asked specifically if he has any headache or throbbing head, he again shook his head. When I reverted to the need, so often expressed, for a case history to be drawn up, something I have requested over several years, he gave me the answer: "I was never ill—there's nothing to be written up." I reminded him of the fractures to his left collarbone and upper arm before his fortress arrest [1923–24], of which I only recently learned by chance. His left arm had in consequence been paralyzed for some time, but he had recovered full use of it by carrying out the most strenuous exercises. He said,

"There's nothing to be written up about that, as it was completely unimportant, and anyway I have regained complete mobility of that arm." Patellar reflex and the others are easily triggered.

April 2, 1945

Easter Monday. At three P.M. I injected him with intravenous Strophantin and Benerva, and carried out electrotherapy on the left arm. *** No complaints, but he has had a lot of serious upsets and slept badly (taking one Tempidorm tablet). Blood pressure 153, plus 66. The military situation is *very* bad, which is why the tremor in his left hand is really pronounced.

During the night (2–3) at 12:30 injected two Omnadin ampoules as a precaution against the many flu and head cold cases around. Pulse 72. Reminded him again of the eye examination (Professor Löhlein) and the electrocardiogram.

April 4, 1945

In the afternoon I injected Strophantin and Benerva as well as Omnadin intravenously (the latter because the cold and rainy weather has left virtually everybody with head colds). Reminded him of Professor Löhlein; he says I can phone him, but the Führer will fix the day and hour of the examination.

April 6, 1945

Three P.M., injected Strophantin and Benerva-forte and Omnadin, intravenously, and performed electrotherapy. Slight conjunctivitis of both eyes, particularly upper left. Says Professor Löhlein should come tomorrow, possibly in the evening.

HITLER'S EYES were duly examined, for the last time, on April 7. "According to the Führer," stated Professor Löhlein in his written report, "the vision of the right eye has gradually grown worse rather than better, while that of the left is as good as ever. But the left eye is impeded by a swelling on the left upper lid, which is tender, causing him to rub it. There is secretion from both eyes of late, which is understandable in view of the dusty atmosphere in the center of Berlin. The Führer," continued Löhlein, "generally leaves the well-ventilated and illuminated bunker only for short periods, for half an hour to two hours daily, and then goes into the Reich Chancery's garden, which is not badly damaged but is of course quite dusty, particularly when windy. He finds himself then very sensitive both to light and the dust-laden wind. It is difficult to arrange a set treatment in view of the irregularity of his existence and the need for him to be constantly available for reports, et cetera. . . . As he hardly ever wears his spectacles he is disproportionately inconvenienced by the bad vision of his right eye. . . . In both eyes there is a moderate degree of chronic conjunctivitis."

As for the right eye. Löhlein confirmed his earlier diagnosis: "The residue of a hemorrhage in the vitreous humor. Lack of macular reflex." He ordered drops of a zinc sulphate supracain solution to be applied three times daily in both eyes, and he prescribed a yellow liniment to be rubbed gently into the left eye before Hitler went to sleep; if this did not result in a rapid reduction of the swelling in the left eyelid this chalazion would have to be excised.

April 7, 1945

In the evening the eyes were examined by Professor Löhlein. Slight conjunctivitis in both eyes, and a chalazion on the left. Slight perturbation of the vitreous humor on the right, similar to before. Pupil reflexes prompt and good on both sides. Pupils no pathology. Lack of right macular reflex. Focal lengths as before. Prescribed warm compresses for left eye, with eye drops of zinc sulphate supracain to be applied twice daily and yellow mercury ointment to be applied beneath the lid each evening. Advised him to wear goggles when he goes for walks in the garden because of the mortar dust.

Later, Professor Löhlein, in conversation with Dr. Stumpfegger and myself, touched on the tremor, which was, he said, now gone from the left leg. He asked if the Führer had ever suffered a speech impediment—which was, however, never the case, apart from the impediment when the polyp had to be excised. The blood vessels in the eyes are narrow rather than wide, and at present there are no indications of any hemorrhaging. I remarked that his blood pressure was constant at 153 mm and for a long time had been even lower, and that a month ago I had again performed a blood-letting.

While his eyes and retina were being examined, the Führer's left hand was held completely motionless (to which I also drew Dr. Stumpfegger's attention).

April 8, 1945

Three P.M. I injected intravenous Strophantin and Benerva-forte and Omnadin, and performed electrotherapy with a large apparatus; his little finger is particularly sensitive to this.

MORELL had loyally followed in his master's footsteps as they led down from the Reich Chancery in Berlin to the underground bunker built by Speer's engineers beneath the garden. The other doctors went also—Stumpfegger and now too Professor Werner Haase, who had treated Hitler some years earlier. Then, on April 15, the final Soviet assault began from the Oder bridge-heads. Hitler had been convinced that Berlin was safe, but within five days the Red Army was within artillery range of the capital. Karl Thöt, the shorthand writer, entered in his diary, "Toward one A.M. on the night of April 20–21 our col-leagues Peschel and Jonuschat came back from the war con-ference into the shelter, where we had gone just before ten P.M. because of the air raid warning, and told us that we are to leave in an hour's time." Hitler had begun sending out his staff. The first shorthand writers left at five A.M. in a Junkers 352 transport plane flying south. Six hours later the Soviet artillery bombardment of the capital's center began, and shells began to rain down on the government buildings. For the next two days, Morell remained, but did not like it.

April 9, 1945

For about ten days the Führer has not gone out; he just goes up to one of the upper floors for one mealtime a day, according to Arndt, but otherwise stays in his bunker. Even the big daily war conference has been held for some time now down in the bunker —for security reasons, as the Führer told me in conversation.

The war conference did not end until five-thirty this morning, and that was followed by tea! Let's hope there's no early morning air raid alert, so he gets enough time to sleep properly. In the afternoon Dr. Stumpfegger brought over Professor Löhlein's report and the thermophore[3] for the Führer's eye.

April 10, 1945

Three fifteen P.M. Injected Strophantin and Benerva-forte plus Omnadin, then applied electrotherapy to the left forearm and hand. Tremor is less. Führer slept from seven-thirty A.M. this morning until two P.M.; his military conferences had lasted until six A.M. and he then had tea until seven. At six A.M. this morning I had to rewrite the prescription Professor Löhlein had provided as he had appended the phrase "For the Führer" and instructed that it was to be collected from some other pharmacy than the Engel Pharmacy. Only the sixth pharmacy tried, the one at the Am Zoo railroad station, could make it up—to be collected tomorrow—as there are evidently no possibilities of obtaining the Supracain anywhere. Drugs are in very short supply and even the central medical stores of the SS main office find difficulty in obtaining them; most of them have been discontinued because of the bombing-out of the factories. After five minutes electrotherapy, pain was felt in the little and index fingers.

I myself have experienced these last few days a great deal of breathlessness and gasping for air (particularly when climbing steps).

April 12, 1945

Midday. Injected Strophantin and Benerva-forte plus Omnadin, intravenously, and electrotherapy.

April 14, 1945

Midday. Injected Strophantin and Benerva-forte plus Omnadin, intravenously, and electrotherapy.

April 15, 1945

As the tremor is a variety of paralysis agitans [*Schüttelläh-*

---

[3] A rubber bag filled with various chemicals that retains its heat for a long time after being placed in hot water; it is used as a warm application.

mung], I am making an attempt at temporarily influencing it by subcutaneous injections of Harmin and administering Homburg 680, a Bulgarian-Italian drug *** [manufactured in?] Kassel.[4]

April 16, 1945

Midday. Injected Strophantin and Benerva-forte intravenously plus Harmin subcutaneously. In the evening one drop of Homburg 680. [*One drop.*]

April 17, 1945

Midday. Injected Harmin subcutaneously; the tremor has slightly improved. Midday also one drop of Homburg 680, and evening the same. [*1 dr + 1 dr.*]

April 18, 1945

Midday, injected Strophantin and Benerva-forte intravenously plus Harmin subcutaneously. Tremor in the left hand somewhat improved, but drowsy.[5] Sleeping at night now only possible with Tempidorms. Since Sunday [April 15] there has been a big Russian offensive at Küstrin and Frankfurt-am-Oder. Administered one drop of Homburg 680 in the morning, at midday and in the evening. [*1 dr + 1 dr + 1 dr.*]

April 19, 1945

Injected Harmin subcutaneously. [*1 dr + 1 dr + 2 dr.*]

April 20, 1945

Injected intravenous Strophantin, Betabion-forte plus Harmin —that is, I had to get Dr. Stumpfegger to do it as I was too shaky. [*1 dr + 2 dr + 2 dr.*][6]

---

[4] See Appendix II on the medicines used. Homburg 680 is particularly indicated in cases of Morbus Parkinson or Parkinson's disease. Morell even provided for the further administering of Homburg 680 after his departure from Hitler's headquarters. In the fall of 1945 Hitler's last desk calendar was found on the floor of the burnt-out Reich Chancery bunker by British Intelligence officers, and removed to London where it still is. Beginning with April 16, 1945, the doses to be administered two or three times daily were penciled in in advance, as noted in the following entries in italics.

[5] *Schläfrig*, which might perhaps mean the hand tended to "fall asleep."

[6] These doses of Homburg 680—evidently to be administered by Dr. Stumpfegger—would rise as follows: on April 22, 2 + 2 + 3 drops; on April

April 21, 1945

Dismissal!

DURING the whole of this final week from April 15 to 21," Morell related a few days later to an American journalist, "I gave him shots of glucose. On Saturday, April 21, he was very dejected— there must have been an important conference on the evening before. I wanted to give him another shot but he grabbed me and lost his temper, shouting that he knew precisely that I was going to inject him with morphine." If this is true, it is probable that Hitler feared his doctor was going to drug him so that the generals could smuggle him out of Berlin to the south against his will. Morell protested his innocence, but Hitler screamed, "Do you think I'm crazy?"

He continued to rant at Morell, threatened to have him shot, and finally ordered him to go home, take off that uniform as the Führer's physician, and "act as if you've never seen me!" "Where-upon," wrote Tania Long, describing this final humiliation of the doctor in the *New York Times*, "the physician collapsed at the feet of his Führer." Again Hitler shrieked at him, "Get out of that uniform, put on some plain clothes and go back to being the doctor of Kurfürstendamm!" With these malevolent words ringing in his ears, Morell fled to the airfield at Gatow.

The patient he left behind was a nervous ruin. Captain Heinz Assmann, who saw Hitler on April 23, retained the pic-ture of a physical wreck who could barely walk, doing so with a stooped back and a shuffling gait, his right leg dragging, his head shaking and his left hand violently trembling on the limply dangling arm. "His handshake was soft and flabby, his gestures were those of an old, old man—only the eyes still had their old flickering gleam and penetrating power. Despite this physical collapse his energy and willpower remained unshat-tered to the very end, and this was astonishing for those of us who witnessed them each day. . . . To the very end he preached fanatically to his staff, urging them to hold on and summon all

---

23, 2 + 3 + 3 drops; on April 24, 3 + 3 + 3 drops; on April 25, 3 + 3 + 4 drops; on April 26, 3 + 4 + 4 drops; on April 27, 4 + 4 + 4 drops, and on the two last days of the calendar, April 28 and 29, 4 + 4 + 4 drops.

their strength, ruthlessness and energy. With incredible tenacity and resolution he fought against his physical decline and set his face against the cruel fate that was closing relentlessly in on him and his people."

April 23, 1945

Took off at two A.M. in a [Focke-Wulf] Kondor for Munich. Flew low over the Russian lines (now at Jüterbog!), saw myriads of burning villages; later crossed the American front line at Partenk[irchen?] and into Bavaria. Here there were a lot of searchlights and flak activity. After looking for some time found and landed at Neubiberg airfield.

EPILOGUE

Morell in Captivity

ONE BY ONE the surviving Hitler doctors were arrested by the Americans. Dr. von Hasselbach had been picked up on April 13, 1945, at Albrechtshaus in the Harz mountains. Dr. Giesing was captured at Amberg on April 23. It was at one A.M. on that same day that Morell had taken the Kondor of Hitler's courier flight and headed south out of Berlin. Among the other VIP passengers singled out for evacuation from the burning capital were Hitler's conference stenographer Herrgesell and a number of wives from the Chancery staff. Karl Koller, the Luftwaffe chief of staff who also left Berlin that night, described in his diary finding "fat old Morell" on the airfield when he landed near Munich.

The flight had not agreed with the portly physician. Of late he had taken the train for all his journeys, because he could not stand flying. It seems that he was on the brink of a fresh heart attack and even some kind of brain damage, because he was driven immediately to a clinic, and on May 1 he was transferred to the city hospital at Bad Reichenhall. Two days later American troops overran the area.

His wife Johanna had arrived at Reichenhall with her friend Aloys Becker on April 30. The director of the new institute where Morell had installed his electron microscope, Dr. Riedel, greeted her with unconcealed ill humor. "Your husband is ill," he told her, "being treated by Dr. Kühne. I suggest you go right on to him."

Frau Morell found her husband in the hospital. "My husband lay weeping in bed," she would describe in a statement in October of that year, "a broken figure. He cried as he told me

277

how the Führer had kicked him out. And he complained about his heart, which had been giving him a lot of trouble the last few years."

She consoled him as far as she was able and promised to visit him every day. Riedel declined to drive her back to the institute—although both the building and its contents belonged to the Morells. In fact that evening two gentlemen of the city council arrived there and indicated to Frau Morell and Becker that they should get out of town. "The local people are talking of storming the building and its bunker," they claimed, "and we can't be responsible for your safety!" The truth was, Frau Morell wrote a few weeks later, that both gentlemen merely wanted to grab as much of Morell's personal property and fortune as possible. Defeat would be bitter for the Morells and for all those who had served Hitler as closely as he.

STILL BEDRIDDEN at Reichenhall, Morell was visited in the hospital on May 18, 1945, by officers of General George S. Patton's U.S. Third Army; they had started a sweep against former SS officers in such hospitals. Morell was questioned but claimed to be suffering from bouts of loss of memory. An American wrote in his diary, "Dr. Morell says he was primarily concerned with scientific research. For this purpose he was collaborating with Dr. Riedel, a chemist. Dr. Morell's main purpose was to work by himself, in order to get away from the permanent scrutiny of the SS. As Dr. Morell himself says, he was a friend of the Jews and that is why he was under constant observation."

But at the same time, he was being incriminated by his former colleagues. Now the doctors dismissed after the intrigue of October 1944 got their revenge. Dr. Karl Brandt, arrested on May 23 when the Flensburg enclave in northern Germany was liquidated by the British army, was questioned many times and spoke volubly about all he knew. Allied doctors described him as "quite handsome in the masculine sense of the word," and noted that "he was at ease and expressed pleasure at the prospect of being interviewed by the doctors on medical subjects." Brandt told the Allies what they wanted to hear. Thus he would tell them, when interrogated in June 1945, a tall story about Morell's alleged narcotics addiction—for which there is not the slightest evidence in Morell's own papers. "I learned," said

Brandt, "from Professor Müller-Hess, a Berlin court doctor, that Morell himself was probably a drug addict (morphine). One of his secretaries was involved in a lawsuit concerning the falsifying of morphine prescriptions. These prescriptions were actually made out by Morell himself. The court files were seized by the Gestapo, however, and the whole case quashed. That was in February 1945."

On May 21 Miss Tania Long of the *New York Times* interviewed Morell. She found Morell a frightened man. "At first his eyes darted about the room like those of a cornered animal, and he explained later that he knew 'they'—the Gestapo, the SS and Heinrich Himmler—were out to get him." But then he warmed to the female interviewer and talked about Hitler. The Führer, he said, had been "an extremely difficult patient," who had refused to be X-rayed and even had answered Morell's quite reasonable request for a complete medical history with the brusque retort, "I have never been ill."

Morell told her bitterly of the angry final parting with Hitler one month earlier in the Berlin bunker: he had wanted to give him a final injection of caffeine (according to Tania Long's recollection), but Hitler had refused it, saying: "I don't need drugs in order to see me through." She tactfully inquired if he had ever given Hitler anything stronger than caffeine—for instance Pervitin, the amphetamine narcotic which had lain behind the suicide of General Ernst Udet and many another human tragedy in Nazi Germany. Morell denied it. His amnesia seemed gone, and he seemed quite coherent. He told her that Hitler's tremors had "reappeared suddenly last September after a violent quarrel with his number two man, Reichsmarschall Hermann Göring."

All this was true enough as we know from the Morell diary. Hitler, he said, "had coronary sclerosis which is not abnormal in men of that age, but a constant threat . . . and toward the end of the war there was always the danger of angina pectoris or an embolism."

A few weeks later things took a nasty turn. On July 17, 1945, Morell was formally arrested by the Americans in the hospital and transferred to the remand prison at Bad Reichenhall. He was incarcerated there at first in a "narrow prison cell with barred windows and opaque glass," and six months later as he lay in Dachau's prison hospital in a bed from which at least he did not have a view of the barbed wire, he would still think back with a shudder to that prison cell. "The wonder is," he would write to his wife, "that I did not get far more mixed-up there than I did."

A week after his arrest, Frau Morell drove with Aloys Becker to Bad Reichenhall to provide moral support, and spoke with an American army captain called Nitz. The captain told her she could speak with the doctor and take him some food if she wished, and she could also fetch their private property. "From him," Johanna Morell wrote a few weeks later, "we went to the prison building. As Captain Nitz had telephoned ahead, we were allowed straight in. Becker went to my husband first, while I waited in a little room. Two young men who apparently ran everything there behaved in such an odious manner toward me that my blood ran cold. When I was then called out, I found my husband sitting in a chair. I will never forget this sight as long as I live—he was old, emaciated, his face was streaked with tears, and he kept repeating over and over again, 'I thought you were dead, I heard you screaming, didn't I!'[1] . . . He wasn't talking much sense. Whenever we tried to explain the real facts of the matter to him, he would say, 'Well, I must have gone mad then.' We consoled him as far as we could. Those two awful young men hovered over us the whole time cracking jokes and making cruel comments. After about a quarter of an hour we had to separate. I could not have remained in control of my feelings longer than that anyway. It was a torture to have to see my husband suffering like that." Before she left, he whispered to her that the Americans had torn out his toe-nails. She could not bear to listen, and quietened him by saying: "Don't get worked up—I don't want to hear it now. Tell me all about it when you are better."

Perhaps Morell's mind was wandering when he said these things. After a while, he was put into the same cell as Karl

[1] The interrogation methods of the Americans preparing the war crimes trials were later laid bare by a commission of inquiry under Supreme Court Justice Simpson, who toured the American internment camps after the so-called Malmédy trial at Dachau. Perhaps the interrogating officers tried on Morell the same device that later became a commonplace in Soviet bloc states; the victim was told that his wife was in the neighboring room and that the screams he was hearing were coming from her.

Brandt, his former colleague and rival at Hitler's headquarters. No doubt hidden microphones recorded every word. Morell certainly had not expected to see Brandt again and was very shocked—according to Brandt, he went pale and began to shake, and stammered a few meaningless words of greeting before sinking onto his bed, curling himself up and beginning to weep again. He later said that he had felt the same when he flew out of Berlin on April 23.

Morell was growing ill—both physically and mentally. Hugh Trevor-Roper, later famous as a historian but at that time still an unknown major in British Intelligence, visited him at the USFET Theater Interrogation Center on September 13, 1945. "Morell," he reported to his superiors, "seemed physically decayed and mentally gaga; he was unsure of most of the facts he gave, and probably genuinely unsure." Six days later Brandt himself confirmed this diagnosis in a private manuscript, writing: "M's state of health is at present not good. Over the last few months he has lost a lot of weight. The earlier symptoms of a chronic heart complaint, and of a gall bladder and possibly also a kidney complaint caused by a hypertrophied prostate, seem to have increased." During the few days he shared a prison cell with Brandt, Morell alternated between complaining of subjective woes and, sometimes, of evil headaches, which might however have emanated from a general but slight urine poisoning; Brandt noted that the professor spent a lot of time sleeping, and that his memory had begun to fail him too. He studied his former colleague with unconcealed curiosity, and wrote: "With regard to his psyche M is at present unstable and, generally speaking, in a state of decay there too. The earlier— often very pronounced—hustle and bustle and the associated craving for admiration and acclaim are no longer there."

Brandt warned the Americans against believing Morell. Perhaps it was Morell's peasant cunning that had instinctively warned him to play the sick man. "Probably he hopes to attract more sympathy that way," he testified. "My distaste for Morell as both a man and a doctor has not been affected by his present stance."

Brandt made no bones of this distaste for his cellmate, and bluntly accused him of shamefully injuring the reputation of the German medical profession by his record. (At that time, neither doctor could foretell that Brandt, and not Morell, would hang.) Morell defended himself lamely. "I wish I were somebody else," he said.

MORELL was transferred to the former Luftwaffe interrogation center at Oberursel, now run by the American army. His nephew was permitted to visit him there, and wrote a few months later: "First he was in this camp at Oberursel, where he was interrogated in the most degrading way: questioned with spotlights beamed on him, overheated cells, et cetera. Then he was transferred successively to Darmstadt, Kornwestheim, Ludwigsburg and Dachau."

Shortly, Johanna learned that Theo was being held at Fürth, near Nuremberg, and she drove over there. "The American in charge there," she would later recall, "rampaged around and complained that my husband would not testify—I couldn't go and see him because he was refusing to testify. That's probably why they were torturing and tormenting him so much." She broke down in tears, and the American relented and gave her two minutes with her husband as being probably the only way of ending this embarrassment. She could see Theo lying in a hospital bed, but was not allowed to speak to him.

The notorious SS concentration camp at Dachau was now run by the Americans with German inmates. When Morell was transferred there, Johanna was again prevented from seeing him. On February 13, 1946, she wrote to the American governor, General McNarney, complaining that she had heard nothing from Theo since July. "I know my husband is seriously ill," she pleaded. "I was particularly alarmed by the state of his nerves when I last visited him at Reichenhall. His speech was so befuddled even then that I suggested he should be transferred to a mental hospital. In the meantime your own investigating agencies must also have come to the conclusion that my husband was only a doctor and refrained from any kind of political activity." McNarney turned a deaf ear on her.

Meanwhile the world's newspapers began to run stories on him. U.S. Intelligence officer Major Cortez Enloe speculated in the mass-circulation *Collier's* weekly on May 4, 1946, "There is some evidence that Himmler, the Gestapo chief, Martin Bormann, Hitler's executive officers and the ill-famed Dr. Morell conspired in a plot slowly to poison the Führer." But he admitted there was no positive evidence yet. More plausibly he added, "It is certain that the daily dose of drugs hastened the collapse of Hitler's personality."

His heart slowly giving up on him, Morell was too ill to defend himself. In June 1946 he was permanently transferred to the prison hospital. The minor cardiovascular episodes which had begun during the latter years now became more frequent; they found expression in a hemiparesis, or state of slight paralysis on one side, particularly affecting the leg. On the prescribed prison stationery Morell scrawled pathetic letters and postcards to his wife. "I am thinking constantly about you and always longing for you," he wrote on July 1, 1946. "I often dream of our earlier beautiful homes. I'm permanently in bed in hospital, but feeling better as that throbbing in my head has gone again. . . . In three weeks I'll be sixty already. . . . How swiftly the years have flown by, and sad to say I have not been able to devote myself more to you. I've often wished I was standing at that turning point again." How much he yearned for those earlier, pre-Hitler times! "My mind keeps going back to those earlier years, around 1920 or so," he wrote to her in mid-July. "Even though I was working from morn to night and you used to go out with me on calls to places like Spandau, those were still the happy times. And then when I grew old and tired and could only carry on with difficulty because of my health, and my heart cried out for peace and tranquility, I was not allowed to have them in our idyllic house in Schwanenwerder, where at your side I could still have had a few more peaceful and happy years. The blame for all this attaches to this accursed war."

That he, Morell, was languishing in a concentration camp now, while his old friend and enemy Heinrich Hoffmann was a free man, rubbed salt into the wound. On September 30, 1946, he mentioned in a letter to Johanna: "Heini Junior is in prison, but is allowed to work by day at his father's—the father is in a suburban villa processing the entire photographic archives [for the Americans]. He's free. . . . There's nothing they can do with me. If only they would realize that and let me out!"

But they still wanted Morell for court testimony. On October 12 a court doctor examined him in the hospital to see if he was fit to testify. Afterward, Morell wrote full of self-pity to Johanna: "As I am unable to raise my right leg or even to answer nature's call without assistance . . . there's probably not much they can do with me. And my head is often very muddled still and my memory has virtually gone, I can't remember anything. I usually wake up around three or four A.M. and stay wide awake until morning. They are massaging my right arm and leg every day."

The big war crimes trial against the German doctors was due to begin on November 15. Twenty-three doctors were in the dock, accused of crimes against humanity; but as Morell—unlike Brandt—was implicated in neither the euthanasia program nor the criminal experiments on concentration camp prisoners, the trial did not affect him. "We'll just have to see what they want from me apart from my treatment of Hitler," he wrote. "Apparently it still hasn't sunk in to these gentlemen that Hitler always kept his thoughts to himself and that he was a very taciturn kind of person. How often did he say that the way he kept his plans secret was one of his great strengths. That I was only his 'private' doctor does not seem to occur to many of these people. Probably they think I had an important position or wielded some kind of influence; they just can't imagine the kind of petty spitefulness I was exposed to."

At the end of October 1946, he tried to write to Johanna once more, but it was agony. After that he could only dictate his letters. Among Morell's papers is one sad attempt at writing a letter to his sister Emilie. "My dearest little sister," he began ten times or more in a spidery scrawl, but each time he got no further with his paralyzed hand, and finally gave up the attempt. The right side of his face was now also paralyzed, and he was in pain from earlier hemorrhages. On June 17, 1947, Morell lost the power of speech as well, but this "temporary aphasia" was, in the opinion of the German doctor who examined him at Dachau, "psychogenic in origin, as are the symptoms of hemiparesis," meaning the partial paralysis.

Be that as it may, the Americans decided he had become an encumbrance and tipped him out of Dachau. Elderly and infirm, Morell was handed a discharge paper No. 52,160 dated June 20, 1947, endorsing him as "Cleared by War Crimes." Then he was just dumped, together with a number of Polish displaced persons (DPs), in the waiting room at Munich station. From there he was taken to a Munich clinic. On June 29, the Dachau doctors sent their report to the clinic, confirming their diagnosis that Morell, like his former illustrious patient, was suffering arteriosclerosis, in his case with damage to the myocardial muscles. He was treated with the same methods as Hitler—with injections; Hanni had reserved a room for him near her home at a Tegernsee clinic, and on June 3 Morell was transferred there, to the "Alpenhof" district hospital. The doctors there restated the myocardial insufficiency diagnosis, and observed too that his memory was severely impaired and that he could no longer read or write.

Theodore Morell never left that clinic. He would die almost a year later, at four-ten A.M. on May 26, 1948. "He died," his assistant Richard Weber would reflect years later, "like a stray dog."

Appendix I

Tests and Checkups, 1940–1945

Dr. Morell's Hitler Dossier. In general, reports that reflect abnormal conditions have been reproduced.

CONTENTS

January 9, 1940 (Blood Test)

Prof. Dr. med. Theo Morell
Berlin W15,
Kurfürstendamm 216

January 9, 1940

Patient A.

Blood pressure: 140/100 (age 50)
Pulse: 72
Blood Group: A
Hbg: 97%
Red corpuscles: 4.7 Mill.
Color Index: 1,03
White corpuscles: 5000
Blood sugar: 110 mg%
Blood sedimentation: 4, 9
    Average value: 6.5

January 10, 1940 (Glandular secretions in Hitler's blood)

Medical Diagnostic Institute
Dr. med. A. Schmidt-Burbach
Berlin NW7, Schiffbauerdamm 3

Reading on calibration with fresh serum: 1467 drum units.
The drum reading for each individual component is the sum of the calibration reading and the catabolic valuation reading listed below.

	CATABOLIC VALUATION (in drum units)	
COMPONENT	Normal	Patient
Hypophysis, pars ant.	13	13
* Hypophysis, pars post.	17	12
Hypophysis, total	14	..
Parathyroid gland	18	18
* Thyroid gland	19	14
Thymus	18	18
* ⎧ Testis	20 ♂	9
⎩	16 ♀	..
⎧ Ovarium	19 ♀	14
⎩	16 ♂	..
Suprarenal gland, cort.	16	18
Suprarenal gland, total	12	11
Cutis	24	..
Lien	12	13
Hepar	11	10
Pancreas	11	12
Kidneys	14	..
Corpus luteum lutin	13	..
Felliculum phase	10	..

*[Pencil notation:] Orchikrin. Hypoph. from Merck. Thyr.
This report on the individual glandular secretions in Hitler's blood was appended to OI/CIR/4, with this introductory explanation: "The process followed involves the use of an interferometer to determine to what degree each of the

January 15, 1940 (Routine VD tests)

Medical Diagnostic Institute
Dr. med. A. Schmidt-Burbach
Berlin NW7, Schiffbauerdamm 3

Lab.-No. 244

To Prof. Morell
Berlin

Result of Examination of Patient A.

Wassermann:	negative
Meinicke (MKRII):	negative
Kahn:	negative
Pallida reaction:	
Complement test for gonorrhea:	
Complement test for tuberculosis:	
Meinicke-tuberculosis-reaction:	

(signed) E. Brinkmann

Berlin, January 15, 1940

December 28, 1940 (Fecal analysis)

Prof. Dr. A. Nissle,   Freiburg i. Br.,
Research Institute,
Freiburg i. Br.   Fürstenbergstrasse 15

Dear Colleague,
    Please find attached my report on your Patient A; I'm glad to see that the
coli bacilli have this time remained typical, in contrast to the last control
tests we made, and that no disruptive subsidiary bacilli have turned up.
Nevertheless I would be glad if, on account of the shortcomings set out in
my report, you would—in order to combat the physical disadvantages of the
extreme overwork of your patient—influence your patient despite the otherwise satisfactory results to prolong the Mutaflor course for as long as this

---

glandular secretions in Hitler's blood serum was affected by catabolic fermentation.
'Normal' destruction of glandular secretions by fermentation is obtained from a
table. . . . The determination is made by preliminary calibration of the interferometer with fresh serum in both chambers: *Units of drum reading* are used to
express the amount of deviation between the two beams. Then the serum in one
chamber of the instrument is substituted for an equivalent amount of serum which
has been incubated for 24 hours at 37° C, after the addition of a predetermined
amount of standardized glandular extract (Organognosto). Then the two beams of
the interferometer are again brought into phase. The amount of change necessary
to accomplish this, again expressed in units of drum reading, indicates the degree
to which the particular glandular secretion involved has been affected by catabolic
fermentation in the blood of the patient." It would be unwise to attach undue importance to these findings, as these 1940 methods were very approximate.

particular work overload continues. I'm convinced that the patient will find the load easier to carry, as I know from tests carried out on my own person under fundamentally similar conditions. One's nervous energy is increased.

With best wishes for the New Year
and Heil Hitler!
(Signed) Nissle

(Attachment to above)

Prof. Dr. A. Nissle,   Freiburg i. Br.,
Research Institute,
Freiburg i. Br.   Fürstenbergstrasse 15

Result of a Routine Examination of a Fecal Sample of Patient A,
received December 23.

Reaction acid. Remarkably sparse growth. Cultures of typical coli bacteria are only moderate in number, and of these only a minority shows any extensive identity with the Mutaflor strain. No other germs or worm eggs present.

It is a satisfactory result inasmuch as only coli bacteria were encountered. The fact that these, which are certainly a derivative of the colonizing Mutaflor bacilli, are losing some of their properties during the time they adhere to and pass through the intestine indicates, as does the relatively bacteria-free quality of the fecal sample, that there is some factor operative, capable of inhibiting the normal colonization process of the Mutaflor strain to a certain degree. The most probable such factor is the patient's current work overload. It is therefore advisable, despite the satisfactory composition of the intestinal flora, to continue with the Mutaflor course.

(Signed) Nissle

August 8, 1941 (Discussion of a fecal analysis)

Prof. Dr. A. Nissle,   Freiburg i. Br.,
Research Institute,   August 8, 1941
Freiburg i. Br.   Fürstenbergstrasse 15

To Professor Dr. Morell . . .
Berlin W 8

Dear Colleague,
Enclosed is the result of the fecal analysis concluded today on your Patient A. For enhanced accuracy the tests were conducted using several enrichment techniques. The presence of paracoli bacteria referred to was only proved with one of the methods.

The test for coli bacteria was carried out on numerous colonies. In only a few were traces of agglutinated Mutaflor serum specifically detected, while no agglutination could be observed in most of the others tested, and the use of the respective cultures for the determination of the coli index showed them to be of quite inferior antagonistic qualities; at any rate they could not be classed as high grade.

There are two ways of interpreting this result: if your Patient A has not been taking any Mutaflor recently it may be the result of a gradual degeneration of the Mutaflor bacilli residing in the body. If on the other hand he has been regularly using Mutaflor then this degeneration must have occurred during the passage through the bowel, in which case external factors must, experience suggests, have caused the damage. As you know such factors include very irregular life-style, hectic professional activity, lack of sleep, aggravation and worry.

Whichever the case, this result indicates a continuation or resumption of the Mutaflor treatment even if the patient's health appears relatively satisfactory. . . .

How I envy you your opportunity of witnessing at first hand world history being made at the Führer's Headquarters. The genius of the Führer, his prompt intervention and his carefully orientated and well-planned reconstruction of our armed forces, are the guarantee that we may look to the future with confidence, even though our fight against the giant Russian army will not be easy. Frederick the Great once said that it's not enough to shoot the Russians dead, you've got to knock them down as well. And the Russians don't seem to have changed much in this respect.

My warmest wishes go with the Führer in his great task. May he be blessed with lasting good health, so that he can retain the strength to achieve his ultimate ambitions for his nation.

Sincerely, and
Heil Hitler!

Nissle

August 14, 1941 (Electrocardiogram)

Balneological University Institute
Director: Prof. Dr. A. Weber   Bad Nauheim

Electrocardiogram I

Date: August 14, 1941
Age: 51   *Clinical Diagnosis:* Coronary Sclerosis
Auricular Rate: 88   *P-QRS Interval:* 0.10–11
Ventricular Rate: 88   *QRS Complex:* 0.08

Rhythm: Pacemaker apparently originates in the uppermost portion
of Tawara node.   *Axis deviation:* Left

Lead I: Slight slurring of Q+R, voltage of T (0.20 mm), slight depression of R–T segment, slight notching of P, small Q-wave present (1.2 mm), R-wave (12 mm), P-wave (0.–0.5 mm).
Lead II: slight slurring of R, voltage of T (0.5 mm), low take off of S–T segment, R-wave 5 mm, P-wave 0.3–0.4 mm.
Lead III: slight slurring of R+S, diphasic P, R-wave 1.8 mm, S-wave 5–6 mm slight arrhythmia.

Note: Standardization present
    Horizontal spacing: 0.04 sec. Vertical sp. 1 mm.
    Actual square spacing: 0.075″

August 20, 1941 (Interpretation of above Electrocardiogram)

Balneological University Institute
Director: Prof. Dr. A. Weber   Bad Nauheim

August 20, 1941

Dear Colleague Morell,

I was glad to hear that you are in good health despite what must be very great responsibility. Let us hope that things progress far enough for us all to enjoy real peace soon.

The electrocardiogram you submitted showed: sinus rhythm, left type. Transition to left retardation. Beginning depression of S—T_I and S—T_{II}. Considerable flattening of S—T_I and S—T_{II}. If these are not the consequence of digitalis or an infection, we must assume primarily that the cause is coronary sclerosis. I recommend making further electrocardiograms at fourteen-day intervals.

In the hope that things continue to go well for you I remain, with best wishes,

and Heil Hitler!
your obedient

A. Weber

May 11, 1943 (Electrocardiogram)

Balneological University Institute
Director: Prof. Dr. A. Weber   Bad Nauheim

Electrocardiogram I

Date: May 11, 1943
Age: 54   *Disease:* Coronary Sclerosis
Auricular Rate: 85–90   *P-QRS Interval:* 0.12
Ventricular Rate: 85–90   *QRS Complex:* 0.08

Rhythm: Pacemaker apparently originating in the uppermost region of Tawara node or in the lowermost region of Sinus node.   *Axis deviation:* Left

Lead I: Slight notching of base of R, low-inverted T, very slight low take-off of R—T segment, P-wave 3 mm, R-wave 9.5 mm, Q-wave 0.75 mm.
Lead II: slurring of R, practically isoelectric T, low take off of RS—T segment, voltage of P 3 mm, voltage of R 3 mm.
Lead III: slight slurring of R+S, low voltage; nearly isolectric T, voltage of R 1 mm, voltage of S 5.5 mm.

Note: Standardization is not present
    Horizontal spacing: 0.04 sec. Vertical sp. 1 mm.
    Actual square-spacing: 0.075″

May 13, 1943 (Morell asks for cardiologist's advice)

Prof. Dr. medicine Theo Morell
Führer's Headquarters

May 13, 1943

To Prof. Weber,
Bad Nauheim

Dear Colleague,

About two years ago I sent to you one of the enclosed electrocardiograms for an opinion, informing you that it was a gentleman in the Foreign Ministry. You expressed the opinion that this was an incipient coronary sclerosis.

Meanwhile I have treated the patient concerned—a man who is subjected to huge burdens and can hardly ever take a respite—from time to time with repeated glucose and iodine injections (frequently giving courses of these injections), in that two or three times a day I inject 10 cc of twenty percent glucose solution and after that 10 cc of Septoiod which always went down very well. I also applied leeches from time to time. There are no heart or angina pains, but a tendency to arterio-spasms with rapid increase in blood pressure (when worked up) and a serious general insomnia. The intramuscular injections of Vitamultin-Calcium have done a lot of good, and I add Tonophosphan-forte on account of the nervous system.

Recently when I gave him a thorough checkup the pulse was 72 and blood pressure 146–154/100 mm, with pure sounds and otherwise completely normal findings, and I made the second attached electrocardiogram. As far as I can see a very minor deterioration has occurred. Would you please be so good as to tell me your opinion on (1) the present result, (2) how it compares with the earlier one, and (3) the proper therapy. If possible in two letters, one I can show the patient and one for me.

I have been holding back with Strophantin and nitroglycerine for the time being.

Thanking you in advance, and with best wishes,

Heil Hitler,

(Morell)

May 17, 1943 (The cardiologist's reply)

Balneological University Institute
Director: Prof. Dr. A. Weber

Bad Nauheim
May 17, 1943

Dear Colleague Morell,

The two takes of May 11 show: sinus rhythm, left type, possibly also incipient left retardation, slight depression of ST_I and ST_{II}. T_I beginning negative, T_{II} on the base line. Compared with the 1941 take, an unquestionable deterioration has taken place inasmuch as the ST depression has become clearer and the T_I, which was at that time still clearly positive, is now negative. The T_{II} which was still clearly positive then now virtually coincides with the base line. The electrocardiogram of May 11 this year reinforces my earlier diagnosis: Coronary Sclerosis, and this is evidently a progressive case.

I would urgently recommend three or four weeks' complete rest. In cases like this you can never make a definite prognosis, but in all probability things will not take a turn for the better while it is not possible to be specific about how much time is left. I recommend treatment either with Teominal or Deriphyllin or Iodine-Calcium-Diuretin, administered for three weeks, then a pause of three weeks and so on repeatedly. Any smoking to be stopped completely, there must be liquid intake and a low-salt diet, and one day per week confined to fruit juices (one liter) provided this does not conflict with his job, and there must be no other eating or drinking during those twenty-four hours and actual work must be cut back to an absolute minimum.

Regular midday rest of at least one hour and as much sleep at night as possible.

I realize that these measures which are absolutely indicated are nowadays hardly possible or completely impossible for a man in a responsible position, but as many of these points as possible should be heeded if his strength is to be maintained.

Heil Hitler!
Cordial best wishes,

yours, A. Weber

June 5, 1943 (Fecal analysis)

Prof. Dr. A. Nissle,   Freiburg i. Br.
Research Institute,
Freiburg i. Br.   Fürstenbergstrasse 15

June 5, 1943

To: Professor Dr. Morell
at present: *Berchtesgaden*
Berghof

Dear Colleague,

Attached please find the analysis after a thoroughgoing investigation of the fecal sample. Unfortunately adequate care is still not being taken with the preparation of all forms of raw food, even though the plants in question are often treated with liquid manure and are for this reason not infrequently exceptionally rich in gastric bacteria and sometimes even in helminthous [worm] eggs. Last year I had this kind of material investigated by one of my Ph.D. students, and we were able to arrive at wholly unsatisfactory results even with the dietary kitchen of the clinic here.

Importance must be attached to staff washing their hands thoroughly with soap and water before handling raw food, and to rinsing each individual salad leaf and the like in running water; the same goes for fruit—apples and pears should always be peeled first, as our examination here shows their peel is invariably filthy with bacteria. No doubt you will in addition to your dietary measures recommend that he continues the Mutaflor cure, and I hope that the masses of aerogenes bacilli, which must have got in with particularly heavily infected material, will soon be displaced from the intestinal flora again; for this reason I would ask you to send me a further fecal sample for investigation after eight or ten days and perhaps a second sample some while after, in case our analysis of the first is not satisfactory.

Chinese medical practice suggests that raw food should always be individually plunged for a few seconds into boiling water; they do it mainly on account of helminthous eggs and dysentery that are widespread there. It is a pretty drastic method, of course, and I only mention it to you in case you want to bear it in mind; obviously the fresh look of the salad leaves is lost.

I would be very pleased if your next news is good news again.

With all good wishes,
Heil Hitler!

Nissle

June 10, 1943 (Fecal analysis, second opinion)

Stool Report II

Material sent in: Stool sample, received on June 2, 1943. Analytical procedure: Set out in detail in the appended report [*not printed*].

Summary of Findings:

The sample submitted had a bright brownish color and showed a rich dash of gall-colored partly emulsified oil (laxative).

In this sample there were found bacteriological traces primarily of intestinal bacteria like the coli communi, enterococci and anerobic (butyric acid) bacilli by culture and microscopic tests, and these were tested with regard to their most important biochemical characteristics.

Particularly noticeable was the presence of numerous coli aerogenes bacilli and a few coli bacteria that weakly fermented in lactose. Verdict: There is evidently a slight dysbacteria of alimentary origin, probably only transitory in nature.

(Signed) Prof. W. Laves

Olmütz, June 10, 1943

January 11, 1944 (Analysis of liquor on Führer's orders)

Prof. Dr. Theo Morell

Führer's Headquarters
January 11, 1944

To the Director,
War Dept. Field Laboratory
Lötzen.

Dear Colleague,

I am sending you herewith a further sample of Slibovicz which is not from the same batch as recently investigated and which I request you to examine immediately particularly for methy alcohol content and other noxious substances.

As this job is at the command of the Führer I request you to expedite it immediately and telephone the result to me at Wolf's Lair 325. Please follow this with a brief written report.

With best wishes
and Heil Hitler!

(Signed) Prof. Dr. Th. Morell
Führer's Personal Physician

January 12, 1944 (Laboratory reply)

Dr. Bickert   War Department Headquarters
Lieutenant-Colonel (medical)   January 12, 1944

To: Professor Dr. Morell
Führer's Headquarters

I am sending you the results of the examination of the two alcohol samples attached [*not printed*].

Qualitative analysis for methyl alcohol and fusel alcohol indicates no grounds against consumption. Quantitative analysis for methyl and fusel alcohol could not be performed as the samples were too small. The slight turbidity of the liquid may perhaps be attributed to having been stored at too low a temperature. It is recommended that the liquid be stored at a constant temperature of about 18° C.

Heil Hitler!

Dr. Bickert

March 2, 1944 (Re eye examination)

To Prof. Dr. Morell

My dear Professor,

As arranged I am sending you (encl.) . . . the result of my examination, which fortunately appears to be comparatively favorable, though it of course indicates the existing danger to the vessel system. I would like in addition to make a few explanatory remarks.

Application of heat twice a day for some 15–20 minutes will surely help to clear up the turbidity of the right eye more quickly. At the same time, I feel that the period of quiet which it makes necessary—even though only twice a day for twenty minutes—offers an opportunity for relaxation which is supplemented by the influence of the heat. Would a similar effect be achieved by a very moderate body massage once a day?

Regarding the use of glasses I should like to say the following: the glasses for distant vision will hardly ever be necessary. The bifocal glasses, on the other hand, would be very convenient whenever it is necessary to shift the eyes quickly between near and distant objects, for example, during a conference in which an individual must be seen clearly while at the same time a letter must be glanced at or followed. The wearer of the glasses thus does not have to put them on and take them off, but looks at distant objects through the upper section of the glasses and at objects near at hand, a document for instance, through the lower.

I consider frequent reexamination of the eyes unnecessary, for psychological reasons undesirable. I do think it advisable, however, to recheck my findings after six or eight weeks, particularly in order to keep current on the conditions of the retinal blood vessels.

I would like to take the opportunity afforded by this letter to express again my sincere thanks for the friendly reception which you have accorded me, and for your advice. It has been a deeply impressive experience for me to be able to have a glimpse into the manifold aspects of your highly responsible activity.

With best wishes,
Heil Hitler!
Your obedient

(Signed) W. Löhlein

March 2, 1944 (Report on an Eye Examination)

The Director   Berlin NW 7,
of the University Clinic   Ziegelstrasse 5–9
for Eye Diseases

1. *Findings of Examination*

The Führer complained that he had been seeing everything as through a thin veil over his right eye for about two weeks. On closer questioning he mentioned that he had experienced a light stabbing pain, of transitory nature, in his right eye recently. He reads, of course, a good deal—especially before falling asleep—and the presbyopic glasses prescribed in 1935 are hardly enough for this purpose now.

Visual acuity was tested under rather unfavorable lighting conditions. Results were as follows:

Right   3/12 (+1.5 sph) 5/6
Left   5/6, glasses rejected

Close vision:

Right   (+4.0) Nieden II in 25–30cm
Left   (+3.0) Nieden I in 5–30cm

Lid apparatus normal. No fibrillation in orbicularis, incidentally no strong defensive reaction to instilling of drops or to tonometry. Motility normal. Anterior eye in good order on both sides in every respect. Pupils of equal diameter, round, and of normal reaction. Anterior chamber shows normal depth. Color of the iris on both sides equally dark blue-gray. After determination of normal inner pressure by palpation, mydriasis of pupils was induced, right with Homatropin, left (currently the eye with better vision) only with Veritol.

Ophthalmoscopy after about thirty minutes gave following results:

Left: Refractive media exceptionally clear. Eye background entirely clear and without pathological findings. Papilla of normal color, exhibiting well-defined physiological excavation. The retinal blood vessels were of normal width and extent. The choroid vessels could not be diagnosed because of the dark shade of epithelial pigment. Posterior pole and periphery also without pathological manifestation.

Right: Background was obscured by a delicate veil. With the use of a magnifying mirror, a very delicate, faintly mobile, diffuse turbidity of the

vitreous humor could be observed, obviously composed of infinitesimal particles. No turbidity of the lens could be observed. The picture of the eye background was therefore not as clear as in the left eye, but still permitted all details to be distinguished: Papilla showed no evidence of pathology. Retinal blood vessels exhibited no noticeable peculiarities, especially no varices of veins or caliber irregularity of arteries. No hemorrhages or white degenerative foci were observed. A faveolar reflex was not distinctly discernible. Periphery showed no pathological conditions.

The tonometric examination (under Psicain) which was performed immediately following resulted in a reading of 8 on both sides with a weight of 7.5, that is to say, a completely normal inner-eye pressure.

Diagnosis: The misty perception with the right eye is explained by a very delicate but diffuse turbidity of the vitreous humor which, since no inflammatory processes can be observed, is to be attributed to minute hemorrhages into the vitreous humor. These hemorrhages do not seem to originate with the blood vessels of the retina. At least no pathological retinal conditions can be observed on either side. Probably a transitory variation in pressure possibly caused by a vessel spasm—the explanation of the presence of blood.

PROPOSAL:

In order to assist in clearing up the turbidity, local application of heat is recommended, perhaps quarter-hour treatments twice a day with electrothermopor or Sollux lamp. Further recommended is instillation of one percent JK [potassium iodide] solution into right eye.

A discussion with Professor Morell was held in the presence of the Führer, during which means of preventing the recurrence of such hemorrhages were evident. Everything contributing to the avoidance of unnecessary excitement, particularly during the period immediately before the night's rest, such as diversion in light reading, was recommended. The use of sedatives is naturally narrowly restricted. Some consideration was given to the use of Luminal tablets.

In addition a change of glasses was prescribed: continuous use of glasses for distant vision is not necessary, but occasional use might be convenient. Therefore the following prescription was made for distant vision: Right +1.5 diopter spher., left plane. The glasses for near vision must be strengthened. Right +4.0 diopter spher., left +3.0 diopter spher. Bifocal glasses of the same strength are also to be provided.

(Signed) Dr. W. Löhlein

September 24, 1944 (Electrocardiogram interpreted)

Balneological University Institute
Director: Prof. Dr. A. Weber   Bad Nauheim

Electrocardiogram I

Date: September 24, 1944
Age: Disease: Switch on A.
Auricular Rate: 85–90   *P-QRS*
        Interval: 0.10–11
Ventricular Rate: 85–90   *QRS Complex:* 0.08

Rhythm: Pacemaker apparently originates in the uppermost portion
of Tawara node. (Conduction
time: 0.10–11.)   *Axis deviation:* Left

Lead I: low-inverted T, slight low take off of R—T segment, notching of P 0.3 mm, small Q-wave (1 mm), voltage of R 8.5 mm.
Lead II: slight slurring of P, isoelectric T, low take off of R—T segment, voltage of P 0.3 mm, voltage of R 3 mm.
Lead III: slight slurring of base of R, voltage of R 1.3 mm, voltage of S 6 mm.

Note: Standardization present
    Horizontal spacing: 0.04 sec. Vertical sp. 1 mm.
    Actual square-spacing: 0.075″

September 24, 1944 (Electrocardiogram interpreted)

Balneological University Institute
Director: Prof. Dr. A. Weber   Bad Nauheim

Electrocardiogram I

Date: September 24, 1944   *Clinical diagnosis:* Coronary sclerosis
Age: *Disease:* Switch on No. 6, apparently
                            affect standardization.
Auricular Rate: 85–90   *P-QRS Interval:* 0.10–11
Ventricular Rate: 85–90   *QRS Complex:* 0.08
Rhythm: Pacemaker apparently origi-
nates in the uppermost portion
of Tawara node. (Conduction
time 0.10–11.)   *Axis deviation:* Left

Lead I: notching of P, low take off of R—T segment.
Lead II: slight slurring of R, isoelectric T, low take off of R—T segment.
Lead III: very slight slurring of R+S.

Note: Standardization present
    Horizontal spacing: 0.04 sec. Vertical sp. 1 mm.
    Actual square-spacing: 0.075″

October 10, 1944 (Urinalysis)

Performed by Infirmary (Corporal Koch), checked by Dr. Weber.

Absolutely normal findings.
Specific gravity: 1.013
Albumen: negative
Sugar: negative
Urobilinogen: no increase*
Sediment:
    Very sporadic leucocytes, one or two in field of view. Otherwise normal. No bacteria.

(Signed) Weber

    * *Author's note:* Note the absence of any signs of damage to the liver, despite the hepatitis a few days earlier.

November 24, 1944 (Blood sedimentation)

Prof. Dr. med. Theo Morell
Berlin W15,
Kurfürstendamm 216

Patient: X (Foreign Ministry)*

Sedimentation Rate of Blood Corpuscles
Westergreen Method

1st hour = 33 mm   Normal value: up to 10 mm
2nd hour = 66 mm
     Average rate mm: 33

[*Handwritten addendum:*] The test was begun about two or three hours after the blood was obtained. N.B.: On November 9, 1944, a course of five Homoseran injections was concluded. On May 11, 1943, the blood sedimentation rate was an average of 2.5 mm.

Dr. M.

* *Author's note:* A camouflage for Hitler. A handwritten annotation indicates who performed the test: "Frau Ruth Krause, medical technical assistant, training 3½ years, Frankfurt am Main; and Dr. (medicine) Richard Weber, assistant to Professor Dr. Morell."

November 24, 1944 (Blood count)

Prof. Dr. med. Theo Morell
Führer's Headquarters

Blood sedimentation	33/66 mm
Hemoglobin:	88%
Blood Count	
Leukocytes	5–600
Erythrocytes	4,380,000
Color Index	1.01
White Blood Corpuscle Differential	
Segment nuclei	56%
Lymphocytes	30%
Eosinophils	3%
Monocytes	4%
{Neutrophils 4% / }Staff nuclei 3%	}7%
Urine:	
Specific gravity	1.017
Albumen	Ø
Sugar	Ø
Urobilinogen	Ø
Sediment:	Inconclusive.

Very small amount of calcium carbonate and a few epithelia.

December 2, 1944 (Morell asks cardiologist's advice)

December 2, 1944
Reich Chancery
Berlin W8

To Prof. Dr. med. Weber
Bad Nauheim

Dear Colleague,

I have several times already submitted to you the electrocardiograms of a foreign ministry gentleman, asking for your opinion. These produced the diagnosis of *coronary sclerosis*. Unfortunately the patient was never able to lay his work aside but has been subject to constant burdens, particularly in recent times, and to major upsets and irritations. These last five years he never went to bed before four or five A.M., as his final conferences and labors were never finished before then. He had become a stranger to the idea of going for walks, as he became accustomed to taking only fifteen minutes' fresh air a day for months on end, spending the rest of his time without natural light in bunkers!

Nevertheless I managed by injecting a lot of 20 percent glucose—in intravenous shots of 10 cc at a time—often for months on end, and by adding iodine from time to time (in the form of Septoiod), to ward off an even more rapid progression of the coronary sclerosis. To fortify him further I frequently administered *Vitamultin-Calcium* (which contains vitamins C, B₁ and nicotinamide, and calcium, et cetera), *Glyconorm* (the extract of cardiac muscles, suprarenal gland cortex, liver and pancreas) and from time to time *liver* extract too. The patient lives a vegetarian existence without nicotine and alcohol, with restricted liquid intake. Iodine-Calcium-Diuretin was not administered, as his stomach is hypersensitive and reacts violently with spasms.

So far there have been no anginal complaints. I would be very grateful to you for any opinion and suggestions for further treatment, if you consider a change is called for. I did recommend massage, but this was not permitted.

I am further enclosing some electrocardiograms of myself. As I informed you earlier, I had my first serious attack of angina pectoris after a miserable airplane flight, with a T₁₁ that stayed strongly negative for some time, and then later regulated again. The QRS opening is gradually getting bigger, and due to the constant responsibility and several hateful intrigues against me, I have begun feeling constantly a little depressed. I perspire at night and get breathless easily. Also the edemas on my lower legs have become more pronounced, so I have been getting massages every few days now. Altitudes of 800 to 1,200 meters do not agree with me at all, and that goes for air that is low in oxygen too. I have had to have a series of Glucadenose injections more than once already, and things go better after that; but as my burdens increase so it becomes evident that I am not getting permanently better. There are unfortunately certain reasons why I cannot take time off.

A few months ago after a sudden upset I had a hemorrhage behind my left eye, but this was rapidly reabsorbed. In the spring of 1942 I had a major upset which caused a frontal hemorrhage, which however rapidly got better, but since then some of my lesser muscles have tired more easily.

A month ago I attended the funeral of my brother at Bad Nauheim for a day—he died of an apoplexy at 61—but I had no time to come and see you as I had to get back urgently. Perhaps I will soon be able to call on you.

I would be indebted to you if you would tell me without pulling any punches how you interpret *my* case too, and give me your suggestions. I've been taking liquid Cardiazol for some weeks and Iodine-Calcium-Diuretin.

Thanking you in advance and wishing you all the best,

Heil Hitler!

yours,

M[orell]

P.S.: Please enclose your account and include your two previous opinions in the bill. Hand your opinion to the courier and give him the electrocardiograms too.

December 4, 1944 (Cardiologist's reply)

Balneological University Institute
Director: Prof. Dr. A. Weber   Bad Nauheim

Dear Professor Morell,

I am replying to your courteous letter from my cellar while hordes of enemy bombers thunder overhead. Please accept my heartfelt condolences on the death of your brother. I would be interested to learn whether it was an apoplexy or a sudden cardiac failure, as he had been suffering from angina for a number of years.

As far as your own electrocardiogram is concerned—and I am not pulling any punches—compared with 1941 the signs of a coronary insufficiency have become clearer. Between July 28, 1944, and October 9, 1944, there was a noticeable improvement, namely in II. S—T is showing an increasing tendency again. I can well understand that your present way of life is not actually good for your coronary arteries. But all of us are wishing that in the foreseeable future there may be a change for the better which will also have a favorable effect on your health. May I suggest adopting a philosophical attitude toward all the petty intrigues that are bound to occur given the position that you occupy. Can't you make one day completely free each week? Taking a day off like that often does more good than all the drugs. I would continue to take the Iodine-Calcium-Diuretin but avoid any kind of sudden physical strain, even if it is only a brief muscular exertion like lifting a piece of heavy furniture, for instance.

And now to the graphs of Patient A [Hitler]: Interpretation of August 14, 1941: sinus rhythm, left type. Flattening of T in all three Leads. A very slight depression of S—T in I and II. Initial complex lasting about 0.09″. Interpretation of May 1943: sinus rhythm, left type. Somewhat more clearly denoted than two years earlier, as is the depression of S—T in I and II. T in I is barely negative. QRS lasting 0.08–0.09″. Interpretation of September 24, 1944: left type, even more clearly marked. Depression of S—T in I, which commencing now is showing a track that is convex upward. T in I is clearly negative. S—T in II is also clearly more strongly depressed. QRS cannot be measured with certainty but apparently lasts longer than in 1943.

There are slowly progressive symptoms of left coronary insufficiency, and probably also of left retardation. In view of everything you set out in your covering letter these changes for the worse should not surprise us.

I recommend primarily that he should if at all possible take complete days of rest and eat a low-salt diet. The vegetarian diet must not be allowed to result in an albumen deficiency. From time to time he should test his weight at morning and night; losing about two pounds or more weight during the day would indicate a disturbed water balance, which can easily occur if there is an albumen deficiency. If Iodine-Calcium-Diuretin does not agree with this patient, then please try administering Deriphyllin, one or two tablets to be taken daily. Of course there is no drug that can make up for the harm done by an unhealthy way of life, but that is just another cost of this war.

I hope it may prove possible for you to come here in the foreseeable future. With the best wishes for your good health, and Heil Hitler, I remain your obedient

(Signed) A. Weber

April 7, 1945 (Eye examination)

The Director
of the University Clinic   Berlin NW 7,
for Eye Diseases   Ziegelstrasse 5–9

Eye Examination of the Führer on April 7, 1945

According to the Führer the vision of the right eye has gradually grown worse rather than better, while that of the left is as good as ever. But the left eye is impeded by a swelling on the left upper lid which is tender and causes him to rub it. There is a secretion from both eyes of late, which is understandable in view of the dusty atmosphere in the center of Berlin. The Führer generally leaves the well-ventilated and illuminated bunker only for short periods, for half an hour or two hours daily, and then goes into the Reich Chancery's garden, which is not badly damaged but is of course quite dusty, particularly when windy. He finds himself then very sensitive both to light and the dust-laden wind. It is difficult to arrange a set treatment in view of the irregularity of his life-style and the need for him to be constantly available for reports, et cetera.

Results:

Visual acuity right (with lens +4.5)
    Nieden II in 25 cm
Close vision: left (with lens +3.0)
    Nieden I in 25 cm
Distant visual acuity:
Right: (+1.5 diopter sph.) 5/10. As he hardly ever wears his spectacles he is disproportionately inconvenienced by the bad vision of his right eye.
Left: 5/5+ glasses rejected.

There is a moderate chronic conjunctivitis on both sides without involvement of the conjunctive bulbi. Secretion very slight. No indications of lachrymal sac involvement.

Quite a large insipid chalazion on left upper eyelid, which provokes rubbing and is bothersome.

Pale conjunctiva on both eyeballs, clear cornea. Anterior chamber shows normal depth, well-shaped iris with prompt reaction by the pupils to light.

Ophthalmoscopy right (after Homatropin): lens clear. In vitreous humor slight delicate turbidity, sluggishly mobile; probably not enough to explain the reduction of vision by itself. Papilla well defined, of adequate color, not paler temporally than on the left where the central vision is good.

But no fovea reflex in contrast to the left. Posterior pole otherwise without pathological manifestation, and in particular no hemorrhages. The retinal blood vessels were not blocked. While the arteries were perhaps a bit thin, there were no marked irregularities. Periphery without pathological manifestation.

Ophthalmoscopy right: (after Veritol): Vitreous humor and lens clear. Eye background without pathological manifestation. Perfect macula reflex.

Diagnosis: Moderate chronic conjunctivitis on both sides. Chalazion on upper left eyelid. Right: The residue of a hemorrhage in the vitreous humor. Lack of macular reflex.

Treatment: On account of the conjunctivitis on both sides: instillation of zinc suprac. drops three times a day on each side. On account of the chalazion left: heat application to left eye for fifteen minutes three times daily (interpose some gauze). In addition before going to bed gently rub two percent yellow mercury ointment into left eye.

If a rapid reduction and amelioration of the chalazion on the left upper lid does not result, it should be excised in an early operation.

Further examination in one week's time, possibly with excision of the chalazion from the left upper lid at the same time.

(Signed) Dr. W. Löhlein

Appendix II

The Medicines

PREPARATIONS ADMINISTERED BY MORELL TO HITLER DURING THE YEARS 1941–1945

The manufacturer is identified where known in brackets. Hamma was the company wholly owned by Morell, with plants in Hamburg and Olmütz.

Acidol-Pepsin
> (Bayer) Indicated for dyspepsia, lack of appetite.

Antiphlogistine-Poultices
> (Lyssia) A paste to be applied by poultice in cases of inflammation of the joints and glands, pleurisy, bruises, knocks and abrasions.

Belladonna Obstinol
> (Dr. Thiemann & Co.) Against constipation in patients with hypersensitive intestinal tracts. For use with patients with vegetative regulatory disorders and tendency to spasms.

Benerva-fortissime
> (Roche) Indicated: Vitamin B_1 deficiency, neuralgia, sciatica, circulatory disorders with vitamin deficiencies; if repeatedly used in some cases it may result in shock, so it must be very slowly injected.

Betabion-forte
> (Merck, Darmstadt) Aneurin chloride hydrochloride. Indicated: vegetative disorders.

Bismogenol
> (Tosse) Bismuth campho-carbonate, used in treating the neck glands.

Boxberger pills (against constipation)

Brom-Nervacit
> (A. Herbert Pharmacy, Wiesbaden) When Hitler became excited or aggravated, which was often, Morell would prescribe one or two tablespoons of Brom-Nervacit, an old and well-known tranquilizer consisting of 4 percent potassium bromide, 0.1 percent sodium phosphate, one percent naphrodyl, diethyl-barbiturate acid, phenyldimethylpyrazolon, alcohol, sweetener and aromatics. To prevent a bromine reaction Morell would however prescribe it only during alternate eight-week periods.

Calcium Sandoz

(Sandoz, Nuremberg) Calcium gluconal actobional. Indicated: disorders of calcium metabolism. Allergic disorders. Hemorrhages.

Calomel

Subchloride of mercury (Hg_2Cl_2). "Used frequently for cleansing enemas, which Hitler administered [to] himself," says OI/CIR/4; and see the diary, September 30, 1944. Once a very popular medication, it was already outmoded in the 1930s and is now obsolete.

Cantan

One tablet contained 0.025 pure l-ascorbic acid. Indicated: vitamin C deficiency.

Cardiazol

(Knoll, Ludwigshafen) In 1941, Morell began administering Cardiazol (chemical designation: pentamethylenetetrazol) to overcome the circulatory disorder evident from the edema observed by Morell on the external and internal malleoli (bony prominences) of Hitler's fibulae and tibia. Normal dosage would be twenty drops taken three or four times a day. Professor Schenck says, "We now know that the effect is relatively short-lived. The drug is still available, but it is not as highly rated as it used to be."

Castor oil

Oleum ricini. A purgative.

Chineurin

(Hamma, Olmütz) Prepared in capsules by Dr. Kurt Mulli. It contained some quinine, and was occasionally used therapeutically against colds, administered orally to Hitler after a meal, in place of Ultraseptyl (q.v.).

Coramin

(Ciba) Well known respiratory and circulatory stimulant: Pyridin-B-carbonic acid diethylamide, used like Cardiazol.

Cortiron

(Schering) Chemical name: desoxycoticosteron acetate. Morell injected this intramuscularly into Hitler on a few occasions, to combat muscle weakness and influence the carbohydrate metabolism and fat resorption.

Dolantin

(Hoechst) Controlled by the Narcotics Act. A powerful and effective analgesic and pain-killer.

Enterofagos ampoules

(Antipiol) Indicated: Acute and chronic diseases of the gastrointestinal tract, constipation caused by bacteria.

Eubasin

A sulfa drug used only once by Morell, since injected intragluteally it caused pain. He used it therapeutically to cure a cold.

Euflat

This was a combined preparation of radix angelica, papaverin, aloe, active bile extracts, coffee, charcoal, pancreas extract. Morell supplied Euflat pills to Hitler to improve his digestion and combat the meteorism.

Eukodal

(Merck, Darmstadt) Dihydro-hydroxycodeinon hydrochloride. Indicated: For use instead of morphine in cases of severe pain and tenderness. Familiar since 1937, a synthetic morphium derivate, controlled by the Narcotics Act. Injected intravenously against epigastric cramps.

Eupaverin

(Merck) Synthetic alkaloid, an anticonvulsant made from poppies. Indicated: Spasms, embolisms, peripheral blood disorders. Used similarly to Eukodal. Morell would mix 0.02 g Eukodal with 0.03 g Eupaverin and inject them as a cocktail intravenously.

Franzbranntwein

An ancient and popular liniment: alcohol, pine needle oil. Still available.

Gallestol

Glucose

Morell injected 20 percent glucose, usually in 10 cc shots, in Hitler from 1937 to the end, to supply calories. He told his American interrogators that he injected it only every second or third day, but the diaries show he used it much more frequently. He wrote on December 17, 1942: "By injecting glucose, I'm doing what I can to strengthen his heart and also to dehydrate the system."

Glyconorm

(Nordmark Works, Hamburg) Containing metabolic ferments like Cozymase I and II, vitamins B_1, B_2 and C, and the amino acids cystein, histidine, tryptophane, and a cocktail of extracts of the cardiac muscle, suprarenal gland, liver and pancreas. Used mainly to prevent pellagra, a nutritional skin disorder, and against vitamin C deficiency, carbohydrate metabolism disorders, intoxication and neuritis. Morell administered 2 cc shots intramuscularly to check Hitler's digestive disturbances.

Glycovarin glucose

Harmin

An alkaloid, one of the family of drugs extracted from deadly nightshade (Solanaceae), used against tremors, but which according to Professor Schenck has no real advantage over other such atropine-based drugs.

Homburg 680

(Homburg) A stabilized extract from the Bulgarian belladonna (deadly nightshade) root. Indicated: all diseases of the Parkinsonism variety, in particular that known as *morbus Parkinson* (paralysis agitans).

Homoseran

(Hamma, Olmütz) A preparation manufactured from placenta, injected by Morell into Hitler for the first time on November 7, 1944.

Intelan

(Ankermann & Co., Friesoythe) Tablets of this contained vitamins A and D and glucose. A typical dragée contained 5,000 international units of vitamin A, 1,000 of vitamin D_2-cholesterin, and 15 milligrams of vitamin B_1-Cyano complex. From 1942 to 1944 Morell administered it like his Vitamultin to induce appetite, to combat Hitler's lack of vitality and ability to concentrate and to increase his resistance to infection.

Karlsbader Mühlbrunnen

A mineral water.

Karlsbader Sprudelsalz

A gaseous mineral water.

Koagovit

A hemostatic.

Dr. Koester's Anti-Gas Pills

These little black spheres contained extra. Nux vom., extr. Bellad., aao.5, extr. Gent. 1.0. Hitler imbibed two to four pills at every meal from 1936 to 1944 to combat his intestinal gas buildup (meteorism). Professor

Schenck states: "As Morell's papers show, this was a completely harmless medicine."

Leo-Pillen

(Leo Works) Laxative.

Lugol's Solution

A compound solution of potassium iodide and iodine used for swabbing the tonsils.

Luizym

(Luitpold Works, Munich) A digestive enzyme preparation containing ferments which split cellulose, hemicellulose and carbohydrates. Indicated: to combat digestive weakness, meteorism, dyspepsia, and the Roemheld syndrome (gaseous buildup in the upper intestine causing painful pressure on the heart); and to render vegetable diets more digestible. Luizym was taken in tablet or dragée form after meals when flatulence was suffered. Still commercially available.

Luminal

(Bayer-Merck) A sedative. Phenyl-ethyl-barbiturate. Indicated: Severe insomnia, spastic and nervous conditions.

Mitilax

(Diwag Chemical Factory) Laxative. Morell wrote in one letter, "It consists of virtually pure paraffin." Its ingredients were liquid paraffin with vanilla or coffee flavoring.

Mutaflor

(Hageda of Berlin) This emulsion of a particular strain of *Bacillus coli communis* was used to colonize Hitler's intestinal tract. On the first day one yellow capsule was taken, followed by a red capsule on the second, third and fourth days and two red capsules a day after that. (See pages 30 and 63.)

Nateina

(Llopis of Madrid) A mysterious hemostatic used on Hitler's middle ear after the Bomb Plot of July 1944. Nateina aroused interest in the medical world in 1930 when it was claimed to have been successfully used on the "bleeders" of the hemophilic Spanish royal family. In Germany it was marketed by Hageda of Berlin, a company close to Morell's business empire.

Neo-Pyocyanase

(Südmedica) Indicated: inflammation of the upper respiratory tract; acute and chronic tonsillitis.

Obstinol

(Dr. Thiemann & Co.) Indicated: Acute and chronic constipation.

Omnadin

(I.G. Farben) Omnadin was a mixture of proteins, lipoid substances of gall and animalic fats, claimed to have antigenic properties and therefore best used at the beginning of infections. It was nearly specific against colds, and Morell preferred to use it (in intramuscular shots of one 2 cc ampoule at a time) instead of Ultraseptyl, as it was nontoxic.

Optalidon

(Sandoz, Nuremberg) Painkiller and analgesic. Morell gave Hitler one or two tablets of this for headaches. It was a proprietary combination of amidopyrine and barbiturate, containing 0.05 Sandoptal (a proprietary hypnotic, iso-butylallyl barbituric acid); 0.125 dimethylamine phenazon (Pyramidon); and 0.025 caffeine.

Orchikrin

(Hamma, Olmütz) A combination of all the hormones of males. Potency
was increased by the addition of extracts of testis, seminal vesicles and
prostata of young bulls. Orchikrin was used in pill form (one pill being
equivalent to three grams of fresh testis) and also injected intramuscularly in ampoules of 2.2 cc. Morell's chemist, Dr. Mulli, claimed it had
been developed to combat cancer of the prostate. Morell suggested to
American interrogators that he had tried it on Hitler only once or twice
to combat fatigue or depression.

Penicillin-Hamma

(Hamma, Olmütz) Morell used this on Hitler on the evening of July 20,
1944, applying it as a powder to a skin wound on his right hand.

Phanodorm

(Bayer-Merck) Cyclobarbitol, a sedative. Indicated: Insomnia or poor
sleep quality.

Profundol

(Promonto) A barbiturate sleeping tablet.

Progynon B Oleosum forte

(Schering) Progynon was an esther of benzoic acid and the dihydro-
follicle hormone. One ampoule was injected intramuscularly, increasing
the circulation of the gastric muscles and preventing spasm of the gastric
wall and vessels.

Prostakrinum

(Hamma, Olmütz) A hormone product—extract of seminal vesicles and
prostata. Manufactured in pill, dragées and ampoules. One pill was the
equivalent of one gram of prostata and seminal vesicles. According to a
letter from Hamma to Morell, on June 6, 1941, the pills had a 0.5 gram
coating of sugar. For a short period in 1943 Morell administered it to
Hitler (two ampoules intramuscularly every second day) to prevent his
depressive moods.

Prostrophanta

(Probably made by Hamma, but unlisted in any codex.) Each ampoule
of Prostrophanta contained 0.3 milligrams of Strophantin (q.v.) in
combination with glucose and vitamin B complex (nicotinic acid).

Quadronox-Tabletten

(Axta) Sedative.

Relaxol

(Fischer) Indicated: for various kinds of constipation.

Sangostop

A hemostatic.

S. E. E. injections

(Merck) Later known as Scophedal, and controlled by the Narcotics Act.
Indicated: pain killer, tranquilizer.

Septoiod

(Diewag Chemical Factory, Berlin) Prescribed against Hitler's respiratory
infections. A solution of three percent iodine, made up of various iodine
salts. The intention was that after instillation, the free iodine would be
released and disinfect inflamed areas and increase bodily resistance.
Morell injected shots of up to 20 cc intravenously. He also expected the
Septoiod to retard the progress of Hitler's coronary sclerosis, and he
occasionally used it as a substitute for the toxic Ultraseptyl.

Spasmopurin suppositories

Used by Morell against Hitler's epigastric spasms.

Strophantin

This crystalline glucoside was used as a powerful heart tonic after the August 1941 electrocardiogram indicated that Hitler was suffering a progressive coronary sclerosis. For two or three weeks at a time Morell injected intravenously with Strophantin daily, and he continued this treatment on several occasions to the end of Hitler's life. It was a powerful and direct-acting stimulant. In order to reduce the risk of inducing a cardiac arrest by injecting too high a concentration too fast, it was usually mixed with 10 cc of glucose (sometimes in the form of the commercially premixed Prostrophanta), and both are injected in one syringe.

Sympathol

(Boehringer) (chemical name: Para-oxyphenylethanolmethylamine.) Used to increase the heart-minute-volume of blood. After 1942 Morell administered ten drops of Sympathol in a solution to be swallowed each day. Sympathol is only one-hundredth as effective as adrenaline.

Tempidorm

(Roland) A barbiturate suppository. Indicated: Insomnia, sleep disorders.

Testoviron

(Schering) Testosterone, the male sex hormone secreted by the testes. Indicated: anginal disorders, depressive conditions.

Thrombovetren

(Promonta) A heart tablet.

Tibatin

A sulphonamide drug.

Tonophosphan

(Bayer) Supplied in 1–2% ampoules or 0.1 gram tablets, Tonophosphan was the sodium salt of dimethyl-amino-methyl-phenyl-phosphinic acid. It was a recognized stimulant for unstriped muscles and was also administered to supply the body with phosphorus. Morell injected Tonophosphan subcutaneously in Hitler frequently during the latter years of the war.

Tonsiosan

(Schwabe)

Trocken-Koli-Hamma

(Hamma, Olmütz) A coli preparation developed by Professor Laves of the University of Graz, in capsules, and used as a substitute for Mutaflor (q.v.) as the Mutaflor supply dried up during the war.

Tussamag

(Tempelhof) Indicated: Expectoration; acute and chronic catarrh of the upper respiratory tract.

Ultraseptyl

(Chinoin, Budapest) A sulphonamide drug. Its chemical designation was 2-(p-aminobenzolsolfanamido)-4-methylthiazol—Morell would administer one or two tablets to Hitler, each containing 0.5 gram, with much fluid, like fruit juice or water, after a meal, against colds and infections.

Vitamultin-Calcium

(Hamma, Olmütz) Its ingredients varied, but in one form it contained ascorbic acid, calcium, vitamin C and vitamin B_1, and was filled into ampoules of 2 cc. Each ampoule thus contained 0.04 gram vitamin C and 0.36 milligrams of B₁ (aneurin)—minimal quantities which would not even remotely approach the daily needs of an adult male. It is interesting to note that Rudolf Franck's pharmacological handbook lists as further ingredients nicotinamide and a minute quantity of p-amido-benzoyldiethylamino-ethanol hydrochloride (otherwise known as procain, the cocainelike alkaloid now marketed as Novocaine).

Vitamultin-forte

(Hamma, Olmütz) Ampoules of this were first injected by Morell on March 14, 1944, to combat Hitler's general fatigue. Not listed in any pharmacological handbook, nor are the ingredients evident from Morell's papers.

Yatren

One tablet of Yatren contained 0.25 grams of chinoiforum iodoxychino-linsulphate. Indicated: amoebic dysentery.